MacBook Pro®

PORTABLE GENIUS
4th EDITION

MacBook Pro®

PORTABLE GENIUS
4th EDITION

Brad Miser

Wiley Publishing, Inc.

MacBook Pro® Portable Genius, 4th Edition

Published by
John Wiley & Sons, Inc.
10475 Crosspoint Blvd.
Indianapolis, IN 46256
www.wiley.com

ISBN: 978-1-118-36361-4

Manufactured in the United States of America

10 9 8 7 6 5 4 3 2

For general information on our other products and services or to obtain technical support, please contact our Customer Care Department within the U.S. at (877) 762-2974, outside the U.S. at (317) 572-3993 or fax (317) 572-4002.

Wiley publishes in a variety of print and electronic formats and by print-on-demand. Some material included with standard print versions of this book may not be included in e-books or in print-on-demand. If this book refers to media such as a CD or DVD that is not included in the version you purchased, you may download this material at http://booksupport.wiley.com. For more information about Wiley products, visit www.wiley.com.

Library of Congress Control Number: 2012946054

WILEY

Credits

Senior Acquisitions Editor
Stephanie McComb

Project Editor
Amanda Gambill

Technical Editor
John Lynn

Senior Copy Editor
Kim Heusel

Editorial Director
Robyn Siesky

Business Manager
Amy Knies

Senior Marketing Manager
Sandy Smith

Vice President and Executive Group Publisher
Richard Swadley

Vice President and Executive Publisher
Barry Pruett

Project Coordinator
Katherine Crocker

Graphics and Production Specialists
Joyce Haughey
Andrea Hornberger
Christin Swinford

Proofreading and Indexing
Penny L. Stuart
Potomac Indexing, LLC

About the Author

Brad Miser has written more than 45 books to help people get more out of their technology, faster and easier. In addition to *MacBook Pro Portable Genius*, Brad has written *Teach Yourself Visually MacBook Pro*, *iPhoto '11 Portable Genius*, *My iPhone*, *My iPod touch*, *Sams Teach Yourself iCloud in 10 Minutes*, and *Sams Teach Yourself Mac OS X Lion in 10 Minutes*. He has also been a co-author, and development or technical editor on more than 50 titles.

Brad is currently a solutions consultant. He has been the director of product and customer services, and the manager of education and support services for several software development companies.

In addition to his passion for silicon-based technology, Brad enjoys his steel-based technology in the form of a motorcycle whenever and wherever possible. Originally from California, Brad now lives in Indiana with his wife Amy; their three daughters, Jill, Emily, and Grace; a rabbit; and a sometimes-inside cat.

Brad would love to hear about your experiences with this book (the good, the bad, and the ugly). You can write to him at: bradmiser@me.com.

Acknowledgments

Stephanie McComb has my emphatic thanks because she is the one with whom this project had its genesis and who allowed me to be involved. Amanda Gambill deserves lots of credit for keeping the project on track and on target; I'm sure working with me was a challenge at times. John Lynn did a great job of keeping me on my toes to make sure this book contains fewer technical gaffs than it would have without his help. Kim Heusel transformed my stumbling, bumbling text into something people can read and understand. Lastly, thanks to all the people on the Wiley team who handle the other equally important parts of the process, such as production, sales, proofreading, and indexing.

On my personal team, I'd like to thank my wife Amy for her tolerance of the author lifestyle, which is both odd and challenging. My delightful daughters, Jill, Emily, and Grace, are always a source of joy and inspiration for all that I do, and for which I'm ever grateful.

Contents

chapter 2

How Do I Manage User Accounts? 50

chapter 3

What Are My Internet
Connection Options? 76

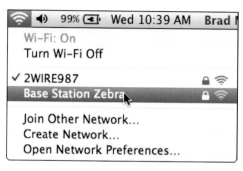

chapter 6

How Do I Take Advantage
of iCloud? 166

chapter 7

How Do I Manage Contacts
and E-mail? 186

chapter 8

How Do I Communicate and Share in Real Time? 220

chapter 9

How Can I Manage My Calendars? 244

chapter 10

How Can I Make Better Use of the
MacBook Pro Audio Features? 266

chapter 11

How Do I Add and Manage
Storage Space? 284

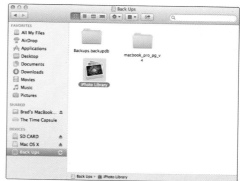

chapter 12

How Can I Run
Windows Applications?   304

chapter 13

How Can I Protect My
MacBook Pro?   318

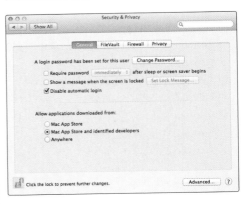

chapter 14

How Do I Solve MacBook
Pro Problems? 350

Introduction

From its distinctive metallic finish to its backlit keyboard, dazzling display, and inviting design, the MacBook Pro is amazing technology that looks as great as it works. Running Mac OS X and including a lot of amazing software, a MacBook Pro allows you to do more right out of the box more easily than any other computer. In fact, a MacBook Pro does so much, it's easy to overlook even more of the great things it can do. That's where this book comes in.

While you probably already know how to turn on your MacBook Pro, you might not know how to create virtual working spaces on the desktop, so that you can keep many applications and windows open at the same time and move among them easily. While you likely know how to use the trackpad to point to objects on the screen and select them, you might not know how to create your own keyboard shortcuts for just about any command in any application that you use. While you have probably thought about how you need to back up your important data, you might not have actually done it. Also, while you've probably surfed the web, you may not have taken advantage of all of the options being connected can give you, from sharing files locally to communicating with people around the world, easily and inexpensively.

The purpose of this book is to provide a resource for you when you are wondering how to do something better, how to do it more easily, or even how to do it at all. You'll find that each chapter is organized around a question. Within each chapter are answers to that question. These answers are task-focused so that you learn by doing rather than just by reading. The steps you'll find are very specific and, hopefully, quite complete. If you start at Step 1 and work through each one in sequence, you'll end up someplace you want to go. Thus, the book's title of *Portable Genius*; it is intended to be your companion, and guide you on your in-depth exploration of your MacBook Pro. Once you've been through a topic's steps, you'll be prepared to go even further by extending what you've learned to other tasks.

This book is designed to cover a broad range of topics in which most MacBook Pro users are interested. There's no particular order to the topics in this book, so you can jump to any chapter without having read the proceeding ones. To get started, I recommend that you take a look at the table of contents and decide which question you want answered first. Turn to the appropriate page and off you go!

How Can I Use My Desktop Space Efficiently?

The MacBook Pro Desktop is the area displayed on its screen. Like a physical Desktop, you place things (in this case, windows) on top to focus your attention on them and use their content. As you work, your Desktop naturally becomes cluttered with windows for applications, documents, and system tools. Keeping control of all of these windows helps you make the most of your Desktop space. With all of the great Desktop management tools Mac OS X offers, it's a lot easier to keep your MacBook Pro Desktop neat and tidy than it is a real desktop.

By default, icons for the MacBook Pro hard drive, external hard drives, DVDs, CDs, and server appear on the Desktop. This is okay if that is your preference, but they unnecessarily take up space on the Desktop because you can get to them more easily by opening a Finder window and using the sidebar.

Genius

The folders and files you see on the Desktop are determined by the contents of the Desktop folder, which is located within your Home folder. If you don't want a folder or file taking up space on your Desktop, move it into a different folder within your Home folder. In addition to having a neater appearance, this also helps you work more efficiently because it's easier to find folders and files if they're here rather than scattered on your Desktop.

Perform the following steps to show or hide Desktop icons:

1. **Choose Finder ⇨ Preferences.** The Finder Preferences dialog appears.
2. **Click the General tab if it isn't already selected.**
3. **Deselect the check boxes for the icons that you don't want to see on your Desktop.**
   For example, to hide the icon for the MacBook Pro internal hard drive or any external hard drive connected to it, deselect the Hard disks check box. As you deselect the check boxes, the related icons disappear from your Desktop.

Genius

To set the size, grid spacing, text size, and other options for the Desktop, click on the Desktop so that no Finder windows are selected. Choose View ⇨ Show View Options, and use the resulting dialog to configure these settings for your Desktop. The title of this dialog indicates the object for which you are configuring the view options, so it should be Desktop. You can use this same command with any folder to set its view options.

Utilizing the Sidebar and Toolbar

Much of the time that you are working on your Desktop will involve Finder windows. Two areas of Finder windows that you will use frequently are the sidebar and the toolbar. You can use these features as they are, but you can also customize them to make your Desktop space more efficient

Using and configuring the sidebar

The Finder's sidebar makes it easy to get to specific locations. It comes with a number of default locations, but you can add items to, or remove them from, the sidebar so that it contains the items you use most frequently.

The sidebar is organized into sections, as shown in Figure 1.1. Favorites are the locations on your MacBook Pro that you visit most frequently. The sidebar includes a number of default locations here, but you can customize this section so that it reflects the places you visit the most. Shared items are locations you are accessing on a network, such as a shared hard drive. Devices includes hard drives and disk images that are mounted on your MacBook Pro.

1.1 Use the sidebar to quickly move to the items that you want to view in a Finder window.

Using the items on the sidebar is simple (which is why it's so useful). Simply click the icon with which you want to work. What happens when you click depends on the kind of icon it is. The following are the potential outcomes:

- **All My Files.** When you click this icon, all of the files you've worked with appear in the Finder window. You can use the view and browse tools to access any file you need.

- **AirDrop.** When you click this icon, any Mac (running Mac OS X 10.7 or higher) with which your MacBook Pro can communicate that also has Wi-Fi on appears with the icon of its current user (given that the user has her own AirDrop folder selected). You can send files to other users by dropping them on the related icon and they can share files with you in the same way.

- **Applications.** If the icon is for an application, the application launches.
- **Documents.** Clicking a document's icon opens the associated application, and you see and work with the document's contents.
- **Folder.** When you click a folder, you see its contents in the Finder window.
- **Shared folder or drive.** When you select a shared network resource, you see either the tools you can use to log in to it or (if your MacBook Pro is configured to automatically log in to the resource) its contents.
- **Devices.** When you select a device, its contents are displayed in the Finder window.
- **Search.** If you click a search icon, the search runs and you see the results in the Finder window.

Note

Each type of sidebar item has a distinctive icon, making what it represents easy to distinguish.

You can show or hide the contents of each section. Point to the section's title and click Hide. The section is collapsed so you only see its title. Click Show to expand a section. Follow these steps to customize the sidebar so that it has the content you want:

1. **Choose Finder ➪ Preferences.** The Finder Preferences window appears.

2. **Click the Sidebar tab, shown in Figure 1.2.**

3. **Select the check box for each item that you want to appear on the sidebar, and deselect those that you don't want to appear.**

4. **Close the Finder Preferences window.**

5. **Open a Finder window.**

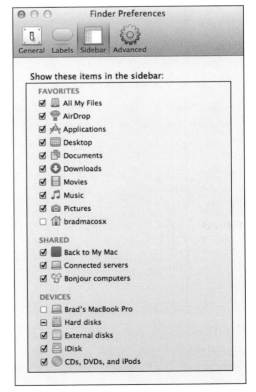

1.2 You can determine the kinds of resources available on the sidebar by setting the appropriate preferences.

Note The Favorites section is the only one that you can manually configure. The content of the other sections is determined by the Preferences settings, to what your MacBook Pro is connected on the network, and the mounted devices or disk images. If you drag an icon onto something in the other sections, it may be copied there instead (such as when you drag an icon onto a disk's icon).

6. **To remove an item from the Favorites section of the sidebar, perform a secondary click on it (the default action is Control+click, but as covered in Chapter 5, you can configure a trackpad gesture for this), and then choose Remove from Sidebar.** The icon disappears. Of course, when you remove something from the sidebar, it's not removed from the computer. It remains in its current location on your MacBook Pro, but is no longer accessible from the sidebar.

7. **To add a folder to the sidebar, drag it from a Finder window or Desktop onto the Favorites section.** As you move the folder onto the sidebar, a blue line appears at the location to which you've moved it. When you're over the location in which you want to place the folder, release the trackpad button. The folder's icon is added to the sidebar, and you can use it just like the default items.

8. **To add a file (document, application, etc.) to the Sidebar, select the item's icon and press ⌘+T.** The item's icon is added to bottom of the Favorites section, and you can use it just like the default items.

9. **To change the order of items in the sidebar, drag them up or down the list.** As you move an item between others, they slide apart to show you where the item you are moving will be. (You can only move items within their sections.)

Genius To move a file to a folder on the sidebar, open a Finder window so it shows the item you want to move. Drag the item's icon onto the sidebar folder in which you want to place it. To copy the file, hold the ⌘ key down while you move the file's icon. If you drop items onto a shared item on the sidebar, it is copied instead of moved. Hold the ⌘ key down to actually move the item.

Using and configuring the toolbar

The toolbar appears at the top of the Finder window and contains buttons and pop-up menus that you can use to access commands quickly and easily. You can configure the toolbar so that it contains the tools you use most frequently. When you open a Finder window, the toolbar appears at the top.

The following default tools appear on the toolbar (as grouped from left to right):

- **Back/Forward buttons.** These move you along the hierarchy of Finder windows that you've moved through (just like the Back and Forward buttons in a web browser).

- **View buttons.** You can change the view of the current window by clicking one of the View buttons. For example, to see the window in List view, click the second button in the View group (its icon has horizontal lines).

- **Action pop-up menu.** This menu contains a number of useful contextual commands. These are the same as those that appear when you perform a secondary click on an item.

- **Arrange menu.** This menu enables you to arrange the contents of the window. For example, you can group items by name, date last opened, size, and so on. Choose None to remove the arrange settings.

- **Share menu.** Use this menu to share a selected item; the options you see depend on the type of item you have selected. Options can include Email, Message, AirDrop, Flickr, and so on.

- **Search bar.** You can search for items on the Desktop by typing text or numbers into the Search bar. As you type, items that match your search term appear in the Finder window.

Perform the following steps to place the tools you prefer on your toolbar:

1. **Open a Finder window.**

2. **Choose View ⇨ Customize Toolbar.** The Toolbar Customization sheet appears, as shown in Figure 1.3.

3. **To remove a button from the toolbar, drag its icon from the toolbar onto the Desktop.** When you release the trackpad button, the selected button disappears in a puff of smoke. The button continues to be available on the sheet if you want to add it again later.

4. **To add a button to the toolbar, drag it from the sheet and drop it on the toolbar at the location in which you want to place it.** When you release the trackpad button, the selected button is added to the toolbar.

5. **On the Show menu, choose how you want the buttons on the toolbar to appear.** Your options are: Icon and Text, Icon Only, or Text Only.

6. **When you finish customizing the toolbar, click Done.** The Toolbar Customization sheet closes and you see your customized toolbar.

1.3 Use the Toolbar Customization sheet to define and organize the tools on your toolbar.

Genius

To return the toolbar to its default state, open the Toolbar Customization sheet and drag the default set of buttons onto the toolbar.

Working with the Dock

The Dock is an important part of your Desktop space. By default, it appears at the bottom of the Desktop, but you can control many aspects of its appearance, including where it is located and, to a great degree, how it works. The Dock is organized into two general sections. The area to the left of the application/document separation line (the white, dashed line that looks like a highway divider a few icons to the left of the Trash icon) contains application icons. The area to the right of this line contains icons for documents, folders, minimized Finder or application windows, and the Trash/Eject icon.

When folders appear on the Dock, they become stacks by default. When you click a stack, it pops up into a fan or appears as a grid (depending on how many items are in the folder), as shown in Figure 1.4, so that you can work with the items it contains. You can disable this feature for any folder so that it behaves more like a normal folder (more on that shortly).

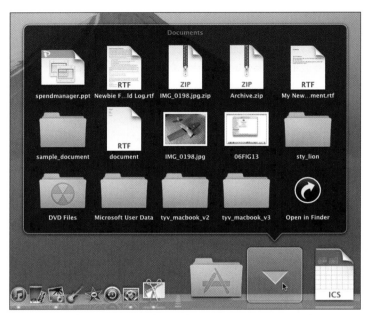

1.4 Clicking a folder's icon on the Dock causes its contents to either appear in a grid or fan out, depending on how many items it contains and your preferences.

You can perform all of the following functions from the Dock:

- **See running applications.** Whenever an application is running, you see its icon on the Dock. If the related preference is set (more details on this a bit later), a small, glowing blue light is located at the bottom of every running application's icon. Application icons also provide information about what is happening with those applications. For example, when you receive e-mail, a badge on the Mail application's icon changes to indicate the number of messages you have received since you last read messages.

- **Open applications, folders, minimized windows, and documents quickly by clicking the related icon.**

- **Quickly switch among open applications and windows by clicking the icon for the item you want to bring to the front.**

- **Be alerted about issues.** When an application needs your attention, its icon bounces on the Dock until you move into that application and handle the issues.

- **Control applications and switch to any open windows within one.** When you perform a secondary click on the icon of an application, a pop-up menu appears. When the application is running, this menu lists commands, as well as all of the open windows related to that application. When the application isn't running, you see a different set of commands (such as the Open command) that you can use to open the application.

- **Customize its appearance and function.** You can store the icon for any item (applications, folders, and documents) on the Dock. You can control how the Dock looks, including its size, whether it is always visible, where it is located, and which applications, folders, and documents appear on it.

Two icons on the Dock are unique and are always there: The Finder and the Trash. When you click the Finder icon (anchored on the left end of a horizontal Dock or at the top of a vertical one), a Finder window opens (if one isn't already open). If at least one Finder window is open, clicking the Finder icon brings the Finder window you used most recently to the front.

The Trash icon is where all folders and files go when their time is done. When the Trash contains files or folders, its icon includes crumpled paper so that you know something is in there. When you select an ejectable item (such as a DVD), the Trash icon changes to the Eject symbol. You can drag a disc, drive, volume, or any other ejectable item onto that icon to eject it.

Unless an application is permanently installed on the Dock (in which case, the icon remains in the same position), the icon for each application you open appears on the right (or bottom) edge of the application area of the Dock. Unlike open applications, open documents don't automatically appear on the Dock. Document icons appear on the Dock only when you manually add them or minimize a document's window. When you open an application's menu in the Dock (by performing a secondary click), you see a list of all open windows within that application.

When you minimize a window, it is pulled by default into the Dock using the Genie Effect. You can change this so that the Scale Effect is used instead. You can also change where the minimized window goes. Minimized windows are marked with the related application's icon in the lower-right corner of the Dock icon so you can easily tell from which application the windows came. If you prefer, you can configure the Dock so that minimized windows move into the related application's icon instead of becoming a separate icon on the Dock.

Note   When you hide an application, its open windows do not appear on the Dock. The hidden application's icon continues to be marked so that you know it is running. You can open a hidden application's Dock menu to jump into one of its open windows.

11

When you quit an open application, its icon disappears from the Dock (unless you have added that application to the Dock so that it always appears there). Minimized windows disappear from the Dock when you maximize them or when you close the application from which they came.

Configuring and using Dock icons

The Dock becomes even more useful when you organize it to suit your preferences. You can move icons around, add or remove applications, and add your own folders and documents to it to make them more easily accessible.

Genius

To move between applications quickly, press ⌘+Tab or ⌘+Shift+Tab. The Application Switcher appears. Click an icon to move into the associated application, or keep pressing ⌘+Tab or ⌘+Shift+Tab to cycle through the list. When you release the keys, you move into the selected application.

To add an application's icon to the Dock, simply drag it from a Finder window and drop it onto the location on the Dock where you want it to be stored, as shown in Figure 1.5. (Application icons must be placed on the left side of the dividing line.) When you add an application icon to the Dock, an alias to it is created. As with the default application icons, you can click an icon to open the application and perform a second click to open its Dock menu.

1.5 Because I frequently use Firefox, I've added its icon to my Dock.

Note

The Dock has two icons that you can't move at all: The Finder and Trash/Eject. Other than these two endpoints, you can change all of the other Dock icons as much as you like. You can't change the location of the dividing line, though; it moves to the left or to the right based on the number of icons on either side of it.

You can rearrange the application icons installed on the Dock by dragging them to the location where you want them to reside. Just as when you install a new icon, when you move an existing icon between two others, they separate so that you can place the icon you're moving where you want it.

You can remove an application icon from the Dock by dragging it up onto the Desktop and releasing the trackpad button. When you do this, the icon disappears in a puff of digital smoke and no longer appears on the Dock. Because the icons on the Dock are aliases, removing them doesn't affect the applications that they represent.

Genius

You can add multiple items to the Dock simultaneously by holding down the ⌘ key while you select each item you want to add, and then dragging them there.

When you place a folder's icon on the Dock, it becomes a stack. A stack has some special characteristics, which is why it isn't just called a folder (however, you can configure a stack to behave like a folder). Two stacks are installed on your Dock by default: Downloads and Documents. You can add any other folders to the Dock just as you would an application; simply drag and drop the icons where you want them. (Remember that folders and documents have to be placed on the right side of the dividing line.) You can also reorganize stack icons by dragging them around on the Dock and (as you probably guessed) you can remove them from the Dock by dragging their icons onto the Desktop.

Stack icons sometimes take on the icon of the most recent file that has been placed into them. For example, if you last downloaded a disk image file, the Downloads stack icon is the one for a disk image. When you place an image into your Pictures folder and have that folder installed on your Dock, its icon is a thumbnail of the last image you placed in it.

When you click a stack icon, its contents fan onto the Desktop if there are only a few of them, or open into a grid if there are many. You can access an item on the fan or grid by clicking it. You can open the folder's contents in a Finder window by clicking Open in Finder.

As mentioned earlier, you can also configure how an individual stack's icon behaves by using its contextual menu. Perform a secondary click on the stack icon and its menu appears, as shown in Figure 1.6.

1.6 Stacks have many configuration options.

Note All Dock settings are specific to each user account (see Chapter 2). One user's Dock settings do not affect another's.

The following options are included on the menu:

- **Sort by.** Choose the attribute by which you want the items in the stack to be sorted. For example, choose Date Added to have the most recently added content appear at the bottom of the fan (if the stack is set to fan, of course).

- **Display as.** Select Stack to have the icon look like a stack or Folder to replace the stack icon with the folder's icon. The only difference is that when you select Folder, you always see the folder's icon on the Dock, as opposed to the icon of the most recently added item, which is what you see when Stack is selected.

- **View content as.** Select Fan to see the default fan layout for the stack (until it contains too many items, at which point it uses the grid instead). Select Grid to have the folder's contents appear in a grid. Select List to display the contents in a list that looks similar to a mini-Finder window, as shown in Figure 1.7. This is useful for folders that contain subfolders because you can select a folder to move into it on another hierarchical menu. Select Automatic to have the Mac OS select the most appropriate view based on the folder's contents.

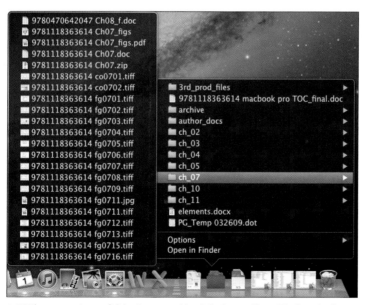

1.7 When you view a folder icon as a List, it behaves like a Finder window in Columns view.

14

- **Options.** Choose Remove from Dock to remove the icon from the Dock. Choose Show in Finder to open a Finder window showing the folder's contents.

- **Open.** Choose this command to open the folder on the Desktop.

Note

Another type of Dock icon is for windows you have minimized. You can move a minimized window icon within the folder side of the Dock, but its location is only temporary (it remains there only until you maximize or close the window). If you drag a minimized window from the Dock, it snaps back to the Dock. You remove minimized windows from the Dock by moving into or closing them.

Changing the Dock's appearance and behavior

The Dock offers several behaviors you can change to suit your preferences. The following steps walk you through how to change various aspects of the Dock's appearance:

1. **Choose Apple menu ⇨ System Preferences.**

2. **Click the Dock icon.** The Dock pane appears.

3. **Drag the Size slider to the right to make the default Dock larger, or to the left to make it smaller.** This sets the size of the Dock when no applications that aren't installed on it are open and no windows are currently minimized. The Dock changes size automatically as you open applications and minimize windows.

Note

When your MacBook Pro is connected to an external display, the Dock always appears on the primary display.

4. **Select the Magnification check box if you want to magnify an area of the Dock when you point to it.** Drag the Magnification slider to the right to increase the level of magnification, or to the left to decrease it. This can make identifying items easier, especially if many items are on the Dock or when it is small.

5. **Select the position of the Dock on the Desktop by clicking Left, Bottom (default), or Right.**

6. **On the Minimize using pop-up menu, select Genie Effect to pull windows down to the Dock when you minimize them, or Scale Effect to shrink them down into the Dock.**

7. **If you want to be able to minimize a window by double-clicking its title bar, select the Double-click a window's title bar to minimize check box.**

8. **If you prefer windows that you minimize to move onto the related application's icon instead of to a separate icon on the right side of the dividing line, select the Minimize windows into application icon check box.** With this setting enabled, you must open the application icon's menu and select a minimized window to move back into it, or move back into the application and use its Window menu to choose the minimized window (unless the minimized window is also the application's active window, in which case you move into it directly).

9. **By default, application icons bounce as the application opens.** If you don't want this to happen, deselect the Animate opening applications check box.

10. **If you want the Dock to be hidden automatically when you aren't pointing to it, select the Automatically hide and show the Dock check box.** If you set the Dock so that it is hidden except when you point to it, you can use more of your display. When this behavior is enabled and you point to the Dock's location, it pops onto the Desktop and you can use it. When you move off the Dock, it is hidden again.

11. **To show the glowing dot icon under running applications, select the Show indicator lights for open applications check box.** These lights are useful because they help you more easily identify open applications when you glance at the Dock (remember, when applications are hidden, you don't see any of their windows).

Genius

You can turn Dock Hiding on or off by pressing Option+⌘+D.

Using the Launchpad

If you've used an iPhone, iPod touch, or iPad, you already know how to use the Launchpad on the Mac because it works in exactly the same manner as the Home pages on those devices. The Launchpad provides one-click access to your applications, and you can organize the Launchpad to make it work efficiently for you.

Note

One difference between the Home pages on Apple mobile devices and the Launchpad is that only application icons can be stored on the Launchpad, whereas on an iPhone, iPod touch, or iPad, you can also store web page icons.

Click the Launchpad icon on the Dock (it is located just to the right of the Finder icon by default) or perform a three-finger pinch (three fingers pinched against your thumb) on the trackpad. This preference is enabled by default on the Trackpad pane of the System Preferences application. The Launchpad then fills the Desktop and you see icons on the current page, as shown in Figure 1.8. To move to a different page, drag two fingers on the trackpad to the left or to the right. As you drag, the page flips to the next or previous page.

1.8 The Launchpad provides easy access to all of your applications.

Note You'll notice that the Dock remains visible if it isn't hidden, or becomes visible if it is hidden when the Launchpad is open. You can also use the Application Switcher while the Launchpad is displayed.

To open an application, click its icon. The Launchpad closes and you move into that application. Click on a folder to access the applications stored within it. The folder then expands and you see the icons it contains, as shown in Figure 1.9. Click the icon you want to use. To close the Launchpad without opening an application, click on it (but not on an application's icon), perform a three-finger unpinch gesture on the trackpad, or press Esc.

1.9 To access an app stored in a folder, click the folder's icon, and then click the application's icon.

Genius

The Launchpad is actually an application. Therefore, you can add its icon to the sidebar, open it by double-clicking its icon in the Application folder, and so on.

By default, the Launchpad contains icons for all of the Mac OS X default applications. When you download and install applications from the Mac App Store application or from the Desktop, those icons are automatically added to the Launchpad. You can organize the icons on your Launchpad to make accessing them easier and faster.

To change the location of icons on the Launchpad, open it and drag the icon you want to move. You can change its location on the current page, or drag it off the screen to the left or right to move it to another page (you have to linger at the edge of the screen until the page changes). As you move one icon between others, they shift to make room for the one you are moving. When the icon is over the location you want, release it.

To create a new folder, drag one icon on top of another. Launchpad creates a new folder and tries to name it according to the type of applications you place together. The folder opens and you see the icons stored there. To change the folder name, select it. When it is highlighted, type its new name, as shown in Figure 1.10.

1.10 You can organize icons on your Launchpad in folders.

You can place icons within existing folders by dragging them on top of the folder in which you want to place them. You can also reorganize icons within folders by dragging them around when the folder is open. To remove an icon from a folder, drag it outside of the folder window until the folder closes. To delete a folder, drag all of its icons outside of it; when you remove the second to last icon, the folder disappears (folders can't contain just one icon).

You can remove applications (if they aren't default Apple applications, that is) by clicking and holding an icon. After a moment, the icons begin to jiggle and the Remove button (x) appears. Click the Remove button and then click Delete at the prompt. Removing an application from the Launchpad also deletes it from your MacBook Pro, so make sure that you don't want it before completing this action. To return the Launchpad to normal without deleting an application, click outside of any application icon.

Note To remove applications that you didn't download from the App Store, run the application's uninstaller or drag it to the trash, and then empty it.

Configuring the Dashboard

The Dashboard is an application that is a collection of mini-applications called *widgets*. By default, the Dashboard application is always running, so its widgets are always available to you.

The following is a list of the default ways in which you can activate the Dashboard:

- **Press Fn+F12 (default).**
- **Click the Dashboard icon on the Dock.**
- **Open the Dashboard Dock icon menu and choose Show Dashboard.**

- **Double-click the Dashboard's icon in the Applications folder.**
- **Open Mission Control and move all the way to the left.**
- **Perform a three- or four-finger swipe all the way to the left.**
- **Double-click a widget's icon.**

When you activate the Dashboard, the widgets that are configured to open when it is activated appear, as shown in Figure 1.11. You can then use those widgets or see their information.

1.11 When you open the Dashboard, you get instant access to a set of widgets.

When you finish using widgets, deactivate the Dashboard again by pressing Fn+F12, performing a three- or four-finger swipe, pressing Esc, or by clicking the right-facing arrow in the lower-right corner of the window. All of the widgets disappear, the Dashboard closes, and you return to your Desktop.

Setting the Dashboard keyboard shortcut and hot corner

You can set a keyboard shortcut that you press and a *hot corner* to which you can point, to open or close the Dashboard. Perform the following steps to configure these:

1. **Open the System Preferences application.**
2. **Click the Mission Control icon.** The Mission Control pane appears.
3. **Click the Hot Corners button.** The Hot Corners sheet appears.
4. **To set a hot corner, use the pop-up menu located next to each corner of the Desktop thumbnail at the top of the pane.** Select Dashboard for the corner you want to make the hot corner. Click OK and the sheet closes.

5. **To change the Dashboard keyboard shortcut, use the Show Dashboard pop-up menu to choose the function or modifier keys you want.** You can also use the menu to the right of the Show Dashboard pop-up menu to set the shortcut to be a secondary or middle mouse-click.

Customizing the Dashboard

One of the nice things about the Dashboard is that you can configure the exact set of widgets that you want to use and how they appear on the screen. Follow these steps to customize your Dashboard:

1. **Activate the Dashboard.** The widgets that are currently configured to open appear.

2. **Click the Add (+) button in the lower-left corner of the screen.** The widget page opens and you see all of the widgets installed on your MacBook Pro. At the bottom of each icon, you see the name of the widget, as shown in Figure 1.12. Widgets are shown in alphabetical order from left to right and top to bottom.

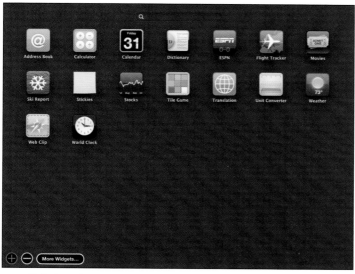

1.12 Click the Add (+) button to open this page and see all of the widgets you have installed on your MacBook Pro.

Genius

Each time you add a widget, a new version of it is added to the Dashboard. This is useful for widgets that you configure with specific information, such as a location, like the Weather widget.

Note Many widgets (such as the Weather and World Clock) require an Internet connection to work. Others, such as the Calculator, do not.

3. **To add a widget to your Dashboard, click its icon.** You move back to the Dashboard and see the widget you added.

4. **Move the widgets around the screen until they are where you want them to be when you activate the Dashboard.**

5. **Close any widgets that you don't want to open when you activate the Dashboard by clicking the Remove (-) button at the bottom of the Dashboard.** Then, click the widget's Close button (the x in the upper-left corner of each widget's window). The widget disappears from the Dashboard but remains on the widget bar.

6. **Click the Remove (-) button when you're finished**.

Configuring widgets

To see if a widget has configuration options, move the pointer over it. If it has options, the Info button (usually a lowercase *i* that is sometimes in a circle) appears, as shown in Figure 1.13. The location of the Info button varies and, sometimes, it is hard to see, so look closely when you hover over a widget.

1.13 Configure a widget by clicking the Info button. In this example, it's in the lower-right corner.

Note On some widgets, it isn't necessary to hover over them to see the Info button.

When you click the Info button, the widget's configuration tools appear, as shown in Figure 1.14. You can use these to make the widget work or look the way you want it to. When you are finished, click Done and the widget is updated accordingly. You should always check out the Info options for any widgets that you use because they can probably make them even more useful to you.

Installing more widgets

The Dashboard includes quite a few widgets, but there are thousands available on the Apple widget website that you can download and install. Follow these steps to get and install new widgets:

1. **Open the Dashboard.**

2. **Click the Add (+) button.**

3. **Click the More Widgets button.** Your default web browser opens and takes you to the Apple widgets web page, shown in Figure 1.15.

4. **Browse or search until you find a widget you want to try.**

5. **Download the widget.** In most cases, the widget is downloaded directly. After it downloads, you're prompted to install it. If this is the case for you, skip to step 7.

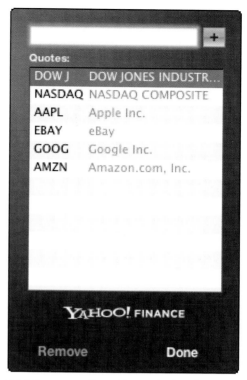

1.14 You can configure the stocks that the Stocks widget tracks for you.

Note If you don't have Gatekeeper set to allow applications to be installed from anywhere, the widget you are trying to download may be blocked. You can temporarily disable the Gatekeeper while you install a widget. See Chapter 13 for more information.

6. **If the file is downloaded to your Downloads folder, move to and open it.** Widget files have the file extension .wdgt. If you don't see this extension, you might have to double-click the file you downloaded to expand it.

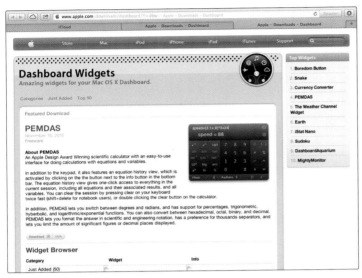

1.15 Got widgets?

7. **Click Install at the prompt.** The widget is added to the widgets page.

8. **Add and configure the new widget to access it from your Dashboard.**

Creating your own web widgets

To create a widget like those you see on the Apple widget website, you have to do some basic programming. However, you can create your own widgets by capturing parts of websites.

Note To create web widgets, you must be using Safari as your web browser.

Follow these steps to create a widget from a website:

1. **Open Safari.**

2. **Move to a web page containing information or tools that you want to capture in a widget.**

3. **Choose File ⇨ Open in Dashboard.** A selection box and capture toolbar appear, as shown in Figure 1.16.

1.16 Use the selection box to choose the part of the web page that you want to capture in a widget.

4. **Make the selection box enclose the part of the page that you want to be a widget by dragging the box to the general area you want to capture.** Next, click the trackpad button to lock the selection box, and then drag its resize handles to enclose the exact part of the page you want.

5. **Click the Add button on the toolbar.** The Dashboard opens and the part of the page you selected becomes a widget, as shown in Figure 1.17.

1.17 I captured a section of a webpage as a widget so I can move back to it easily.

6. **Click the new widget's Info button.**

7. **Use the resulting tools to select a theme.** The theme determines the border of the widget.

8. **If the clip has audio and you want it to play only while the Dashboard is open, select the Only play audio in Dashboard check box.**

9. **Click Done.**

10. **Place the widget on your Dashboard.**

The web capture selection tool captures a defined portion of the web page, based on what you select. If the structure of the web page changes, it might shift what's shown in the widget. You then must re-create the widget to fix any problems. You can remove a web widget the same as other widgets. Unlike the others, though, when you close a widget you've captured, it's gone forever.

Genius If the widget isn't exactly what you want it to be, open the Info panel and click Edit. You can resize the widget's window to capture the part of the page you want to appear.

Managing Your Desktop with Mission Control

Mission Control is a tool that enables you to see and access anything on your Desktop. You can also create multiple Desktops (or *spaces*) that contain different collections of open windows. To activate Mission Control, click its icon on the Dock or swipe four fingers up the trackpad (the default gesture; see Chapter 5 for more information). You then see the thumbnails for the following items at the top of the screen, as shown in Figure 1.18:

- **Dashboard**

- **Your spaces, named as Desktop X (where X is a sequential number)**

- **Applications open in Full Screen mode**

1.18 Mission Control shows all of the open windows on your Desktops.

In the center part of the window, you see all of the windows open in the applications within the current Desktop. Windows are organized by application and you see the application's icon and name with its group. The Dock appears in its default location and you can use it just as you would when working outside of Mission Control. Mission Control also enables you to manage windows on a specific Desktop.

Managing windows on a Desktop

As you work on documents, move to websites, check your e-mail, choose tunes to listen to, and all of the other things you do on your MacBook Pro, you can accumulate a lot of open windows on your Desktop. This makes it easy to multitask so that you don't have to stop one activity to start another. The downside, though, is that it's easy to lose track of where the specific window you want is located, or you might have a hard time getting back to the Desktop.

Mission Control helps you manage screen clutter from open windows with the following three modes:

- **Hide all open windows**
- **Show an application's windows**
- **Show all windows on the current Desktop, all Desktops, the Dashboard, and Full Screen apps**

Each of these modes has a specific use and you access them in slightly different ways.

Hiding all open windows

Hiding all open windows is useful when the Desktop on which you are working is so cluttered, you have a hard time finding anything. To clear away all of your windows in one sweep, press the keyboard shortcut (in most cases, the default is Fn+F11; I cover how to set this later in this chapter). All of the windows are moved off the screen, leaving an uncluttered Desktop. If you look carefully at the shaded edges of the Desktop shown in Figure 1.19, you see the edges of the windows that have been moved off to the side.

1.19 Where, oh where, have all of my windows gone? If you look carefully at the shaded edges of the screen, you'll see them.

You can return your Desktop to its cluttered condition by pressing the keyboard shortcut (usually Fn+F11) again, or by clicking anywhere in the shaded borders of the Desktop. The windows slide back onto the visible part of the Desktop where you can use them again.

Showing application windows

When you are working with multiple windows in the same application, it can be tough to get back to a specific window if you can't see all of them at the same time. Press the keyboard shortcut (Control+down arrow, by default) or swipe down with four fingers (the default gesture) to see all open windows for the current application, as shown in Figure 1.20.

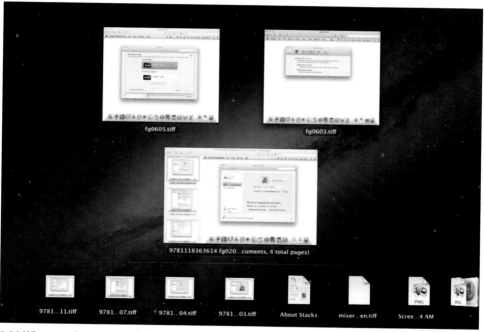

1.20 When you have many windows open in an application, Mission Control makes it easy to move into a specific one.

At the top of the screen, you see the windows that are currently open on the Desktop. Under these, you see the windows that are hidden or those that you worked with previously that are now closed (such as documents you have edited). To move into a window, click it; it is highlighted in blue when you move over it. The window becomes active (if it is for a closed document, the document opens) and moves to the front so that you can use it. The rest of the open application windows then move to their previous positions.

Genius

When you have all of the windows for an application showing, press Tab to quickly move through them. You can also press ⌘+Tab to open the Application Switcher bar, which shows all open applications, and then press ⌘+Tab to move to the application on which you want to focus. When you release the ⌘ key, the windows for the selected application appear.

Showing all windows

In this mode, you see Mission Control, as shown in Figure 1.21, which shows your Desktops, applications running in Full Screen mode, and the windows open in the active Desktop. The details of using Mission Control in this mode are provided later in this chapter.

1.21 In this mode, Mission Control enables you to access any open window and the Dashboard.

Using Desktops

As you use your MacBook Pro, it's likely that you'll develop sets of tasks that you work on at the same time. For example, you might use Word to create text and a graphics application to write a book. These kinds of activities invariably involve a lot of windows. While you can use Mission Control to manage all of the open windows for an application, it's not very efficient because you can only focus on one window at a time, so it can still take some work to get to the windows you want to use.

You can use Mission Control to create collections of applications and their windows on separate Desktops. This way, you can jump between sets easily and quickly. For example, if you use several Internet applications, you can create an Internet Desktop specifically for those, such as an e-mail application and web browser. To use your Internet applications, just open that Desktop and the windows are all in the positions you last left them. You might have another Desktop that contains Contacts and Calendar. You can then use these applications by switching to their Desktop. Multiple Desktops make moving to and using different sets of windows fast and easy. They also improve the efficiency with which you work.

Note Desktops are also referred to as *spaces*. Other spaces include applications in Full Screen mode and the Dashboard.

Configuring Mission Control

Now that you have a good understanding of Mission Control, you can configure it by setting your Mission Control preferences, and then creating the Desktops you want to use.

The following steps walk you through the process of configuring your Mission Control preferences:

1. **Open the Mission Control pane of the System Preferences application, as shown in Figure 1.22.**

2. **Deselect the Show Dashboard as a space check box if you don't want the Dashboard to be accessible via Mission Control.**

3. **If you don't want Mission Control to automatically rearrange spaces based on the ones you've used most recently, deselect that check box.**

4. **Deselect the When switching to an application, switch to a space with open windows for the application check box if you don't prefer that.** If you select this option, when you change applications, you also move into the Desktop in which the application has windows open.

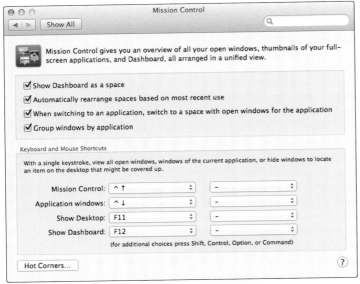

Configure Mission Control preferences to tweak how its features work.

5. **In the Keyboard and Mouse Shortcuts section, configure the keyboard shortcuts and mouse clicks to activate Mission Control and all application windows, and show the Desktop and Dashboard.** Use the menus on the left to set key combinations (the defaults are Fn+F9 through Fn+F12) and the menus on the right to set mouse-clicks.

6. **Click the Hot Corners button to open the Hot Corners sheet.** Use this sheet to set an action to occur when you point to that corner of the screen. For example, if you want the Launchpad to open when you move the pointer to the upper-right corner of the screen, select Launchpad on the menu in that location.

Genius

To add keyboard modifiers to the shortcut keys or hot corners, press a key (such as the ⌘ key) while you have a menu open. The symbols for the keys that you press are then shown next to the function keys. If you select one of these combinations, you need to hold down the same modifier keys when you click the appropriate function key to activate the command.

Once you have set the Mission Control preferences, you are ready to set up the Desktops you want to use. First, create a Desktop, and then add the applications you want to include in that space.

Follow these steps to get set up:

1. **Open Mission Control, such as by swiping four fingers up on the trackpad.** The Dashboard (if included), current Desktops, and applications in Full Screen mode are shown at the top of the screen. The applications and windows open in the current Desktop are shown in the center of the screen.

2. **Point to the upper-right corner of the screen until the Add Space button (+) appears, and then click it, as shown in Figure 1.23.** A new space called Desktop *X* (where *X* is a sequential number) appears. Repeat this step until you have created all the Desktops you want to be available.

1.23 When you click the Add button, a new space (Desktop) is created.

3. **Click the icon for one of the Desktops you created, as shown in Figure 1.24.** It becomes active and ready for you to configure. You see any open applications that are configured to be available in all Desktops.

1.24 Click the Desktop you want to configure.

4. **To add an application to the Desktop, perform a secondary click on its Dock icon and the resulting menu.** Choose Options, and then select one of the following choices:

   • **All Desktops.** This adds the application to all Desktops so it is available no matter which one you are using.

   • **This Desktop.** This adds the application to the current Desktop.

   • **None.** This removes the application from all Desktops so it behaves independent of the Desktop you are using.

Note

If the application is already assigned to a space, you also see Desktop *X* (where *X* is a sequential number) on the menu indicating to which space the application is assigned.

5. **Repeat steps 3 and 4 until you've configured all of the Desktops you want to use.**

6. **To remove a Desktop you no longer need, open Mission Control, point to the Desktop, and then click the Remove button (x).** The Desktop is deleted, and any applications assigned to it are set to All Desktops.

Managing your Desktop

After you have configured Mission Control, you can perform any of the following to manage your Desktops:

- **To change spaces, swipe three or four fingers (depending on your trackpad's settings) to the left on the trackpad to move to a later space, or to the right to move into an earlier space.** As you drag, you switch between Desktops and applications open in Full Screen mode. When you move all the way to the left, you open the Dashboard (unless you disabled the preference that includes the Dashboard as a space). When you stop on a space, it becomes active and the windows open within it appear the same as they were the last time you used that Desktop.

Note

The gestures or keyboard combinations you use to work with Mission Control depend on the preferences you set using the Trackpad, Mission Control, and other panes of the System Preferences application.

- **To open Mission Control, swipe four fingers up the trackpad.** Mission Control opens, and the thumbnails of the spaces you configured are at the top of the screen. The current space is highlighted with a white box. You can jump into a space by clicking its thumbnail (you move into the window you last used in that space), or by clicking in a window that is open in the current space.

- **To move into a specific window, move to the space in which it resides.** Click inside the window into which you want to move.

- **When you switch to an application that is part of a space, you move into that space unless you disabled the default preference.**

- **When there are too many Desktops and Full Screen applications for the names of each to be displayed, point to a Desktop or application; it is magnified and its name appears.**

- **To use an application in all spaces, configure it for All Desktops.**

- **To close Mission Control without changing spaces or windows, swipe four fingers down the trackpad or press Esc.**

Genius

You can reorganize your spaces by dragging their icons at the top of the Mission Control screen.

Using Applications in Full Screen Mode

Many applications, such as Safari, iMovie, Aperture, and so on, need all the Desktop room they can get to work more efficiently. As mentioned previously, applications can appear in Full Screen mode. In this mode, the application takes over the entire screen and its menu bars are hidden, as shown in Figure 1.25.

1.25 Using an application in Full Screen mode gives it the most screen real estate possible.

Explore Full Screen mode in applications that you use frequently and see if it helps you use them more efficiently. The following pointers may help you:

- **Activate Full Screen.** Choose View ➪ Enter Full Screen or press Control+⌘+F. The application's current window fills the screen and the menu bars are hidden.

- **Reveal the menu bars.** Hover at the top of the screen. After a few seconds, the menu bars appear and you can access them just as you do when you aren't working in Full Screen mode.

● **As covered earlier in this chapter, applications running in Full Screen mode appear as spaces in Mission Control.**

● **Exit Full Screen mode.** Choose View ⇨ Exit Full Screen or press Control+⌘+F.

Configuring Notifications

Many applications use notifications to communicate information to you. For example, Mail notifies you when you receive new messages, Calendar alerts you to upcoming events, Reminders reminds you about various things, and so on. The Mac OS X Notification Center provides a central point of control for, and configuration of, the notifications with which you work.

Working with the Notification Center

To view the collection of notifications you have received, click the Notification Center menu located on the right end of the menu bar. The Notification Center pane appears, as shown in Figure 1.26. Notifications are grouped by the application from which they come. You can scroll the list to see all of the notifications you have received. The order in which the groups are shown is determined by a preference setting (which is covered later in this chapter). When this is set to Manually, you can drag sections up or down the list.

To see the details of a notification, click it. You then move into the related application and

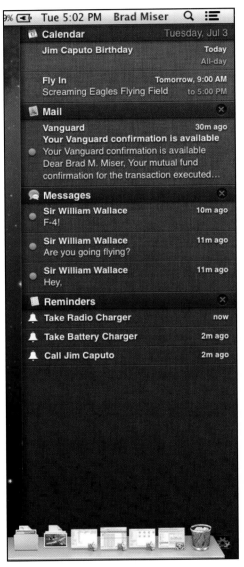

1.26 The Notification Center provides a one-stop shop for the information that various applications are managing for you.

can work with the information. For example, if you click an e-mail notification, you move into Mail and can read the full message.

As covered later in this chapter, you can enable or disable notifications, and configure them for specific applications. Applications also send individual notifications to the Desktop, such as when Calendar sends an alert about an event. The following are several options you can configure for these notifications:

- **Badges.** These are counters that appear on an application's icon to let you know how many of something you have, such as e-mail messages, texts, updates for applications, and so on.

- **Banners.** These are small messages that appear in the upper-right corner of the screen, as shown in Figure 1.27, when something happens, such as when you receive a message. Banners contain the icon of the app from which they come, and they can also show you a preview. They are nice because they don't inter-

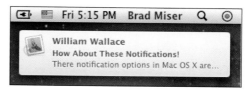

1.27 Banners are good because they don't require any action on your part.

fere with what you are doing. If you ignore a banner, it disappears after a few seconds. If you click it, you move into the application that produced the banner. If you receive a new banner while a previous one is still visible on the screen, the second one displaces the first so that the latest one is displayed.

- **Alerts.** This is another means that applications use to communicate with you. There are alerts for many types of events, such as texts, reminders, missed call notifications, and so on. The main difference between a banner and an alert is that alerts remain on the screen until you take some action, such as clicking Close or Snooze to dismiss an alert for an event, as shown in Figure 1.28.

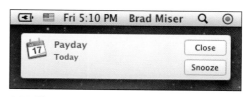

1.28 Alerts require action to get rid of them.

- **Sounds.** These are audible indicators that something has happened. For example, when something happens in the Game Center, you can be notified via a sound.

Configuring notifications

You can configure your notifications on the Notifications pane of the System Preferences application, shown in Figure 1.29. The applications for which you can configure notifications are shown in
the pane on the left side of the window. When you select an application, its notification options are
shown in the right pane of the window. You can configure each application's options individually.

1.29 The Notifications pane enables you to configure how applications notify you.

The following are some highlights and suggestions about configuring notifications:

- **Use the alert style buttons to configure the type of notifications the application
  uses.** The options are: None, Banners, or Alerts.

- **Use the Show in Notification Center check box and menu to determine if the application's
  notifications are shown in the Notification Center, and if so, how many are shown.** If this is
  not selected, notifications from the application do not appear in the Notification Center.

- **If you want the application's icon on the Dock (or elsewhere) to display a badge when
  you have new information, such as new messages, select the Badge app icon check box.**

- **To disable the sound associated with an application's notifications, deselect the
  Play sound when receiving notifications check box.**

- **Use the Sort Notification Center menu to determine how applications are listed in
  the Notification Center pane.** Choose By time if you want the most recent information
  to appear toward the top of the pane, or Manually if you want to manually configure the
  order by dragging application sections up or down the pane.

Genius

To disable alerts and banners, scroll to the top of the Notification Center and set the Do Not Disturb switch to the On position. All alerts and banners are suppressed until you set the switch to the Off position again.

Working with Displays

Current MacBook Pros have 13- or 15-inch displays. No matter which display size you have, more is always better. Fortunately, you can maximize the amount of information you see on your MacBook Pro screen by configuring its display. For even more working room, you can attach and use an external display, or broadcast your MacBook's output to an Apple TV using AirPlay. For the ultimate in Desktop space, you can connect your MacBook Pro to a projector. When you use an external display or projector, you can display the same image on the MacBook Pro and the external device, or you can expand your Desktop over both displays. You can also configure the Desktop picture on your displays to make your MacBook Pro's appearance more interesting.

Configuring the MacBook Pro display

While the physical size of the MacBook Pro screen is fixed, the amount of information that can be displayed on it (its *resolution*) is not. Setting the appropriate resolution is a matter of choosing the largest that you can view comfortably with no eyestrain. There are standard resolutions you can use, but which of these are available to you depends on the specific MacBook Pro you are using. For example, the 13-inch model has a different set of resolutions than the 15-inch model. Likewise, models with Retina displays support yet a different set of options. Follow these steps to find your maximum resolution:

1. **Open the System Preferences application.**

2. **Click the Displays icon.** The Displays pane appears, as shown in Figure 1.30. The name shown at the top of the pane matches the display it configures.

3. **Click the Display tab if it's not already selected.**

4. **To use the resolution that is optimal for the internal display, select Best for built-in display and skip to step 7.** The display's resolution is set to what Apple considers optimal for the display's size.

5. **To manually select a resolution, select Scaled.** In the Resolutions section, you see all of the resolutions supported by your MacBook Pro display. Resolutions are shown as the number of horizontal pixels by the number of vertical pixels, such as 1024 × 768. Larger values have a higher resolution. Some resolutions are stretched so that they fill the screen (the MacBook Pro has a widescreen format display).

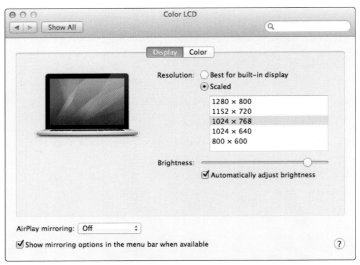

1.30 Use the Displays pane to maximize the amount of room you have on your Desktop, while still being comfortable for you to view.

6. **Click a resolution.** The screen updates to the resolution you selected.

Genius

If you see a warning prompt when you select a resolution, it's usually a good idea to heed it. This prevents problems with viewing your Desktop or returning to a previous resolution.

7. **Drag the Brightness slider to the right to make the screen brighter, or to the left to make it dimmer.**

8. **To have your MacBook Pro automatically adjust the brightness based on the ambient light, select the Automatically adjust brightness check box.**

9. **Hide the System Preferences application by pressing ⌘+H.**

Note

MacBook Pros with Retina displays don't support resolutions in the same way as those without them. On a machine with Retina displays, you can choose the Scaled option, but instead of selecting an actual resolution, you choose different scales. They look like different resolutions because the text and images change relative size the same as they do when you change the resolution.

10. **Open several windows on the Desktop.**

11. **If you can see the information on the screen comfortably, move back into the System Preferences application and select a higher resolution.**

12. **Look at the open windows again.** If you can still see the information comfortably, repeat steps 10 and 11 until the information gets too small to read comfortably, or you reach the maximum resolution.

13. **If the information in the windows is too small to read comfortably, move back to a lower resolution.**

Connecting and configuring an external display with a cable

One truth about working with computers is that you can never have too much screen space. In addition to making your documents and windows larger so that you can see more of their contents, more screen space helps you work more efficiently because you can have more windows open at the same time.

As I covered earlier, one way to gain more display space is to make the resolution as large as you can comfortably view it to maximize the number of pixels on the screen, and thus, the amount of information displayed there. At some point, you'll reach a maximum amount of information on the screen due to the maximum resolution of the MacBook Pro or because the information at a higher resolution becomes too small for you to view comfortably.

To add more screen space to your MacBook Pro (which can support many different displays and resolutions), you can connect an external display. You can use it in two ways: As an extension of your Desktop so that you can open additional windows on it, or you can use *video mirroring*, which means the same information appears on both displays.

When choosing an external display, the two most important considerations are size and cost. Larger displays are better because they give you more working space. However, they also tend to be more expensive, depending on the specific brand you choose. In most cases, if you choose the largest display you can afford from a reputable manufacturer, such as Apple, ViewSonic, or Samsung, you'll be in good shape.

To add an external display, you connect it to the MacBook Pro Thunderbolt port. To do this, you need a Mini DisplayPort to DVI adapter that converts the Thunderbolt connection to the standard

DVI connector used on most modern displays. You can also use the Mini DisplayPort to VGA adapter to use your MacBook Pro with older displays.

Follow these steps to attach an external display to a MacBook Pro:

1. **Connect one end of the display's video cable to the Mini DisplayPort to DVI, and the other end to the DVI port on the display.**

2. **Plug the Mini DisplayPort to DVI Adapter into the Thunderbolt port.**

3. **Connect the display to a power source.**

4. **Power up the display.**

Note Apple makes a display that is designed to work with your MacBook Pro. In addition to having a Mini DisplayPort connector, it also has additional USB ports, a power adapter, speakers, and a camera. This display converts your MacBook Pro into a Desktop workstation.

Once an external display is connected to your MacBook Pro, follow these steps to configure it:

1. **Open the System Preferences application.**

2. **Click the Displays icon.** A Displays pane opens on both the MacBook Pro and external displays. The name of the pane on the MacBook Pro internal display is Color LCD. The name of the pane on the external display is the name of that display. Also, notice that the Displays pane on the primary display (by default, the MacBook Pro display) contains the Arrangement tab.

3. **Click the Arrangement tab, shown in Figure 1.31, on the Displays pane on the MacBook Pro screen.** You see an icon representation of each display. The display marked with the menu bar at the top is the primary display which, by definition, is the one on which the menu bar appears.

4. **Drag the external display's icon so that it is on the left or right side of the MacBook Pro display's icon.** This should match the physical location of the display compared to the MacBook Pro.

5. **If you want the external display to be the primary one, drag the menu bar from the MacBook Pro display's icon onto that of the external display.** When you release the trackpad button, the menu bar jumps to the external display. Windows that were open on the MacBook Pro display move onto the external display, and vice versa.

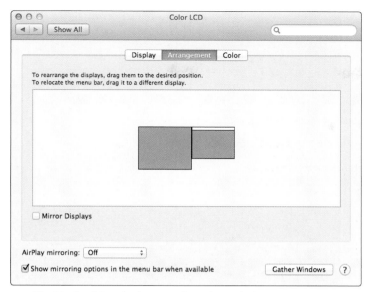

1.31 The MacBook Pro display is on the right (with the menu bar at the top), indicating that it is the primary display), while the external display is on the left.

6. **Select the Display pane for the external display.**

7. **Select the resolution for the external display from the list of those available.**

8. **If the Refresh rate menu appears, choose the highest rate available.**

9. **Quit the System Preferences application.**

You can now use the space on the external display like you use the internal display. To place a window on the external display, drag it from the MacBook Pro display onto the external one. You can move windows, the pointer, and other items from one display to the other just as you can move them around the MacBook Pro internal display. You can configure windows on each display so that you can see many at the same time. For example, you might want your primary documents open on the external display and your e-mail application open on the MacBook Pro display. The menu bar remains on the primary display, so if you do most of your work on the external one, you might want to make it the primary display to make menu access easier.

Genius

If you click Gather Windows on the Display pane, each pane is moved onto the primary display.

If the resolutions are significantly different between the two displays, you see a big change in appearance when you move a window between them. You might have to resize a window on one display that was the right size on the other. To stop using the external display, disconnect it from the MacBook Pro. If it was the primary display, the MacBook Pro display becomes the primary one. Any open windows on the external display move onto the MacBook Pro display.

Note Applications in Full Screen mode don't work that well with multiple displays. When in Full Screen mode, an application takes over both displays. One shows the application's windows while the other just has a background. However, you can move elements of the application, such as the media browser in Apple applications, onto the secondary display. This enables you to use all of the primary display for documents on which you are working.

Connecting and configuring an external display with AirPlay

AirPlay enables a MacBook Pro to wirelessly broadcast its video to an Apple TV. This is a great way to display your MacBook Pro's output on a larger display, such as an HDTV. To use AirPlay, your MacBook Pro must be on the same network as the Apple TV. When this is the case, using AirPlay is a snap.

Follow these steps to set up an external display with AirPlay:

1. **Power up the Apple TV and configure the display to which it is connected.** If your MacBook Pro and the Apple TV are on the same network, they will find each other automatically.

Note AirPlay requires that the devices be on the same network and that the network have the specifications required to transmit AirPlay. If your MacBook Pro and Apple TV are on the same network, but no AirPlay devices are detected, odds are that the router providing the network is not configured to support AirPlay. You'll need to reconfigure the router or use a different network. Also, AirPlay has to be enabled on the Apple TV (Settings ⇨ AirPlay ⇨ AirPlay On).

2. **On the Displays pane, choose Apple TV on the AirPlay mirroring menu.** Your MacBook Pro Desktop appears on the Apple TV display.

3. **Open the AirPlay Mirroring menu shown in Figure 1.32.**

4. **To set the image size on the Apple TV display to match the resolution of your MacBook Pro, choose This Mac.** To fit the resolution to the display's size, choose Apple TV.

When you use AirPlay, anything that appears on your Desktop also appears on the Apple TV display. To stop using AirPlay, choose Turn Off AirPlay Mirroring on the AirPlay Mirroring menu.

Using a projector

If you make presentations, conduct training, or just want a really big display, a projector is

1.32 Use this menu to configure your MacBook's output to an Apple TV.

the way to go. With one of these, you can broadcast your MacBook Pro display to very large sizes for easy viewing by an audience. Using a projector is similar to using an external display, so if you can work with those, you can work with a projector.

Genius If you are using an unfamiliar projector, set the MacBook Pro resolution to a relatively low value, such as 1024 × 768. If the projector doesn't display, reduce the resolution to see whether it starts displaying. Once it displays, increase the resolution until the projector is no longer capable of displaying the image.

Purchasing a projector is a bit more complicated and, usually, more expensive than purchasing a display. The following list includes a few of the many things to consider when buying a projector:

- **Size.** A smaller projector is easier to carry and, as you move through airports and such, this is very important. Smaller projectors of the same quality are more expensive than larger ones, so find a balance between portability and price.

- **Resolution.** There is more variability in the resolution of projectors than displays. At the lower end of the price range, you'll find projectors that are capable of only 800 × 600 resolution. Many Mac applications can't even run at a resolution this low. The lowest resolution you should consider for a projector is 1024 × 768 (also called XGA). Higher resolutions are better, but also more expensive.

45

- **Brightness.** The brightness of projectors is specified in lumens. Projectors with higher lumen ratings are generally able to throw larger and brighter images farther. How many lumens you need depends on a lot of factors, most of which are probably beyond your control (such as the brightness levels of the location in which you'll be using the projector).

- **Throw range.** This measures the closest and farthest distances at which the projector can be used.

- **Video interface.** Like displays, the options for projectors include DVI or VGA. However, most projectors provide a number of other input options, such as component, composite, and S-video. These are important if you use the projector with other sources, such as a DVD player.

- **Bulb life.** Like all other bulbs, the one in a projector eventually fails and must be replaced. Unlike bulbs for lights, you can expect to pay hundreds of dollars for a replacement projector bulb, so try to get one with a long life.

- **Cost.** Expect to pay several hundred dollars for a good-quality projector that has at least 1024 × 768 resolution.

Note

Some projectors automatically select the appropriate input source and some don't. If the projector isn't projecting an image, use its source menu to select the source to which your MacBook Pro is connected. You can also use the Detect Displays command on the Displays menu or on the Display pane of the System Preferences application to see if that restores an image on the projector.

Using a projector is very similar to using an external display. You connect a projector to the MacBook Pro using a Mini DisplayPort to DVI or Mini DisplayPort to VGA adapter, and then use the Displays pane to set the projector's resolution. However, in most cases, you want to use video mirroring so that the image being projected is the same as that you see on the MacBook Pro Desktop. This is the usual arrangement for presentations because you can face the audience and view the MacBook Pro display, while the audience sees the same image through the projector.

You can activate video mirroring by opening the Displays menu and selecting Turn On Display Mirroring. The projector then takes on the same resolution as the MacBook Pro internal display.

Caution

You can use the Show mirroring options in menu bar menu on the Display pane to determine when the menu is shown on the menu bar. Choose one of the following options: Automatically to have Mac OS X automatically display the menu options; Always to have them always displayed; or Never to hide the menu.

Setting a Desktop picture

I confess that this section has nothing to do with efficiency. However, there's more to life than being efficient. Because you stare at your Desktop so much, you might as well have something interesting to look at, which is where Desktop pictures come in. You can set any image to be your Desktop picture. You can use the default images included with Mac OS X, image files you create or download from the Internet, or (best of all) photos from your iPhoto or Aperture libraries. You can also configure your MacBook Pro so that the Desktop picture changes over time to keep it even more interesting.

Perform these steps to configure your Desktop picture:

1. **Open the System Preferences application.**

2. **Click the Desktop & Screen Saver icon.** The Desktop & Screen Saver pane appears.

3. **Click the Desktop tab.** The Desktop picture tools appear. On the center-left side of the pane are the sources of images from which you can select pictures for your Desktop, including Apple (default images), iPhoto (images from your iPhoto library), Aperture (images from your Aperture library), and Folders (your Pictures folder plus any others you add).

Genius

When your MacBook Pro is connected to an external display, the Secondary Desktop pane appears on that display. You can use that pane to set the Desktop pictures on the external display as you can for the internal display. You can have the same Desktop picture settings, or completely different images and display options.

4. **Expand the source of images you want to work with by clicking its Expansion triangle.** The contents of that source appear. For example, if you expand the Apple source, you see its folders. If you expand the iPhoto source, you see Events, Photos, photo albums, and so on.

5. **Select a source of images in the left pane of the window.** Thumbnails of the images in that source appear in the right pane of the window. For example, if you select the Nature folder under the Apple source, you see thumbnails of the nature images included by default.

6. **Click the image that you want to apply to the Desktop.** The image fills the Desktop and you see it in the image well at the top of the Desktop pane, as shown in Figure 1.33.

1.33 I've selected an image from my iPhoto library as my Desktop picture.

Genius

You can set a different Desktop picture for each of your Desktops. Use Mission Control to move to the Desktop for which you want to set a picture, set it, and then switch to the next Desktop.

7. **If the image you selected isn't the same proportion as your current screen resolution, use the pop-up menu that appears just above the thumbnail pane to choose how you want the image to be scaled to the screen.** For example, choose Fit to Screen to have photos scaled so that they fit the screen, Fill Screen to have photos scaled to fill the screen, Tile to have images that are smaller than the Desktop fill the Desktop space as tiles, and so on.

8. **If the image doesn't fill the screen, click the Color button that appears to the right of the menu when it can be used.** The Color Picker opens.

9. **Use the Color Picker to choose the background color that appears behind photos when they don't fill the Desktop.**

10. **To change the Desktop picture automatically, select the Change picture check box.** This causes the images in the source selected on the Source list to be applied to the Desktop according to your settings.

Note

When you configure the picture to be changed automatically, the image in the image well is replaced by the recycle symbol.

11. **On the pop-up menu, choose how often you want the picture to change.** The options include different time intervals or when certain events occur.

12. **If you want images to be selected randomly instead of by the order in which they appear in the source, select the Random order check box.** A new image from the selected source is applied to the Desktop according to the timing you selected.

13. **To make the menu bar translucent so that you can see the Desktop picture behind it, select the Translucent menu bar check box.** When this option is not selected, the menu bar becomes a solid color.

14. **Quit the System Preferences application.** Enjoy your Desktop.

Genius

You can use any folder as a source of Desktop pictures by clicking the Add (+) button located at the bottom of the source list. Use the resulting dialog to move to and select the folder containing the images you want to use. After you click the Choose button, that folder appears as a source on the list and you can work with it just like the default sources.

How Do I Manage User Accounts?

Mac OS X is a multiuser operating system, meaning that your MacBook Pro is designed to be used by multiple people. Each person has his own user account that includes a Home folder for storing files; system preferences for options such as Dock configuration, the Desktop picture, and screen resolution; application preferences; and security settings. When a user logs in, Mac OS X configures itself based on that user's specific preferences and, in effect, becomes personalized. Understanding how to create and manage user accounts is an important part of getting the most out of your MacBook Pro.

Working with User Accounts

You use the System Preferences application to create and manage most of the user accounts on your MacBook Pro. Before jumping in, make sure that you understand all of the following types of user accounts:

- **Administrator.** This is the second most powerful type of user account. When logged in under an Administrator account, you have complete access to the System Preferences application and can make changes to the operating system, including creating and managing user accounts or changing network settings. Administrators can also install software at the system level, where it can be accessed by all users. The user account that you create the first time you start your MacBook Pro is an Administrator account.

- **Standard.** When logged in under a Standard user account, a user can only make changes related to that specific account. For example, someone using a Standard user account can change her Desktop picture and application preferences, but she can't install applications that are available to all users or create other user accounts. Standard user accounts can install applications using drag and drop in the Applications folder within their Home folders.

Note   By default, your MacBook Pro uses the Automatic Login feature. This automatically logs in the default user account (the one you created when you first started your MacBook Pro, unless you've changed it) as soon as you start your computer, which can disguise that you are accessing a specific user account.

- **Managed with Parental Controls.** The Mac OS X Parental Controls feature enables you to limit the access that a user has to various kinds of content, such as e-mail and websites. When you manage this kind of account, you determine specific types of content, applications, and other areas that the user can access. People using this type of account are prevented from doing all actions not specifically allowed by the Parental Control settings.

- **Sharing Only.** This type of account can only access your MacBook Pro to share files across a network. It has no access to the operating system or any files that aren't being shared.

- **Group.** Access to folders and files on your MacBook Pro is determined by each item's Sharing and Permissions settings. One of the ways you can assign privileges to an item is by configuring a group's access to it. A group user account is a collection of user accounts that is used only to set access privileges. You create a group, assign people to it, and then use the group to set access permissions for files and folders.

Authentication

Some tasks require you to confirm that you have access to an Administrator user account. This is called authentication. When you work with an area that requires this, the Authentication status Lock icon is visible in the lower-left corner of the window. If the Lock is closed and some buttons or commands are grayed out (inactive), you need to authenticate before you can perform an administrator action. If the Lock is open, you are authenticated and can proceed with the action you want to perform.

To authenticate, click the Lock icon. The Unlock dialog appears and, if you are logged in using an account with Administrator rights, the full name associated with the current account appears in the Name field. If the Name field is empty, you are logged in under an account without Administrator rights. If the full name isn't for the Administrator account you want to use or the Name field is empty, type the full name for the account you want to authenticate with (for example, Brad Miser) or the name of an Administrator account (such as bradm).

Type the account password, and then click Unlock. You are authenticated as an Administrator and returned to the pane of the System Preferences application with which you were working. The Lock icon is now open and you can perform administrative tasks.

- **Root.** Mac OS X is built on the UNIX operating system, so it has an extensive security architecture that specifically controls what each user account can do and the resources it can access. The Root user account is unique in that it bypasses all of the limitations inherent to the other types of accounts (even Administrator accounts). When you log in under the Root user account, the system doesn't limit anything you try to do. Because of this, the Root user account is the most powerful and, also, the most dangerous because you can do things that might damage the system or files that it contains. You typically only use the Root user account during troubleshooting tasks. Unlike the other accounts, you don't administer the Root user account using the System Preferences application. I cover how to use the Root account later in this chapter.

Creating Administrator or Standard user accounts

Follow these steps to create a new Administrator or Standard user account:

1. **Choose Apple menu ⇨ System Preferences.**

2. **Click the Users & Groups icon.** The Users & Groups pane opens (see Figure 2.1). In the list on the left side of the pane, you see the current user accounts. The user account under which you are logged in appears at the top of the list, and its details appear in the right pane of the window along with the tools you use to configure that account. At the bottom of the user list are the Login Options button, and the Add (+), Remove (–), and Action menu (the icon shaped like the sun) buttons.

2.1 In the Users & Groups pane in the System Preferences application, you can create and manage user accounts on your MacBook Pro.

3. **Authenticate yourself if needed (make sure the Lock icon is open).**

4. **Click the Add (+) button.** The New Account sheet appears.

5. **On the New Account pop-up menu, choose Standard to create a Standard user account or Administrator to create an Administrator account.** After it is created, you can change a Standard user account into an Administrator account or vice versa.

6. **Type a name for the account in the Full name field.** This can be just about anything you want, but usually a person's actual name works best. The Full name is one of the names that a user types to log in to or authenticate the account (if it is an Administrator account). Mac OS X creates an account name based on the full name you type.

7. **Edit the account name if you want to change it.** This name appears in a number of places, such as the path to the user's Home folder. It's a good idea to keep the account name short. Also, it can't include any spaces or some special characters.

8. **If you want to create a password yourself, type it into the Password box and skip to step 12; if you want to use the Password Assistant to help you create a password, click the Key icon.** The Password Assistant appears, as shown in Figure 2.2.

9. **Choose the password type from the Type pop-up menu.** There are a number of options, such as Memorable and Letters & Numbers. After you choose a type, the Assistant automatically generates a password of that type for you and enters it in the Password field on the New Account sheet.

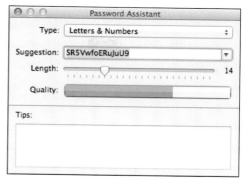

2.2 The Password Assistant helps you create secure passwords.

Note

While it isn't a good practice from a security standpoint, a user account doesn't have to have a password. If you leave the Password and Verify fields empty, the user will have a blank or empty password. He leaves the Password field empty and clicks the Login or other button to complete the action he is performing. While this is more convenient, faster, and easier than typing a password, it is also much less secure.

10. **Drag the slider to the right to increase the length of the password, or to the left to decrease its length.** The longer a password is, the more secure it becomes. A good password should include numbers or special characters to make it harder to crack. As you make changes to a password, the Quality gauge shows you how secure the password is.

11. **When the password shown on the Password Assistant is what you want to use, leave the Password Assistant open and click back in the New Account sheet.**

12. **Retype the password in the Verify field and type a hint about the password in the Password hint box.** This hint helps a user log in to his account when he can't remember the correct password.

13. **Click Create User.** The user account is created and appears on the list of accounts. You are ready to customize it by adding an image and configuring other elements.

Note

The Mac OS X FileVault feature is a way to protect the information stored under a user account so that it can't be used without the appropriate password. I go into more detail about this feature in Chapter 14.

An image, such as a photo or other graphic, can be associated with a user account. User account images appear in various locations, such as the Login window. Mac OS X automatically chooses an image for each user account from the default images it has. You can leave this as is, or you can use the following steps to customize the user account with an image of your choice:

1. **Move to the Users & Groups pane of the System Preferences application and authenticate yourself, if necessary.**

2. **In the Accounts list, select the user account with which you want to associate an image (this can be your own account, too).**

3. **If you want to use an image already stored on your MacBook as the user's image, drag the file onto the image well, which is the box located to the left of the Change or Reset Password button; if you don't want to use a file for the image, click the image well.** (When you select the account currently logged in, the button is Change Password; when you select a different account, the button is Reset Password.) The image sheet appears; if you dragged an image file onto the well, you see the image you placed there ready to

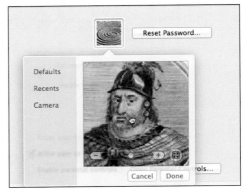

2.3 An image you associate with the user account appears in several locations, including the Mac OS X Login window.

be edited (see Figure 2.3) or you see the image that previously appeared in the well. The image sheet has three tabs: Defaults, which shows you the Mac OS X default images; Recents, which enables you to choose an image you've applied recently; and Camera, which enables you to use the MacBook Pro camera to create a new image.

4. **If you placed an image file in the well, it is ready to be edited and you can skip to step 9.**

5. **To choose one of the default images, click Defaults, and then click the image you want to use (scroll the window to see all of the default images available to you).** To change how the image appears, click Edit and skip to step 9, or click Done and go on to step 6.

6. **To use an image that you can have previously applied, click Recents, and then click the image you want to use.** If you want to change how the image appears, click Edit and skip to step 9 or just click Done to use the image as it is and skip the rest of these steps.

7. **To capture an image with the MacBook Pro camera, click Camera.** Position the camera so the image you want to use is shown, and then click the Camera button. After the countdown, the image is captured and ready for editing.

8. **Set the size of the image that is displayed by dragging the slider to the right to include less of the image or to the left to include more of it.** The portion of the image that will be displayed is shown within the preview window.

9. **Drag the image inside the box until the part you want to be displayed is contained within the box.** You may need to use the slider in conjunction with this step to get the image just right.

10. **Click Done.** The sheet closes and you see the image you configured in the image well on the Users & Groups pane.

Genius

To apply special effects to a user account image, edit it, and then click the Effects button located just above the Done button. You see various effects that can be applied. Click the arrow buttons to scroll through all of the effects. Click the effect you want to apply and you return to the sheet where you see the image with the effect applied. Resize and place the image as needed, and then click Done.

If the user has an Apple ID, click Set, type the user's Apple ID in that field on the resulting sheet, and click OK. This associates the user's Apple ID account with the Mac OS X user account. An Apple ID is used for many purposes, including shopping in the iTunes or Apple Online Stores and, in most cases, working with iCloud. This is optional, and the user can add this information after she logs into her Mac OS X user account.

To allow the user to reset his Mac OS X user account password by using his Apple ID, select the Allow user to reset password using Apple ID check box. This gives the user another way (in addition to using the hint you configure) to regain access to his Mac OS X user account should he forget his password.

If you selected the Standard account type but change your mind and want to make the user an Administrator, select the Allow user to administer this computer check box. This changes the account type to Administrator. This enables you to configure Parental Controls for the user account, which is covered in the next section.

The user account you created now appears on the list of accounts, as shown in Figure 2.4, and is ready to use.

2.4 Because this is an Administrator account, William can perform Administrator tasks, such as creating other user accounts.

Setting Login Items for a user account

Any application or file added to the Login Items list for a user is automatically opened when a user logs in to her account. For example, if a user opens Safari and Mail every time she uses the MacBook Pro, you can add these applications to the user's Login Items so that they open when she logs in. Here's how you can make life easier for users (including yourself):

1. **Log in under the user's account.** Log in to your own account to set the Login Items for your own account.

2. **Open the System Preferences application and click the Users & Groups icon to open the Users & Groups pane.**

3. **Select the current user and click the Login Items tab, as shown in Figure 2.5.**

4. **Add items to the list by clicking the Add (+) button at the bottom of the pane.**

5. **Use the resulting dialog to move to and select the files you want to add to the list.** Hold the ⌘ key down to select multiple files at the same time.

6. **Click Add.**

7. **Select check boxes for any items on the list that you want to be hidden by default.**
For example, if you want Mail to open but be hidden, select its check box. The next time the user logs in, the files on the Login Items list open. Those you elected to hide do open, but are hidden.

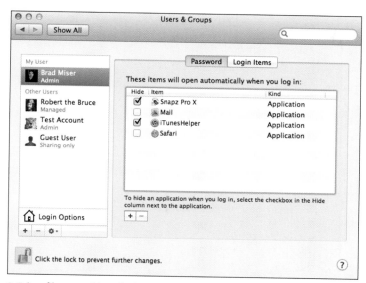

2.5 Any file you add to the Login Items tab opens automatically when a user logs in.

Configuring e-mail, contacts, and calendar accounts

Many services require a user account to access, such as e-mail, calendars, and contacts. You can configure such accounts on the Mail, Contacts & Calendars pane of the System Preferences application. Any accounts you configure there are immediately available in the applications that can use them, including Mail, Calendar, Messages, Contacts, and so on. Managing these accounts from one place is much easier than doing so in each individual application.

Follow the steps below to add an account:

1. **Open the Mail, Contacts & Calendars pane.** The accounts currently configured are shown on the Account list on the left side of the pane.

2. **To add an account, click the Add (+) button at the bottom of the Account list.**

Note

Accounts you create within an application, such as Mail, automatically appear on the Account list in the Mail, Contacts & Calendars pane.

59

3. **Select the type of account you want to add from the following options: iCloud, Microsoft Exchange, Gmail, Yahoo!, AOL, Twitter, Flickr, and so on.** If the account is not provided by one of the named services, such as Gmail, select Other. The configuration sheet for the type of account you selected appears.

4. **Follow the on-screen prompts to complete the creation of the account.** For most of the named services, this requires typing the full name, account name, and password, and then clicking Set Up. After typing this information, you select the applications you want to be able to use the account (such as Mail, Contacts, or Calendar). If you select Other, you first choose the type of account you are creating, such as a Mail account, and then follow the on-screen prompts to complete the account configuration. After you complete the process, the account appears on the Account list on the left side of the pane.

You can change an account by selecting it on the list. Information about it then appears in the right part of the pane. You can select or deselect an application's check box to allow or prevent the application from using the account. You can click Details to change the account's configuration. To delete an account, select it and click the Remove (–) button at the bottom of the Account list.

Creating Sharing Only user accounts

Typically, you create Sharing Only user accounts for groups of people who need to get to files on your MacBook Pro. Creating a Sharing Only user account is similar to creating other types of accounts. To create a new account, choose Sharing Only on the New Account pop-up menu and complete the New Account sheet. When you finish with the creation process, you see that the only tools for the Sharing Only account are for the full name, image, password reset, and Apple ID.

You don't use a Sharing Only user account from your MacBook Pro; its purpose is to enable people to log in to your MacBook Pro from other computers. Provide the username and password to each person whom you want to allow access to your MacBook Pro. Those users can then log in to access files that you share. However, make sure that the files have sharing permissions set for the sharing user account.

Creating Group user accounts

Creating a Group user account is much simpler than the other types of accounts. Follow these steps to create one:

1. **Open the System Preferences application.**

2. **Click the Users & Groups icon.**

3. **Click the Add (+) button.**

4. **On the New Account pop-up menu, choose Group.**

5. **Type the group name in the Name field.**

6. **Click Create Group.** You move to the group's screen, on which you see all of the user accounts on your MacBook Pro (see Figure 2.6).

2.6 Select a user's check box to add him to the group.

7. **Select the check box for each user whom you want to be a member of the group.** The group is ready to be used to assign access permissions to each member of the group.

Changing accounts

You change existing user accounts using the same set of tools that you use to create accounts. To make changes, follow these steps:

1. **Open the System Preferences application.**

2. **Click the Users & Groups icon.**

3. **Select the user whose account you want to change.**

4. **Use the tools in the right part of the pane to make changes to the user account, such as resetting a user's password or changing her Apple ID.**

Note   The safest way to change an account's username is to delete the account and re-create it with a different username. However, when you delete a user account, you might delete all of its files, so be careful about doing this.

Deleting accounts

If you no longer need a user account, you can delete it. Follow these steps to do so:

1. **Open the System Preferences application and click the Users & Groups icon.**

2. **Select the account that you want to delete.**

3. **Click the Remove (–) button at the bottom of the user list.** A sheet appears with three options for handling the user's Home folder:

   - **Save the Home folder in a disk image.** All the files in the user's Home folder are saved into a disk image located in the Deleted Users folder under the Users folder. You can access the files in the disk image by opening it.

   - **Don't change the Home folder.** If you choose this option, the Home folder remains in its current location in the Users folder, but its permissions are changed so that you can access it from an Administrator user account.

   - **Delete the Home folder.** If you choose this option, all traces of the user are removed from your MacBook Pro. (To make the deletion even more permanent, select the Erase home folder securely check box.)

4. **Click OK.** The user account is deleted and the user's Home folder is handled according to the option you selected.

Limiting access with Parental Controls

The Mac OS X Parental Controls feature enables you to limit the access a user has to the following functionality and content:

- **Simple Finder.** When you limit users to the Simple Finder, they can only access their own documents and specific applications that you choose.

- **Limited applications.** You can use Parental Controls to create a list of applications to which the user has access.

- **System functions.** You can prevent users from administering printers, burning CDs or DVDs, changing their passwords, or changing the icons on the Dock.

- **Hide Profanity.** You can hide profanity in the Mac OS X Dictionary application.

- **Websites.** You can prevent users from visiting specific websites.

- **People.** You can specify the people with whom the user can exchange e-mail or messages or connect with the Game Center.

- **Time Limits.** You can determine when the user is able to access her user account.

Using Parental Controls is a two-step process. First, create the user account that you want to limit. You can use Parental Controls with the Standard or Managed with Parental Controls accounts. The only difference between these is that a Managed with Parental Controls account is set for restrictions from the start, while you have to select an additional check box for a Standard account. Second, configure the controls you want to use with the account. All of these controls are covered in detail later in this chapter.

Creating Managed user Accounts is similar to creating Standard or Administrator user accounts. Just choose Managed with Parental Controls from the New Account pop-up menu. When you are done with the creation process, you see that the Enable Parental Controls check box is selected. To set limits on a Standard user account, select the account, and then select the Enable Parental Controls check box (when you do so, the account type becomes Managed instead of Standard).

You are now ready to use the Parental Controls pane to configure restrictions for the user account. The following are the two ways in which you can start this process:

● **Open the System Preferences application and click the Parental Controls icon.** Select the user account that you want to limit on the list of accounts in the left part of the window, and then click the Enable Parental Controls button.

● **Open the System Preferences application and click the Users & Groups icon.** On the Users & Groups pane, select the user account you want to manage, select the Enable parental controls check box, and click the Open Parental Controls button.

After you open the Parental Controls pane with the appropriate user selected, you can configure that user's limitations by using the tabs at the top of the pane.

Genius

You can manage Parental Controls from a different computer on the same network. To do this, open the Action menu on the Parental Controls pane and choose Allow Remote Setup. On a remote computer (one that is on the same network), open the Parental Controls pane. Select the computer on which the account for which you want to set Parental Controls exists. After you log in with an Administrator account, you will be able to remotely configure Parental Controls.

Restricting system resources

With this setting, you can determine the Finder's behavior, the applications a Managed user can access, and whether the user can change the Dock by clicking the Apps tab.

Follow these steps to access this control:

1. **Click the Apps tab.** The Apps controls appear, as shown in Figure 2.7.

2.7 Use the Apps tab to configure a user's access to applications installed on the Mac.

2. **To enable the Simple Finder for the user, select the Use Simple Finder check box.**
   When the user logs in, he sees a very simple Desktop. The Dock contains only three folders; when the user clicks one, it opens on the Desktop and he has access only to the applications that you enable and the documents that he creates. Within Finder windows, everything opens with a single click.

3. **To limit the user's access to specific applications, select the Limit Applications check box.**

4. **Deselect the check boxes for the categories or individual applications that the user is not allowed to use.** Select the check boxes for those the user is permitted to use.

5. **To limit the rating of applications that have been downloaded via the Mac App Store that the user can access, open the Allow App Store Apps pop-up menu and choose a level.** The options are Don't allow, which prevents the user from opening any App Store applications; up to age (where age is 4+, 9+, 12+, or 17+), which limits the

applications to those rated by the age category you select; or All, which allows all App Store apps to be used.

6. **If you don't want the user to be able to change the Dock, deselect the Allow User to Modify the Dock check box.** If you selected the Simple Finder option in step 2, this option is disabled.

Restricting content

You can limit the user's access to various kinds of content by clicking the Web tab. You then see the Web controls in the pane, as shown in Figure 2.8. There are two ways in which you can limit the user's access to websites. The first is by clicking the Try to limit access to adult websites automatically radio button, and then clicking Customize. On the resulting sheet, add the URLs you want the user to be able to visit to the top pane by clicking the upper Add (+) button and typing the URL, or block access to specific sites by clicking the lower Add (+) button and typing the URLs you want to block. Click OK. The user can visit the sites you added to the allow list and can't visit sites you typed on the prevent list. Access to other sites (such as adult websites) may be blocked, too.

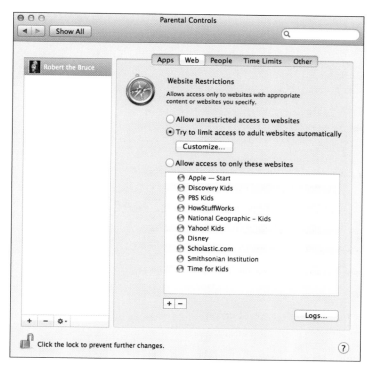

2.8 If you don't want the user to access selected websites, use the Web controls.

The second way in which you can limit a user's access to websites is by clicking the Allow access to only these websites radio button. When you choose this option, the list of allowed websites (bookmarks) at the bottom of the pane determines the sites the user will be able to visit.

To add a site to the list (so the user is able to visit it), click the Add (+) button at the bottom of the list, choose Add bookmark, create the bookmark you want to add, and then click OK. To organize the bookmarks on the list, click the Add (+) button at the bottom of the list and choose Add Folder. Name the folder, and then add bookmarks to it. To remove a bookmark from the list so that a user can't access the related website, select the bookmark and click the Remove (–) button.

Limiting people

On the People tab, shown in Figure 2.9, you can limit the people with whom the user of the Managed user account can interact via e-mail, messages, and the Game Center. You can define specific e-mail addresses and chat accounts with which the user can communicate. To provide more flexibility, you can also set the system to notify you when someone who is not on the approved list attempts to communicate with the user. On the notification, you can choose to allow the contact, and the person is added to the approved list. If you choose to reject it, the communication is blocked.

2.9 Use the People tab to control with whom a user can e-mail, chat, or play games.

To prevent the user from joining multiplayer games in the Game Center application, deselect the Allow joining Game Center multiplayer games check box. To allow the user to add friends in the

Game Center, select the Allow adding Game Center friends check box. To limit the user to e-mailing only specific people, select the Limit Mail check box. To limit the user to messaging only with specific people, select the Limit Messages check box. To define the people with whom the user can e-mail or message, click the Add (+) button. The Contact sheet appears, as shown in Figure 2.10.

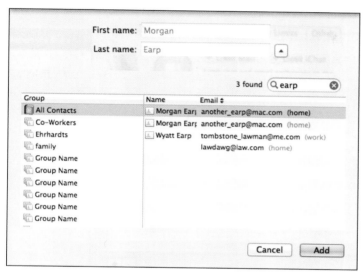

2.10 Configure the Contact sheet to allow the user to communicate with someone via e-mail or messaging.

Type the first and last name, and e-mail or chat address. Next, choose Email or AIM from the pop-up menu to identify the type of address you entered and click Add. You add a contact from your Address Book by clicking the triangle next to the Last Name box. Choose Email or Instant Messaging on the pop-up menu at the top of the contact list and select the contact you want to add. Select the address from which you want to allow communication, and click Add; all the addresses for the contact you select are added to the allowed list.

If you want to receive e-mail requiring your permission when someone who is not on the list is involved in an e-mail exchange, select the Send permission requests to check box (see Figure 2.9) and type your e-mail address.

Caution The e-mail and chat controls only work with Mail and Messages. If the user can access other applications for these functions, the controls won't limit her access. Use the Apps controls to set limits to ensure she can only access Mail for e-mail and Messages for messaging.

Setting time limits

You can use the Time Limits tab to limit the amount of time for which the user can use the MacBook Pro. When a time limit is reached or when the time is outside of an allowed window, the user can't log in to his user account. If he is already logged in when the time limit is reached, he is logged out after a brief warning that allows him time to save any open documents. Follow the steps below to set time limits:

1. **Click the Time Limits tab, as shown in Figure 2.11.**

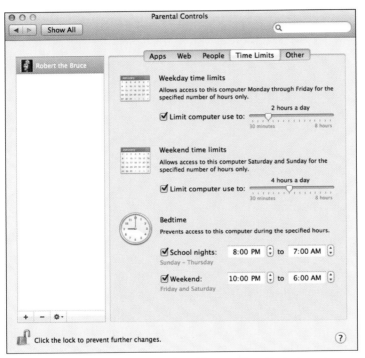

2.11 Using a MacBook Pro can be a lot of fun; use Time Limits to make sure it doesn't replace other important activities.

Note When a user has been logged out because of time limits, a red circle with a hyphen in it appears next to the user's name in the Login window. The time at which the user can log in again is also shown.

2. **To set the amount of time for which the user can be logged in on weekdays and/or weekends, select the Limit computer use to check box in the corresponding section.** Set the time limit using the related slider.

3. **To prevent the user from being logged into the user account for specific periods of time Sunday through Thursday, select the School nights check box.** Type the time period during which user activity should be prevented.

4. **To prevent the user from being logged in to the user account for specific periods of time on Friday and Saturday, select the Weekend check box.** Type the time period during which user activity should be prevented.

Note Time limits apply only to the Managed user account. If the user can log in under another user account, he can continue using the MacBook Pro regardless of the limits set on his own account.

Setting other limits

You can limit the following actions by selecting or deselecting the related check boxes on the Other tab:

- **The use of Dictation**
- **Access to profanity in the Dictionary application**
- **Administering printers**
- **Burning DVDs and CDs**
- **Changing the user account's password**

Checking Up on Managed Users

Using the Logs button (which appears on the first three tabs), you can view a Managed user's activities, such as websites visited, websites blocked, messaging sessions, and applications used. To see user activity, click Logs (see Figure 2.9). Use the Show activity for pop-up menu to set the timeframe of the logs you want to view. Use the Group by pop-up menu to determine how the events are grouped.

In the Log Collections list, select the kind of activity you want to see, such as Applications. In the right area of the pane, you see the activity related to that category. For example, when you choose Applications, you see a list of all the applications the user has accessed. To see each instance of application use, click the expansion triangle next to the application name. Under its icon, you see each date and time that the application was used, and the amount of time it was used. When you select an application or activity, click Block to change the permissions for that application or activity, or click Open to open the application or website.

Using Automatic Login

The Mac OS X Automatic Login feature does just what it says. You can choose to log in to a specific user account each time your MacBook Pro restarts. Follow these steps to enable Automatic Login:

1. **Open the System Preferences application and click the Users & Groups icon.**

2. **Click Login Options.** The Login Options pane appears, as shown in Figure 2.12.

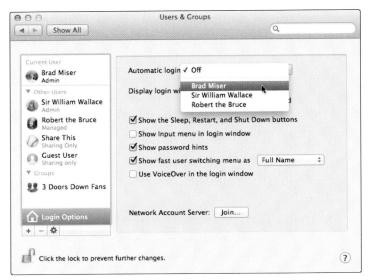

2.12 Use the Automatic Login pop-up menu to select a user account to automatically log in to your MacBook Pro.

3. **From the Automatic Login pop-up menu, choose the name of the user that you want to be automatically logged in.**

4. **Type the user's password and click OK.** Each time your MacBook Pro starts or restarts, the user you selected is logged in automatically.

Caution Enabling Automatic Login makes your MacBook Pro less secure. Anyone who has access to it can use it because no additional information is needed to log in. While this feature is convenient, you should only enable Automatic Login if your MacBook Pro is in an area where you can control it and people won't be able to use it without your knowledge.

Configuring the Login Window

The Login window appears to prompt a user to log in. If Automatic Login is disabled, it appears when your MacBook Pro starts up. If a user logs out of her user account, the Login window also appears. You can also make it appear by choosing Login Window in the Fast User Switching menu (this is covered in the next section). Follow these steps to configure options for the Login window:

1. **Open the System Preferences application and click the Users & Groups icon.**

2. **Click Login Options.** The Login Options pane appears.

3. **Select a Login window option by clicking one of the following two radio buttons:**

   ● **List of users.** When this option is selected, each user account's name and picture is shown on the Login window. The person logging in can click the appropriate user account to be prompted to type the password for that account. This option is more convenient because the user only has to recognize her user account and remember her password to be able to log in.

   ● **Name and password.** When this option is selected, the Login window contains empty Name and Password fields. The user must type the account's name (full name or account name) and password to be able to log in.

4. **If you want to be able to restart your MacBook Pro, put it to sleep, or shut it down from the Login window, select the Show the Restart, Sleep, and Shut Down buttons check box.**

Caution If you've enabled Automatic Login, don't select the Show the Sleep, Restart, and Shut Down buttons check box. If you do, someone can gain access to your MacBook Pro when the Login window is displayed without having a user account by clicking the Shut Down button and then restarting the MacBook Pro.

5. **If you want to be able to be able to choose the language layout from the Login window, select the Show Input menu in login window check box.** This is useful if people who use different languages share your MacBook Pro.

6. **To show a hint when a user forgets his password, select the Show password hints check box.** The user can click the Forgot Password button to see the hint for his account.

7. **To have your MacBook Pro read the text in the Login window, select the Use VoiceOver in the login window check box.**

Working with Fast User Switching

The Fast User Switching feature is great because it allows multiple users to be logged in at the same time. Instead of having to log out of your account for someone else to log in, the other user can log in by using the commands on the Fast User Switching menu. This is good because when you log out of an account, all processes may be shut down, meaning that all open documents and applications are closed. If you have a lot of ongoing work, this can be a nuisance. With Fast User Switching, other users can log in while your account remains active in the background. When you log back in to your account, it is in the same state as when the other user logged in, and you can get back to what you were doing immediately.

Fast User Switching is disabled by default; follow these steps to enable it:

1. **Open the System Preferences application and click the Users & Groups icon.**

2. **Click Login Options.**

3. **Select the Show fast user switching menu check box.**

4. **On the menu, choose how you want the Fast User Switching menu to be identified.**
   You are given the following options:

   - Full Name (of the current user account)

   - Short Name (of the current user account)

   - Icon

To use Fast User Switching, open the Fast User Switching menu on the menu bar by clicking the name of the current user, the account name, or the icon. The Fast User Switching menu appears, as shown in Figure 2.13.

On this menu, you see the options listed below:

- **List of user accounts.** Each user account configured on your MacBook Pro appears on the list.

- **Login Window.** Choose this command to cause the Login window to appear.

2.13 The Fast User Switching menu makes it easier to share your MacBook Pro with others.

● **Users & Groups Preferences.** Choose this command to move to the Users & Groups pane of the System Preferences application.

To switch to a different user account, select it on the menu. The password prompt appears. If the password is entered correctly, that user account becomes active. The current account remains logged in but is moved to the background.

You can have as many user accounts logged in simultaneously as you want. However, remember that each account that is logged in can have active processes, all of which use the MacBook Pro resources—you don't want to get too carried away.

Genius

To quickly secure your MacBook Pro without logging out, choose Login Window from the Fast User Switching menu. The Login window appears, but you remain logged in (you see a check mark next to your username). For someone to use your MacBook Pro, she must know a valid password to be able to log in (unless you've configured a user account to not require a password, which is not a good idea).

Working with the Root User Account

Because Mac OS X is based on UNIX, it includes the Root user account. In a nutshell, the Root user account is not limited by any security permissions. If something is possible, the Root user account can do it. This is both good and bad. It's good because you can often solve problems using the Root user account that you can't solve any other way. It's bad because you can also cause problems from which it can be difficult, if not impossible, to recover. By contrast, when you use an Administrator account, you have limited access to certain system files, and so there is no way you can delete them; however, under the Root user account, anything goes, and it's possible for you to do things that cause your MacBook Pro to be unusable.

You should only use the Root user account for troubleshooting. While you shouldn't use the Root user account often, when you need to use the Root user account, you'll really need it.

By default, the Root user account is disabled. You must enable it before you can log in to use it. By following these steps, you can enable the Root user account with the Directory Utility application:

1. **Open the Users & Groups pane of the System Preferences application, select Login Options, and click Join.**

2. **At the resulting prompt, click Open Directory Utility.**

3. **Click the Lock icon.** (Skip this step and the next one if you are already authenticated.)

4. **Type an Administrator username (if necessary) and password, and then click OK.**

If you're comfortable using UNIX commands, you can also enable and use the Root user account by opening the Terminal application and entering the appropriate commands to enable the Root user account, set its password, and log in.

5. **Choose Edit ⇨ Enable Root User.** You're prompted to create a password for the Root user account.

6. **Type a password in the Password and Verify fields, as shown in Figure 2.14.** I recommend using a different password from the one you use for your normal user account so that it's more secure.

7. **Click OK.** The sheet closes, but nothing else appears to happen. Don't worry— the Root user account is now enabled and you can use it.

2.14 Create a secure password for the root account to prevent unintended access to it.

8. **Quit the Directory Utility application.**

Because it has unlimited permissions, you can add or remove files to any directory on your MacBook Pro while you are logged in under the Root user account, including those for other user accounts. You can also make changes to any system file, which is where the Root user account's power and danger come from.

Note The full name of the Root user account is System Administrator. Therefore, you see that term instead of Root wherever the full account name appears.

To log in to the Root user account, start from the Login window by choosing Login Window on the Fast User Switching menu, logging out of the current account, or restarting your MacBook Pro (if Automatic Login is disabled). If the Login window is configured to show a list of users, scroll down and select the Other username; the Name and Password fields appear. If the Login Window is configured to show name and password, you don't need to scroll because these appear immediately.

Type *root* as the name, type the password you created for the Root user account, and click Login. You log in as the Root user account (or under root, as UNIX aficionados would say). The Root user account's Desktop appears, and you can get to work.

Genius To disable the root account, open the Directory Utility application and choose Edit ➪ Disable Root User. You can change the Root user account's password by choosing Edit ➪ Change Root Password.

When you are logged in to the Root user account, you can use your MacBook Pro the same as you do with other user accounts, except—and this is a big exception—you have no security limitations. You can place files into any folder, delete any files, or complete any other action you try, regardless of the potential outcome. Additionally, if you use the System Preferences application, you see that you no longer have to authenticate because all possible actions are always enabled for the root account.

Caution Be careful when you work under the root account. You can cause serious damage to Mac OS X, as well as to data you have stored on your MacBook Pro. You should be logged in under the root account only for the minimum time necessary to accomplish specific tasks. Log in, do what you need to do, and then log out of the root. This minimizes the chance of doing something you didn't intend.

What Are My Internet Connection Options?

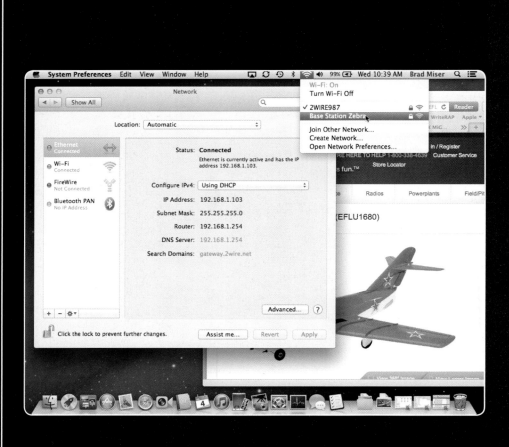

Being able to take advantage of the Internet is a skill that is almost as important as being able to read (of course, you have to be able to read to use the
Internet, so reading still wins on the importance scale). Fortunately, your
MacBook Pro is a perfect tool for getting the most out of the Internet. To use
the Internet, you must be able to connect to it, which is where this chapter
comes in handy. It covers how to connect in a variety of ways, and it is likely
that you will use several of them.

Setting Up a Local Network

There are many ways to connect your MacBook Pro to the Internet. Fortunately, one of the great things about using a MacBook Pro and related Apple technology is that you don't have to worry about all the technical details involved. It's quite easy to create and manage a local network that provides Internet access and other services, such as file sharing, to multiple computers.

This chapter focuses on networks built around an Apple AirPort Extreme Base Station or Time Capsule. Either of these makes managing a network easy, while providing all of the features most people need for a local network (a Time Capsule also provides wireless backup, which is ideal for MacBook Pro). MacBook Pro networking technology supports wireless and wired networking standards. This means you can use just about any network component designed to the same standards to accomplish the same tasks. However, that requires a bit more effort and complexity, and who needs that?

There are two general steps to creating a local network. First, install and configure the AirPort Extreme Base Station or Time Capsule. Second, connect devices (such as computers and printers) to the wireless or wired network provided by the base station.

Installing an AirPort Extreme Base Station or Time Capsule

An Apple AirPort Extreme Base Station is a relatively simple device. It contains a transmitter that broadcasts the signal over which the wireless network is provided, and it has four Ethernet ports. One, the WAN (Wide Area Network) port, connects to a broadband Internet connection, which is most commonly connected to a cable or DSL modem. The other three ports connect to an Ethernet network or to Ethernet-equipped devices, including computers, printers, and Ethernet hubs. Along with the power adapter port, the base station offers a USB port to which you can connect a USB printer. This is also where you would connect a USB hard drive to share a printer or hard drive with the network.

A Time Capsule is an AirPort Extreme Base Station with the addition of an internal hard drive. You can use this drive to store any kind of data, but it is ideal for backing up your MacBook Pro using Mac OS X Time Machine (backing up with a Time Capsule and Time Machine is covered in Chapter 14). Because this chapter focuses on the network aspects of these two devices, you should henceforward consider them equivalent (that is, the same steps covered here work for either device). Therefore, going forward, you'll see the more generic term *base station*, which refers to either device.

Got Internet?

I assume that you already have an Internet account that uses a cable or DSL (Digital Subscriber Line) modem to connect to the Internet. There are other ways you can connect, such as with a satellite or even with a dial-up connection, but cable or DSL are ideal for most people. Fortunately, unless you live in a rural area, you probably have one or more of these options available to you. If you have cable TV service in your area, it is highly likely that cable Internet service is also available. To see whether DSL is available to you and to find service providers in your area, check out http://dsl.theispguide.com. After you obtain an Internet account and install the appropriate modem, you're ready to create a local network to provide Internet access to your MacBook Pro, as well as any other computers that share your space.

If possible, set up the base station in a central area so that it provides the maximum amount of wireless coverage where you install it. In most houses, a base station provides adequate signal strength, even if you position it at one end of the house and place computers that you want to network at the other end. However, the closer the computers are to the base station, the stronger the signal will be. A stronger signal means a faster, more reliable connection.

After you place the base station in its location, attach its power adapter to the base station and plug it into a wall outlet. Use an Ethernet cable to connect the cable or DSL modem to the base station's WAN Ethernet port. You can connect an Ethernet device to each of the three LAN (Local Area Network) Ethernet ports on the base station, shown in Figure 3.1. For example, you can connect a network printer, a Mac, or a Windows computer. To add more than three devices, you can connect one of the ports to an Ethernet hub, and then connect additional Ethernet devices to that hub.

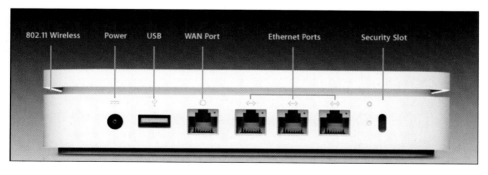

3.1 The three Ethernet ports enable you to create a wired network to go along with the wireless one.

If you want to share a USB printer with all the computers that can access the network, connect the printer's USB cable to the USB port on the base station. Likewise, you can connect a USB hard drive to the base station's USB port to share that drive on the network.

After you install the base station, you need to configure it. You can do this via the AirPort Utility application. You must configure the base station from a computer with which it can communicate, either through Wi-Fi or an Ethernet network. To wirelessly configure the base station, make sure that Wi-Fi is enabled on your MacBook Pro (connecting via Wi-Fi is covered later in this chapter). To configure the base station through Ethernet, connect your MacBook Pro to one of the Ethernet ports on the base station or to a port on an Ethernet hub connected to the base station.

The following steps show you how to configure a base station that has been previously used. If you're starting with a brand-new base station, the details might be slightly different. For example, you'll be prompted to name a new base station, whereas one that was previously used already has a name. However, the overall process is the same. Follow these steps to configure the base station's identification and configuration password:

1. **Open Applications ⇨ Utilities ⇨ AirPort Utility.** The base stations with which your MacBook Pro can communicate are shown in a diagram displaying how they are connected to each other and the Internet. You see all of the base stations currently within range of the MacBook Pro you are using, and whether they communicate wirelessly or over an Ethernet connection.

Note Colored dots indicate the current status of the base station. A green dot means the base station is successfully communicating with the network, while an orange dot means there is a problem or the base station is restarting. If a base station's software needs to be updated, its icon is marked with a red badge. Click the base station's icon and follow the on-screen instructions to update its software.

2. **Select the base station you want to configure.**

3. **Click Edit.** You're prompted to type the base station's password (unless you've accessed the base station previously and set MacBook Pro to remember the password; in that case, it is automatically entered for you).

4. **If you were prompted to do so, type the password and click OK.** You next see a sheet that has several tabs. You select a tab to configure the related area of the base station. For example, you would select the Internet tab to configure how the base station accesses the Internet.

Note Two passwords are associated with a base station: One that enables you to administer the base station, and another that enables you to join the wireless network provided by the base station. You should use different passwords for these because you may be providing the network password to people whom you don't want to be able to configure the base station.

5. **Click the Base Station tab, as shown in Figure 3.2.**

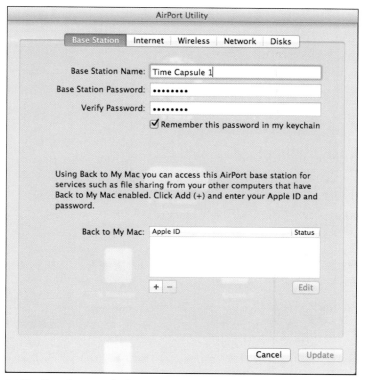

3.2 The Base Station tab allows you to configure basic attributes, such as the name and password.

6. **Type the name in the Base Station Name field.** This is the name of the base station, not the name of the network it provides.

7. **Type the administration password in the Base Station Password and Verify Password fields.** Again, this is the password you use to configure the base station, not the one you use to access the network it provides.

8. **Select the Remember this password in my keychain check box.** This causes your MacBook Pro to remember the password so that you don't have to type it each time you configure the base station from your MacBook Pro.

Perform the following steps to configure the wireless network that the base station provides:

1. **Click the Wireless tab.** On this tab, you configure the wireless network provided by the base station (see Figure 3.3).

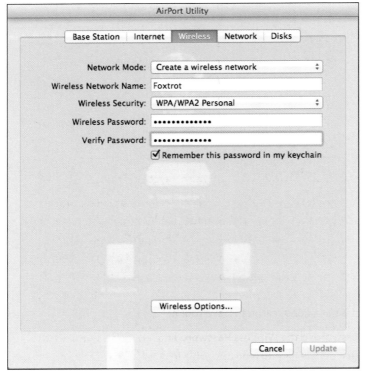

AirPort Utility

| Base Station | Internet | Wireless | Network | Disks |

Network Mode: Create a wireless network ⬍

Wireless Network Name: Foxtrot

Wireless Security: WPA/WPA2 Personal ⬍

Wireless Password: ••••••••••••

Verify Password: ••••••••••••

☑ Remember this password in my keychain

Wireless Options...

Cancel   Update

3.3 Use the Wireless tab to create the wireless network provided by the base station.

2. **Use the Network Mode pop-up menu to choose Create a wireless network.**

3. **Type the name of the wireless network in the Wireless Network Name field.** This is the name that you choose to access the network being provided by the base station.

Note

WDS (Wireless Distribution System) is a way to link base stations together to create larger networks. If you choose Extend a wireless network on the Network Mode pop-up menu, you can set up the base station to communicate with other base stations.

4. **Use the Wireless Security pop-up menu to choose one of the following security options:**

   - **WPA/WPA2 Personal or WPA2 Personal.** WPA (Wi-Fi Protected Access) is the most secure encryption technique supported on an AirPort network. However, using WPA can limit the access of some devices to the network. Use this option for a network that includes only Macintosh computers unless you're sure the other devices (including Windows computers) that you want to connect can support WPA. If you have older devices on your network, choose WAP/WPA2 Personal. If all of the devices you use can support WPA2, choose WPA2 Personal.

   - **WEP.** This is an encryption strategy that attempts to provide wireless networks with the same level of protection as wired networks. This option provides a good level of security, while being more compatible with Windows and other devices. For networks that include older Macs or Windows computers, select this option.

   - **None.** If you select this option, your network won't be secure and anyone within range can join it without a password. You should not use this option unless you are very sure that unauthorized users cannot access your network. This option leaves your network and all devices connected to it vulnerable to attack and I don't recommend that you use it. There isn't a good reason to have an unsecured network. After all, you only have to type a network's password the first time you join it; not wanting to type a password is not a good reason to leave your network open.

5. **Type the network password in the Wireless Password and Verify Password fields.** This is the password that people have to type to be able to connect to the secured network.

6. **Select the Remember this password in my keychain check box.** This causes your MacBook Pro to remember the network password so that you don't have to type it when you connect.

7. **To do more advanced configuration of the base stations, click Wireless Options.** This is unusual, but you should know what these options are should you ever need to use them.

8. **To change the country with which the base station is associated, choose it on the Country pop-up menu.** This can impact some of the other options on the base station; you should select the country in which you are using the base station if it isn't selected by default (it usually is).

9. **If you do not want the network name to be broadcast and appear on network selection screens, select the Create hidden network check box.** In order to use a hidden network, the user must know the network name rather than selecting it from a menu. I cover how to access a hidden network later in this chapter.

10. **Use the Radio Mode pop-up menu to determine the wireless standards supported on the network.** The more standards you allow, such as 802.11n (802.11b/g compatible), the more types of devices are able to connect to the network. However, when slower devices are connected, the overall speed of the network may decrease. You must allow the type of connection supported by the devices you want to connect to the network. Modern Macs all support 802.11n, which is currently the fastest standard.

11. **Use the Radio Channel pop-up menu to select the channel over which the base station communicates.** Generally, the default channel works fine, but if you are having trouble communicating with devices, you can try different channels to improve signal transmission and reception. If you have multiple AirPort networks in the same area, you can use the Channel pop-up menu to have the networks use different channels so that they don't interfere with one another.

12. **Click Save.** The sheet closes and your options are set.

Note

There are many ways an Internet connection can be configured; the details of each are different. However, most cable and DSL Internet accounts are configured using details similar to those shown here. Review the information you received from your provider for the details you need to use to configure the base station to access your Internet account. Most of the time, you simply connect the base station to the modem and it connects to the Internet with the default settings.

Dynamic Host Configuration Protocol (DHCP) means that the device controlling the network (the modem, in this case) provides Internet Protocol (IP) addresses to each device on the network, including the base station. It manages all of the addresses to ensure that the one for each device is unique. As you connect different devices, the modem automatically assigns an address, which is great because you don't have to think about configuring a network address. To configure the way the base station gets its IP address, click the Internet tab and choose DHCP on the Connect Using pop-up menu, as shown in Figure 3.4.

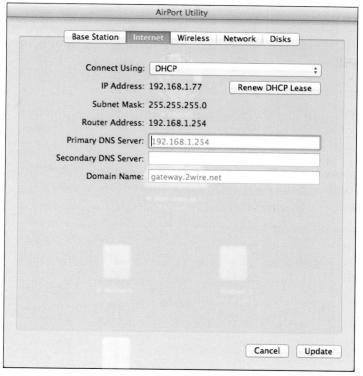

3.4 Use the Internet tab to configure how the base station gets its IP address.

Note

The other option for configuring how a base station gets its IP address is static. When you choose this option, you must get the addresses from your Internet service provider and type all of them in the fields. This is very unusual unless you are setting up a base station in a large organization that doesn't use DHCP and instead configures a specific address for each device.

You can configure how the base station manages the network using the Network tab. How you configure this depends on the modem you are using to connect to the Internet. If the modem provides the wireless network you want to use and manages all of the IP addresses on the network, you enable the base station to simply act as a bridge between the modem and other devices. If the modem doesn't provide a wireless network or you want the base station to manage the IP addresses for all devices, configure the base station to manage the IP addresses on the network.

Caution

Make sure you have only the modem or the base station managing the IP addresses on the network or the devices may conflict with each other. If you do allow both devices to manage the IP addresses, make sure that you configure a different range of IP addresses than those provided by the modem.

Perform the following steps to configure the network:

1. **Click the Network tab.**

2. **If the modem to which you connected the base station provides a wireless network, choose Off (Bridge Mode) on the Router Mode pop-up menu and skip the rest of these steps.** If you want the base station to manage the addresses, choose DHCP and NAT (Network Address Translation) on the Router Mode pop-up menu.

Note

NAT shields devices that are connected to the base station from Internet attacks. To hack a device, you need its IP address, and NAT hides the addresses of the devices connected to the base station so that only the base station's IP address is available. Make sure that NAT is enabled for your network if the base station is providing the IP addresses for it. NAT is covered in more detail in Chapter 13.

3. **To configure the range of addresses that the base station assigns to devices, use the DHCP range pop-up menu and fields to configure the range, such as 10.0.1.2 to 200.** You want to make sure that the range you configure does not conflict with other DHCP servers.

4. **Ensure the Enable NAT Port Mapping Protocol check box is selected.**

Note

There are additional options on the Network tab, but unless you are managing a complicated network in a large organization, you aren't likely to ever need them.

After you configure all of the settings you want the base station to use, click Update. The base station is configured according to the settings you entered. When the process is complete, the base station restarts and its wireless network becomes available.

Building a local network

The base station and modem are the heart of the local network. In addition to providing an Internet connection to the other devices on the network, they make many other services available, such as file and printer sharing. To add devices to the network, build it by connecting wireless devices to it, connecting a USB printer or hard drive to the base station's USB port, connecting a network printer to one of its Ethernet ports, or adding an Ethernet router and connecting more Ethernet devices to it.

In most cases, adding a device to your network is simple. You first make the physical or wireless connection between the network and the device, and then configure the device to connect to and use the network's resources, such as its Internet connection.

Connecting via Wi-Fi

To be able to connect to a Wi-Fi network, such as one provided by a Time Capsule, you first enable Wi-Fi on your MacBook Pro. Once Wi-Fi is enabled, you can find and connect to a wireless network. Follow these steps to configure your MacBook Pro to use Wi-Fi:

1. **Open the System Preferences application and click the Network icon to open the Network pane.**

2. **Click the Wi-Fi option in the list of available network options in the left part of the pane.** The Wi-Fi tools appear in the right part of the pane.

3. **If Wi-Fi is currently off, turn it on by clicking the Turn Wi-Fi On button.** Wi-Fi services start and your MacBook Pro begins scanning for available networks (you see radiating waves at the top of the Wi-Fi menu if it is enabled). If you've previously connected to an available network, you join that network automatically and its name appears on the Network Name pop-up menu.

4. **If you want to be prompted to join new networks, select the Ask to join new networks check box.** When your MacBook Pro is in an area with networks you've not previously connected to, you're prompted to connect to them.

5. **Select the Show Wi-Fi status in menu bar check box to put the Wi-Fi menu on your menu bar.** You can use this menu to quickly select and control your Wi-Fi connection.

6. **Click Advanced.** You see the Advanced options sheet, which you can use to configure additional aspects of your Wi-Fi connection.

7. **Click the Wi-Fi tab shown in Figure 3.5.**

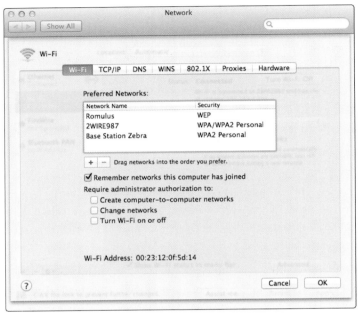

3.5 This sheet provides several useful options that you should configure to make working with Wi-Fi networks even faster and easier.

8. **If you don't want your MacBook Pro to automatically remember previously used networks, deselect the Remember networks this computer has joined check box.** Networks that the MacBook Pro remembers become your preferred networks and you automatically join these by default.

Genius   If multiple networks are remembered, you can drag them up or down in the list of Preferred Networks on the Wi-Fi tab to determine the order in which they are joined. Put the network you want to use first at the top of the list, and your MacBook Pro connects to that one first when it is available. If not, it looks for the second network on the list and continues this process until it finds an available network.

9. **Select or deselect the check boxes to prevent or allow changes without administrator authorizations.** For example, if you don't want nonadministrator users to be able to turn Wi-Fi on or off, select the Turn Wi-Fi on or off check box.

10. **Click OK.** The Advanced sheet closes. Your MacBook Pro is ready for wireless communication.

To manage your wireless network connections, open the Wi-Fi menu, as shown in Figure 3.6. The following information can be accessed in the Wi-Fi menu:

- **Signal strength of the current network.** When you are connected to a wireless network, the number of dark waves at the top of the menu indicates the strength of the signal.

3.6 The Wi-Fi menu is a fast and easy way to identify wireless networks in range of your MacBook Pro.

- **Wi-Fi status.** The first two items relate to Wi-Fi status. If it is turned on, you see Wi-Fi: On at the top of the menu with the command Turn Wi-Fi Off underneath it. If your MacBook Pro is searching for a network to which to connect, the status is Scanning. If Wi-Fi is not enabled, the status is Wi-Fi: Off and the command is Turn Wi-Fi On.

- **Available networks.** The second section of the menu shows you all the networks within range of your MacBook Pro. If you are currently connected to a network, it is marked with a check mark. If a network is marked with the Lock icon, it is secure, and you need a password to join it.

- **Join Other Network.** You use this command to join a hidden network for which you must know the network name and password.

- **Create Network**. This option enables you to create a network with the MacBook Pro as the hub to which other devices can connect. For example, if you are working in a group that doesn't have access to a network, you can create one to allow the group to share files.

- **Open Network Preferences.** This command opens the Network pane of the System Preferences application.

If a network is open, meaning that its information is broadcast publicly, then it appears on the Wi-Fi menu. To join an open network, perform the following steps:

1. **Open the Wi-Fi menu.**

2. **Select the network you want to join.** If no password is required (which is not usually the case), you join the network immediately. Its name is checked on the list of networks, you see the signal strength at the top of the Wi-Fi menu, and you can skip the rest of

these steps and start using the network's resources. If a password is required, you're prompted to provide it.

3. **Type the network password, as shown in Figure 3.7.**

4. **If you want to see the password you typed, select the Show password check box.** This can be useful because sometimes network passwords are convoluted and it can be hard to tell whether you typed it correctly.

5. **Select the Remember this network check box.**

6. **Click Join.** You join the network and its resources become available to you.

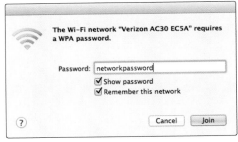

3.7 If you select the Remember this network check box, you see this dialog only the first time you connect to a network.

Genius

You can also join wireless networks from the Network pane of the System Preferences application. Choose the network you want to join on the Network Name pop-up menu and type the password at the prompt.

To control access to a network more tightly, it can be hidden. This means that its name doesn't appear on the Wi-Fi menu because its identity or existence isn't broadcast. To be able to access a hidden network, you need to know it exists, what its name is, the kind of security it uses, and its password. If you have all of that information, you can join it by doing the following:

1. **Open the Wi-Fi menu.**

2. **Select Join Other Network.** The Find and join a Wi-Fi network dialog appears (see Figure 3.8).

3. **Type the network name in the Network Name field.**

4. **Choose the kind of security the network uses in the Security pop-up menu.**

5. **Type the network password.**

6. **Click Join.** You join the network and its resources become available to you.

3.8 Use this dialog to join closed networks.

Connecting via Ethernet

Ethernet connections are fast; in fact, your MacBook Pro may perform better with an Ethernet connection than it does with a wireless one. This might not be too noticeable for Internet activity, but transferring files within a local network is much, much faster. Ethernet connections are also more secure because their signals travel over a cable. Because you have to be physically connected to the network with a wire, this makes it much harder for someone to intercept or interfere with the signal. Of course, keeping your MacBook Pro physically connected to the network can be limiting. Some MacBook Pro models don't have an Ethernet port, so you must have an Ethernet adapter to be able to connect the computer to an Ethernet network.

If you've installed an AirPort Extreme Base Station or Time Capsule and it has at least one open LAN port, you can use that port to access the network, including its Internet connection. You can also connect your MacBook Pro to an Ethernet hub that is connected to the base station, or directly to a modem via its Ethernet port.

Caution You can connect a cable or DSL modem directly to the Ethernet port on your MacBook Pro to provide it with an Internet connection. However, this exposes the MacBook Pro to attacks from the Internet. If you do connect it directly, make sure that you enable the Mac OS X firewall by opening the Security & Privacy pane of the System Preferences application, clicking the Firewall tab, and clicking Start before you connect the computer to the modem.

When you travel, Ethernet ports into a network are generally available in businesses, schools, and hotels. In hotels, ports are enabled, but in businesses or schools, most open ports are disabled for security. If a port isn't enabled, you need to contact someone in the IT department to have it enabled for you. Perform the following steps to connect your MacBook Pro to an Ethernet network:

1. **Connect one end of an Ethernet cable to an available Ethernet port on the network.**

2. **Connect the other end to the Ethernet port on your MacBook Pro; if your MacBook Pro doesn't have an Ethernet port, you need to use an Ethernet adapter to do this.**

3. **Open the System Preferences application and click the Network icon.** The Network pane appears.

4. **Select Ethernet from the list of available connections.** Status information is shown at the right (see Figure 3.9). If you see Connected, your MacBook Pro is connected to an active network. If the status is something else, such as Not Connected, check the connections to make sure the cable is plugged in correctly. If the status continues to be something other than Connected, the Ethernet port may not be active.

3.9 Select Ethernet on the list of available connections to see the connection status.

5. **Select Using DHCP on the Configure IPv4 pop-up menu.**

6. **Click Apply.** The MacBook Pro begins using the network's resources, such as an Internet connection.

Note It's a good idea to carry an Ethernet cable and adapter (if needed) with you as part of your MacBook Pro toolkit, as some locations that offer a connection don't always provide a cable.

Connecting via Cellular Modem

Using a cellular modem, you can get a high-speed Internet connection from anywhere within the service area covered by the device and service plan you are using. If you travel regularly, a cellular modem can be a much more convenient way to connect to the Internet while you are on the move. Because the connection is the same for you no matter where you are, you don't have to find and sign onto networks in various locations, making a cellular modem much easier to use. A cellular modem can also be less expensive to use than purchasing temporary accounts multiple times in the same time period.

The primary downside of cellular modems is that the networks they access aren't available in every location. Like cell phones, you need to be within a covered area to be able to access the service provided on the network. The other downside of a cellular modem is that its connection can be a bit slower than some wireless or wired connections that may be available to you. Even with this usually minor limitation, you may find a cellular modem to be an indispensable part of your MacBook Pro travel toolkit.

Caution

Almost all cellular modem accounts include a specific amount of data transfer under the monthly fee. If you go above this limit, it gets very expensive. Most service providers enable you to access your data usage or even send warnings when you are getting close to the limit on your service plan. Because of this, it's usually a good idea to connect to other networks (such as a Wi-Fi network that provides free access) when moving large amounts of data.

Obtaining a cellular modem is a lot like buying a cell phone; you need to purchase the device you use to connect to the wireless network and also sign up for a service plan. One of the best options for a cellular modem is a MiFi device. These are mobile Wi-Fi hotspots that connect to the cellular network and provide Internet access for your MacBook Pro. They are great because you can connect multiple devices (usually up to five) to them simultaneously without using up a USB port just to connect to the Internet (you can place the device itself in a backpack or computer bag).

The terms for these devices are similar to other kinds of cellular modems, so they are definitely worth checking out. The primary downside to MiFi devices is that because they aren't connected to your computer, the Internet connection lasts only as long as the device's battery does. However, in some cases, you can connect the device to your computer via a USB port to charge it while you use it, thus removing the battery limitation but requiring you to deal with a cable. Most major cell phone providers also offer cellular modems, so research devices on their respective websites. Consider the following factors when choosing a cellular modem:

- **Mac compatibility.** Most USB devices are compatible with Mac OS X. All MiFi devices are compatible because they provide a wireless network to which a Mac can connect.

- **Coverage areas.** Check that the network's coverage area matches the locations in which you use your MacBook Pro. Make sure that you focus on the coverage area for cellular modem connections (most maps also include cell phone network coverage).

- **Connection speed.** The download speed is the most important because when you use the Internet, you primarily download data. Of course, faster is better. In the United States, 3G connections are standard, but faster 4G connections are becoming widely available. You should try to get a 4G device if your provider has a 4G network because a faster device can always connect to a slower network if that is all that is available to you.

- **Terms.** There are a number of costs to factor into your decision, including the cost of the device itself (in many cases, this is free for a new account), the monthly cost of the account (usually dependent upon the amount of data allowed per month), contract requirements (such as an annual commitment or by month), and possible activation fees.

Caution

Trying a cellular modem is a bit of a gamble in terms of the coverage area and performance that you'll actually experience. For example, even if you primarily use your MacBook Pro in covered areas, your location and objects in those areas can interfere with the performance of your connection. Ask for a trial period when you purchase a device so that you can return it if it doesn't work for you. Some providers allow this and some don't.

After you obtain a cellular modem, you need to install and configure it. The details depend on the specific device and the service provider that you use. Refer to the following general steps to set up your device:

1. **Install the cellular modem's software.** This software includes the drivers and other software associated with the operating system and the application you use to connect to the network.

2. **Connect the device to your MacBook Pro.** For example, when you use a MiFi device, you connect it to your Mac using a USB cable.

3. **When prompted, restart your MacBook Pro.**

Once the cellular modem is installed and configured, connecting to the Internet is usually pretty simple. Again, the details depend on the specific device and service you use.

Refer to the following general steps to connect your device to the Internet:

1. **Launch the cellular modem's connection application.** In the application's window, you see the types of wireless connections that are available to you, including those available through Wi-Fi.

2. **Select the connection you want to use.**

3. **Click Connect.**

Using a MiFi device is even easier than other types of cellular modems. After you configure it to provide a Wi-Fi network, you simply power it on. When its network starts up, you connect your MacBook Pro to it just as you would with any other Wi-Fi network you use.

Connecting via iPhone or iPad Tethering

If you have an iPhone or iPad and a service provider that supports it, you can connect your MacBook Pro to the Internet via your device's cellular data network (such as the AT&T network for iPhone users who live in the United States). This is convenient because an iPhone or iPad can connect to the Internet in many locations, and you don't need another device because the iPhone or iPad becomes the cellular modem.

The specific steps you follow to connect to the Internet via tethering depend on the particular network that you use. However, the following general steps should help you get set up:

1. **Add tethering capabilities to your iPhone or iPad services.** You can usually do this via your account's website. In most cases, adding this capability requires additional fees based on the amount of data that is allowed per month.

2. **Access the tethering settings on the iPhone or iPad by tapping Settings ⇨ General ⇨ Network.**

3. **Tap Set Up Personal Hotspot.**

4. **Follow the on-screen instructions to complete the configuration.**

5. **Use one of the following options to connect your MacBook Pro to an iPhone or iPad Internet connection:**

   - **Wi-Fi.** Connect your MacBook Pro to the iPhone or iPad Wi-Fi network, which provides the connection coming through the device's cellular connection.

● **Bluetooth.** Connect your MacBook Pro to the iPhone or iPad via Bluetooth so the MacBook Internet connection is via the Bluetooth connection. See Chapter 5 for information about connecting your MacBook Pro to other devices via Bluetooth.

● **USB.** Connect your MacBook Pro to your iPhone or iPad using a USB cable, just like when you sync your device. If the tethered connection isn't detected and available on your MacBook Pro immediately, use the Network pane of the System Preferences application to select it, choose Using DHCP on the Configure pop-up menu, and then click Apply. The MacBook Pro should be able to access the Internet via the device's network.

Managing Multiple Network Connections

With Mac OS X, you can have multiple connections active at the same time. You can also determine which connection option your MacBook Pro uses first. In this section, I cover how to configure the connections that you use. You can also use locations to create sets of connections so that you can easily reconfigure your MacBook Pro for connectivity by choosing a location.

Configuring network connections

You use the Network pane of the System Preferences application to manage your MacBook Pro's connections. Follow these steps to configure network connections:

1. **Open the Network pane of the System Preferences application.** Along the left side of the pane, you see all of the connections configured on your MacBook Pro, as shown in Figure 3.10. Connections marked with a green

3.10 You can monitor the status of your connections in the Network pane.

dot are active and connected, and those marked with a red dot are not. Connections marked with a yellow dot are active, but not connected to anything. The connection at the top of the list is the current one.

2. **Select a connection.** Detailed information about the connection and the controls you use to configure it appears in the right of the pane. You've used some of these controls already to configure Wi-Fi and Ethernet connections. Configuring other kinds of connections is similar.

3. **Remove a connection that you don't use by selecting it and clicking the Remove (–) button located at the bottom of the connection list.**

4. **Open the Action pop-up menu (the gear icon) and choose Set Service Order.** The Services sheet appears.

5. **Drag services up and down in the list until they are in the order that you want your MacBook Pro to use them, starting at the top of the list and moving toward the bottom.** Typically, you want the fastest and most reliable connections at the top of the list. Each connection is tried in turn until one works. If you order them by their speed and reliability, the best available connection is always used.

6. **Click OK.** Your changes in the Services sheet are saved and the sheet closes.

7. **Click Apply.** The changes that you've made on the Network pane are saved and take effect.

Managing network connections with locations

In addition to having multiple connections active, you can use locations to define different sets of connections so that you can easily switch between them. For example, you may use one Ethernet configuration to connect to the Internet at home and a different one to connect when you are at work. Creating a location for each set of connections makes switching between them simple because you only have to configure them once. After they are configured, you can switch between them by simply choosing a different location. Without locations, you may have to reconfigure the Ethernet connection each time you are in a different place with your MacBook Pro.

As covered earlier, you can have multiple connections active at the same time. If you use only one configuration for each connection, you don't need to use locations. Rather, you want to use locations when you use different configurations of the same type of connection (such as an Ethernet). Your MacBook Pro includes one default location called Automatic. You can create new locations when you need them, or change and delete existing ones. Perform the following steps to configure a new network location:

1. **Open the Network pane of the System Preferences application.** The current location is shown on the Location pop-up menu at the top of the pane.

2. **On the Location pop-up menu, choose Edit Locations.** The Locations sheet appears. In the top pane of the sheet, you see the current locations that are configured on your MacBook Pro.

3. **Click the Add (+) button at the bottom of the sheet.** A new location called Untitled appears.

4. **Type a name for the new location and press Return.**

5. **Click Done.** The new location is saved and you return to the Network pane. The location you created is shown on the Location pop-up menu, as shown in Figure 3.11.

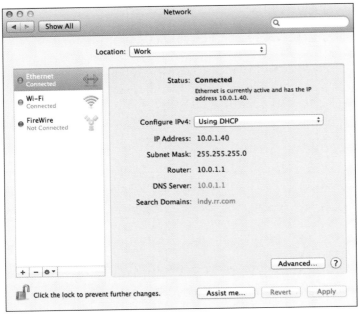

3.11 The location called Work is currently selected on the Location pop-up menu and is ready to be configured.

6. **Perform any of the following actions to configure the location:**

   - **Select a connection and configure it.**

   - **Delete a connection that you don't want to include in the location.**

   - **Add a connection by clicking the Add (+) button at the bottom of the list of connections.** On the resulting sheet, select the interface you want to use on the Interface pop-up menu, type a name, and then click Create. The connection is added to the list and you can configure it.

   - **Set the order in which you want the connections in the location to be used.**

7. **Click Apply.** Your changes are saved and the location becomes active.

Genius

If one of the current locations is similar to the one you want to create, select it on the Locations sheet, open the Action drop-down menu, choose Duplicate Location, and then give the copy a different name. This is faster than re-creating a location from scratch.

Perform one of the following actions to change the location you are using:

- **Open the Network pane of the System Preferences application and choose the location you want to use on the Location pop-up menu.** If the Apply button becomes active, click it to apply the location (some configuration changes require this, while others do not).

- **Choose Apple menu ⇨ Location ⇨ *locationname* (where *locationname* is the name of the location you want to use).** After you select a location, it is marked with a check mark on the menu to show you that it is active. Note that the Location menu doesn't appear unless you have at least two locations configured on your MacBook Pro.

Perform the following steps to edit or remove locations:

1. **Open the Network pane of the System Preferences application.**

2. **Choose Edit Locations from the Location pop-up menu.** The Locations sheet appears.

Genius

If you have created at least one location, you can quickly jump to the Network pane by choosing Apple menu ⇨ Location ⇨ Network Preferences.

3. **Perform any of the following tasks:**

   - To rename the location, select it, open the Action drop-down menu, choose Rename Location, type the new name, and press Return.

   - To delete a location that you no longer use, select it, and then click the Remove (–) button at the bottom of the sheet.

   - To duplicate a location, select it, open the Action drop-down menu, choose Duplicate Location, type the new location's name, and then press Return.

4. **Click Done.** You return to the Network pane.

Troubleshooting an Internet Connection

The time will come when you try to connect to a website or send e-mail and you see error messages instead, like the one shown in Figure 3.12. While this probably won't happen often, you do need to know what to do when a good Internet connection goes bad. In general, the solutions to most connection problems are relatively straightforward.

3.12 Houston, we have a problem.

One of the difficulties in solving an Internet/network problem is that there are typically a number of links in the chain, including your MacBook Pro, other computers, an Ethernet hub, and printers, to name a few. There are, however, three general sources of problems: Computers and other devices connected to the network (clients), an AirPort Extreme Base Station or Time Capsule, or the cable or DSL modem that you use to connect to the Internet.

Because there are multiple devices, the first step in solving an Internet/network issue is to determine the source of the problem. The three sources of problems can be classified into two areas: Client devices or the network. To determine which area is the source of an issue, try the same action that resulted in an error on your MacBook Pro on a different computer that uses the same connection (such as a Wi-Fi connection) and is on the same network. If the problem also occurs with other computers, you know that it is network-related, which is discussed in the next section. If the problem doesn't occur on a different computer, you know it's specific to your MacBook Pro, which is discussed later in the chapter.

Solving a network connection problem

Solving a network connection problem can be tricky because there are a number of potential sources of the problem both within and outside of the network, the latter of which are out of your control. Start with basic steps and try to determine which part of the network is causing the problems so that you can begin to solve them. Perform the following steps, working from the first element in the chain:

1. **Check the status of the modem.** Most modems have activity lights that indicate whether they are powered up and have a working connection. If the modem appears to be working, move on to step 2. If the modem doesn't appear to be working, move on to step 7.

2. **Check the status of the AirPort Extreme Base Station or Time Capsule.** It also has a light that uses color and flashing to indicate its status (see Figure 3.13). If the light indicates that the base station is working (in the current version, the status light is a solid green), move on to step 3. If not (for example, if the status light is flashing amber), move on to step 5.

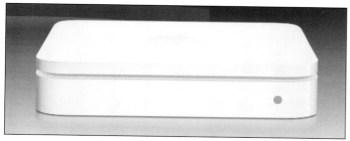

3.13 If the status light on the base station is green, all systems are go.

3. **Disconnect power from the base station and the modem.** Wait at least 20 seconds, and then reconnect power to the base station and modem. This resets the network and often solves the problem. Try what you were doing when you first encountered the problem. If it's successful, you're finished. If not, continue on to the next steps.

4. **If the modem's power light is on (which it probably is) but the connection light is not, contact your Internet service provider to make sure service is available.** Periodically check the modem status lights until the normal status lights appear; when they do, you should be good to go. If service is available, the provider can run some diagnostics from the source to determine if your modem is connected, and whether the problem lies between your modem and the provider, or is an issue with the modem and

its configuration. If the source of the problem is the modem itself, the provider can help you troubleshoot and solve the issue.

Genius

If Internet connectivity is critical to you, consider adding a backup connection that you can use if your primary one goes down. One choice for this is a cellular modem, which is useful for other purposes as well. Another option is to be aware of available hot spots in your area so that if your primary Internet connection goes down, you can take your MacBook Pro to a hot spot to work until your connection is restored.

5. **Remove power from the base station, wait 10 seconds, and reconnect it.** If the base station's status light turns green, the problem is solved; if not, you need to further isolate the problem.

6. **Ensure that the firewall is set on your MacBook Pro (see Chapter 13).**

Caution

Never connect a computer directly to a cable or DSL modem without some sort of firewall protection. To enable the Mac OS X firewall, open the Security & Privacy pane of the System Preferences application, click the Firewall tab, and then click Start. Even with this option enabled, it's not a good idea to leave the computer directly connected for more than a minute or two.

7. **Connect the MacBook Pro directly to the cable or DSL modem using an Ethernet cable.**

Note

To get a connection directly from the modem, your MacBook Pro must have the Ethernet connection enabled, which is covered earlier in this chapter.

8. **Try an Internet activity.** If it works, you know the problem is with the base station, and you can continue with these steps. If you can't get an Internet connection directly from the modem, you know that the problem is with the modem or the Internet connection; contact your provider for assistance.

9. **Troubleshoot the base station until you solve its problem.** You might need to reset and reconfigure it. See the documentation that came with the base station or use the Apple support website at www.apple.com/support/airport for help.

Solving a MacBook Pro connection problem

When you know the network is performing and other devices have connectivity, you can focus on the MacBook Pro to solve the issue. Perform the following steps to troubleshoot MacBook Pro connection issues:

1. **Try a different Internet application.** If one works but another does not, you know the problem is related to a specific application and you can troubleshoot that application. If no Internet application works, continue with the following steps.

2. **Open the Network pane of the System Preferences application.**

3. **Check the status of the various connections.** If the status for a connection is Not Connected, as shown in Figure 3.14, you need to reconfigure it to get it working.

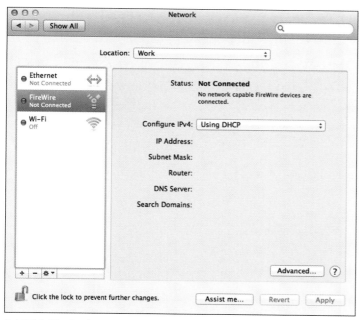

3.14 This MacBook Pro isn't connected.

4. **If the status is Connected, choose Apple menu ⇨ Restart.**

5. **Click Restart at the prompt.**

6. **After the MacBook Pro restarts, try the activity again.** Restarting when you have a problem is always a good idea because it's easy to do and solves a lot of different issues.

Note

When you can't access a web page because of a network issue, applications such as Safari (the Mac OS X default web browser) present the Network Diagnostics button. Click it to start the diagnostics application, and follow its instructions to try to solve the problem.

Finding help for Internet connection problems

While the steps in this section help with many Internet connection problems, they certainly won't solve them all. When they don't work, you have a couple of options. First, find a computer that can connect to the Internet and go to www.apple.com/support or www.google.com. Search for the specific problem you are having and use the results you find to solve it. Second, disconnect everything from your network, make sure that the firewall is on, and then connect your MacBook Pro directly to the modem. If the connection works, you know the problem is related to the network. Start with the base station, and then add other devices one-by-one until you find the source of the problem. If the connection doesn't work, you need help from your Internet service provider to solve the problem.

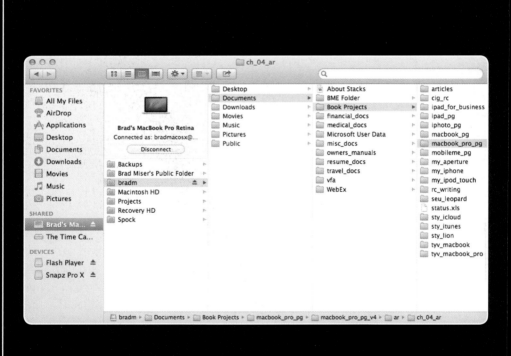

If you connect your MacBook Pro to the Internet with an AirPort Extreme Base Station or Time Capsule, as described in Chapter 3, you create a local network at the same time. Any devices connected to your local network through either a wireless or Ethernet connection can communicate with the other devices on your network. This is ideal because Mac OS X includes a lot of very handy network features. Perhaps the most useful of these is the ability to share files but, as you'll soon see, there are plenty of other powerful network features to explore and use.

Sharing Files

If you have more than one computer on your local network, the ability to share files among them is really useful. Not only can you easily move files between them, but you can also store files on one computer and work on them using any other computer on the network. In this section, I cover all of the MacBook Pro general sharing capabilities.

Sharing files with AirDrop

AirDrop is the Mac OS X file sharing feature that enables you to easily share files with other people. To do so, you simply drop the files you want to share on an icon representing the person with whom you want to share it. Unlike the other sharing techniques covered in this chapter, AirDrop requires little configuration and works automatically as long as the computers sharing files are all running Mac OS X Lion or later, and have Wi-Fi turned on.

To use AirDrop, open a Finder window and select AirDrop on the sidebar, as shown in Figure 4.1. AirDrop automatically identifies all of the other Macs in range of your MacBook Pro that have Wi-Fi turned on (they appear at the bottom of the window), and the AirDrop icon selected (if a user hasn't selected AirDrop, she won't be visible to you).

4.1 When you select AirDrop on the sidebar, you see all of the other Macs in range of your MacBook Pro that also have AirDrop selected.

The Macs don't have to be on the same Wi-Fi network to use AirDrop. They just have to have Wi-Fi turned on.

To share a file with someone, simply drag it onto his AirDrop icon. At the prompt, shown in Figure 4.2, click Send.

4.2 Here, the file called 0402.tiff is dropped onto Brad Miser's AirDrop icon to be shared.

The person with whom you are sharing the file has to accept it by clicking either Save or Save and Open, as shown in Figure 4.3. When the user clicks Save, the file is saved in the Downloads folder in his Home folder. If the user clicks Save and Open, the file is saved in the same location and opens in the associated application. If the user clicks Decline, the file isn't copied, and you see a message stating that the user has declined your request; click OK to dismiss it.

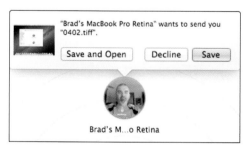

4.3 Clicking Save saves the file being shared to the user's Downloads folder.

Using AirDrop is a great way to easily move files between computers. Its limitation is that each computer has to have AirDrop selected. This means that action is required on both sides to share files, unlike the other sharing techniques covered in this chapter. Also, someone has to send you a file in order for you to get it; you can't access it otherwise. However, if you want to quickly get a file to someone else, it is a great option.

Genius

If you regularly use your MacBook Pro near other people with whom you want to share files, open AirDrop in a dedicated Finder window and minimize that window on the Dock. That way, your AirDrop will always be available to others and you won't be taking up valuable Desktop space with its window. If someone sends you a file, the AirDrop window and prompt jump onto your Desktop automatically.

Sharing your files with others

Mac OS X has file sharing features that provide more control and functionality for sharing files than AirDrop offers. Using file sharing enables you to provide other users with access to any location on your MacBook Pro so they can use that location as if it were on their own computers. Likewise, you can use the files and folders other users share on the network.

Complete the first two (the third is optional) of the following tasks to enable other computers to access files stored on your MacBook Pro:

- Configure user accounts to access your MacBook Pro from other computers.
- Configure file sharing services on your MacBook Pro.
- Set specific security privileges on the files and folders you share.

Configuring sharing user accounts

To be able to access files on your MacBook Pro, a user must have a valid user account on it that he uses to log in to access the files that you are sharing. Group is the only type of user account you can't use to share your files. Any Administrator, Standard, Managed with Parental Controls, or Sharing Only user accounts can access your MacBook Pro. The Sharing type of user account is especially intended to provide only sharing access to your MacBook Pro, while the access that the others have depends on the type. For example, an Administrator user account has administrator access to your MacBook Pro when logged in across the network.

If sharing files is all you want the user to be able to do while logged in to your MacBook Pro, create a Sharing user account, as shown in Figure 4.4. If you want to provide broader access to your computer, create a Standard or Administrator account instead. See Chapter 2 for more help on creating and managing the user accounts on your MacBook Pro.

4.4 A Sharing account (like the Share This account highlighted here) is ideal for enabling people to access the files on your MacBook Pro.

Note

By default, a user account called Guest User exists on your MacBook Pro (and every Mac, for that matter). This is a Sharing Only account that doesn't require a password for use. Initially, it provides access only to the Public folders in each user's Home folder. However, when you provide permissions to Everyone (more on this later), those permissions also apply to the Guest User account, and provide more access to files and folders.

Configuring file sharing

The second part of enabling file sharing is to configure your MacBook Pro to share its files, choose the folders you want to share, and determine the user accounts and permissions with which you want to share those folders. Perform the following steps to get it set up:

1. **Open the System Preferences application.**

2. **Click the Sharing icon.** The Sharing pane opens.

3. **To set the name by which your computer is recognized on the network, type a name for the computer in the Computer Name field.** The default name is *yourname*'s MacBook Pro (where *yourname* is the name you entered when you configured your MacBook Pro for the first time during the start-up process). You can leave this as is or create a different name.

Note

The name you see in the Computer Name field is a nickname. Your computer's real name is shown in the text below Computer Name. It is created based on the name you typed, but it is translated into acceptable syntax, and the extension .local is added to it. For example, any spaces are replaced with a hyphen and prohibited special characters are transformed. If you click Edit, you can edit the *true* name of your computer on the network.

4. **Select the On check box next to the File Sharing service in the left pane of the window.** File sharing starts up, you see its status change to On, and you see your computer's address and name just below the status text, as shown in Figure 4.5. Below this, you see the Shared Folders section, which lists the folders currently being shared. By default, the Public folder (with each user account's Home folder) is shared. In the Users section, you see the user accounts with which the selected folder is shared and the permission each user account has to that folder.

4.5 Use the Sharing pane of the System Preferences application to configure file sharing services on your MacBook Pro.

5. **To share a folder, click the Add (+) button at the bottom of the Shared Folders list.** The Select sheet appears.

6. **Move to and choose the folder you want to share.** You can only share folders for which you have Read & Write access.

7. **Click Add.** You return to the Sharing pane, and the folder you selected is added to the Shared Folders list. You see the default user accounts and associated permissions for that folder in the Users section. Initially, you see that your user account has Read & Write permissions; the other users and permissions will differ depending on the user accounts you have on your MacBook Pro.

Caution

One user is called Everyone. This *does* actually mean what it says. It represents absolutely everyone who uses your MacBook Pro or can access it over the network. When you set a permission for Everyone, it is applied to all user accounts except those for which you set specific access permissions, so be careful with this option.

8. **To allow a user account to access the folder, click the Add (+) button at the bottom of the Users list.** The User Account sheet appears, showing all of the user accounts configured on your MacBook Pro and all of your contacts (see Figure 4.6).

9. **Select Users & Groups, and then select the user accounts with which you want to share the folder.**

10. **Click Select.** You return to the Sharing pane and see the users on the Users list. After you add users to the list, you set the permissions that each user has to the folder you are sharing.

4.6 Choose the users with whom you want to share the selected folder on this sheet.

Genius

If you click the Address Book option (or any of the groups in your Address Book) in the User Account sheet, you can access any person in your Address Book. If you select a contact in your Address Book, you're prompted to create a password for that person to allow him to share files on your MacBook Pro. This creates a Sharing Only account for that person on your MacBook Pro.

11. **With the folder for which you want to allow access selected, select a user from the Users list on the Sharing pane.**

12. **On the pop-up menu at the right edge of the Users list (see Figure 4.7), choose from the following list which permissions the selected user account should have for the folder:**

- **Read & Write.** The user can open and change the contents of the folder.

- **Read Only.** The user can see and open the items in the folder, but can't change them.

4.7 Robert the Bruce will be able to see and change items in the Pictures folder when his permission setting is Read & Write.

- **Write Only (Drop Box).** The user can't see the contents of the folder or change them. All he can do is place files within the folder.

- **No Access.** This option (available only for Everyone) prevents any access to the folder by anyone except the users shown on the Users list.

Genius

If you'll be accessing files on your MacBook Pro from other Macs, it's a good idea to create a user account with the same name and password on each computer. This makes it much easier for you to log in.

13. **Repeat steps 11 and 12 for each user on the Users list.**

14. **To remove a user's access to the folder, choose the user, click the Remove (–) button at the bottom of the Users list, and then click OK in the warning sheet.**

15. **To unshare a folder, choose it on the Shared Folders list, click the Remove (–) button at the bottom of the Shared Folders list, and then click OK in the warning sheet.**

After you complete these steps, all that remains is to provide the user account information to the people with whom you'll be sharing your files.

Say Hello to Bonjour

Bonjour is the name of the Apple technology introduced way back in Mac OS X version 10.2 that makes it possible for devices on a network to automatically find each other. This means you don't have to bother with addresses or browsing though various paths to find the device you want to work with. Bonjour enables you to automatically find all the Macs on your network. Many other devices, such as printers, are also easily found with Bonjour. Even Windows computers can use Bonjour as long as they have the Apple Bonjour for Windows software installed.

Setting sharing permissions from the Finder

As I mentioned earlier in this chapter, you can share folders from the Sharing pane of the System Preferences application. You can also view and set sharing information for files and folders from within Finder windows. Follow these steps to check it out:

1. **Open a Finder window.** Move to the folder or file for which you want to get (or set) sharing information, and then select it.

2. **Choose File ⇨ Get Info.** The Info window appears.

3. **Expand the Sharing & Permissions section, as shown in Figure 4.8.** You see each user account and the permissions it has to the file or folder you selected in step 1.

4. **To set permissions for the folder, authenticate yourself under an Administrator account by clicking the Lock icon, and then providing the required user account and password.**

5. **Use the Add (+) button to add users to the folder or select users.** Click the Remove (–) button at the bottom of the window to remove users from the folder.

6. **Use the Privilege pop-up menus to set the access permission for each user.**

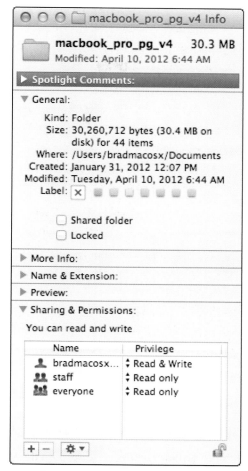

4.8 In the Sharing & Permissions section, you see and can set the access that users have to a folder or file.

Genius

To quickly apply a set of permissions to everything within a folder, open the Info window and set the sharing permissions as explained earlier in this chapter. Open the Action menu (the gear icon) and choose Apply to enclosed items. Click OK at the prompt. All of the files and folders within the selected folder will have the same sharing settings.

Accessing shared files

While it is better to give than to receive, there's also the expression *share and share alike*. You can access files being shared with you in one of the following ways:

- Browse using the sidebar
- Go directly to a shared source by its address

Both of these methods work, but the browsing option is the quickest and easiest. If you are accessing a device that supports Bonjour, browsing is definitely the way to go.

Using the sidebar to access shared files

Thanks to Bonjour, as soon as your MacBook Pro is connected to a network, any computers that are sharing files are immediately recognized and mounted on your Desktop, making it easy to access the files they are sharing. Perform the following steps when you want to access shared files:

1. **Open a Finder window in the Columns view.** Use this view for consistency with these steps and easier access to the shared files.

2. **In the Shared section of the sidebar, select the computer with the files that you want to access.** In the first pane, you see the computer's name, its icon, your current connected status (as Guest, which happens automatically), and the Public folders for each user account on that computer (along with the Public folders under other user accounts on your MacBook Pro).

Genius You don't need to log in to access Public files and folders. This is because you are automatically logged in under the Guest User account as soon as your MacBook Pro detects another computer on the network that has file sharing enabled.

3. **Click Connect As.** The Login dialog appears. The Registered User option is selected automatically.

Note The other two options in the Login dialog are Guest (under which you are signed in automatically as soon as you select the computer) and Using an Apple ID. If you choose the latter, you can select your Apple ID to log in to the file-sharing computer. This is especially useful if you are accessing files on a computer that is already set up with your Apple ID.

4. **In the Name field, type the name of the user account you want to use to log in.** This should be the name of the user account created for you to access the files you are allowed to share.

5. **Type the account password in the Password field.**

6. **Select the Remember this password in my keychain check box.** This enables you to log in automatically in the future.

7. **Click Connect.** Your MacBook Pro connects to the computer and mounts all of the folders being shared with you in the Finder window, as shown in Figure 4.9. The resources you see are those for which the account you are using has Read, Write Only (Drop Box), or Read & Write permissions.

4.9 I've logged in to the computer called Brad's MacBook Pro Retina under the bradmacosx@mac.com account.

8. **Select the folder containing the files with which you want to work.** The files in that folder become available to you only if you meet the following conditions:

   - **You have Read Only permission to a folder.** You can view the files it contains (you can't, however, save any changes you make to the files) or drag them to a different location to copy them. You can't move any files into the folder, delete files from it, or save any files there.

- **You have Read & Write permission to a folder.** You can do anything you want with the files it contains, including making changes, copying, or deleting them.

- **You have Write Only (Drop Box) permission to a folder.** You can't see its contents. All you can do is drag files into the folder to copy them there.

Genius

If you copy a file from a folder for which you have Read Only permissions to a new location, it is copied in the Locked state. If you try to make changes to it, you are warned that it is locked. If you click Overwrite, a new version of the file is created that contains the changes you made. From that point, it behaves the same as a file you created on your MacBook Pro.

Accessing shared files using a URL

For computers that are not using Bonjour, you can move directly to a computer that is sharing its files by using its address on the network. Follow these steps to connect to a computer via its URL:

1. **If the computer you want to access is a Mac, open the Sharing pane of the System Preferences application and select File Sharing.** You see the computer's address (starting with afp://) under the File Sharing status information. Use the address to log in to the computer.

2. **From the MacBook Pro Desktop, choose Go ⇨ Connect to Server.** The Connect to Server dialog appears, as shown in Figure 4.10.

3. **Type the address of the computer you want to access in the Server Address field.**

4. **Click Connect.** The Login dialog appears.

4.10 Using the Connect to Server command, you can log in to a file-sharing computer through its network address.

Note

If your network uses Dynamic Host Control Protocol (DHCP), which most do, the address of the computer can change. If you can't connect to a computer to which you've successfully connected before, check its address to see if it has changed. If you use Bonjour to connect to a computer, you don't have to worry about this, because the address changes are managed automatically.

5. **In the Name field, type the name of the user account with which you want to log in.**

6. **Type that account's password in the Password field.**

7. **Select the Remember this password in my keychain check box.** This enables you to log in automatically in the future.

Genius

If you regularly connect to a certain computer, add it as a favorite by clicking the Add (+) button in the Connect to Server dialog. It is then added to the list of favorites shown under the Server Address field. You can move back to an address by selecting it, and then clicking Connect. You can also return to a recent server by opening the Recent pop-up menu (clock) located at the right edge of the Connect to Server dialog.

8. **Click Connect.** The Volume Selection dialog appears. In this dialog, you see the folders and volumes that are available to your user account on the computer to which you are logging in.

9. **Select the volumes you want to use.**

10. **Click OK.** Your MacBook Pro connects to the other computer, and each volume you selected is mounted on your Desktop. You can then use the contents of the volume according to the permissions the user account has for each item.

Note

If you have Finder preferences set so that Connected servers appear on your Desktop, you see an icon for each volume you're accessing on the sharing computer. You can access a shared volume by simply opening its icon. You can also always access shared volumes by choosing Go ⇨ Computer.

Sharing files with Windows PCs

If your network includes both Macs and Windows PCs, you can share files between them. The process is similar to sharing files between Macintosh computers, but (as you probably guessed) there are some differences.

Sharing files on a MacBook Pro with a Windows PC

The process of configuring files to share with Windows PCs is very similar to the one for sharing files with Macs.

First, you must follow these steps to enable Windows file sharing:

1. **On the Sharing pane of the System Preferences application, click Options.** The Options sheet appears, as shown in Figure 4.11.

2. **Select the Share files and folders using SMB (Windows) check box.**

3. **Select the On check box for a user account that you want to be able to access files on your MacBook Pro from a Windows PC.** The Password dialog appears.

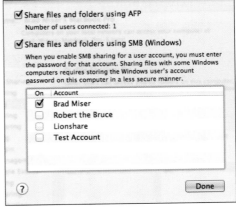

4.11 You can activate Windows file sharing on the Options sheet.

4. **At the prompt, type the password for the user account in the Password field.** This is the same password you created when you set up the user account.

5. **Click OK.** The dialog closes and you return to the Options sheet.

6. **Click Done.** Shared files are available from Windows PCs on the network.

Genius

You configure Windows sharing by user account, but you control the folders that are shared using the tools on the Sharing tab. You can't share some folders with only Windows or only Macs. If you want to configure a folder to limit sharing only to Windows PCs, create a unique user account for Windows PC users.

Accessing files from a Windows PC

After you configure your MacBook Pro to share files with Windows computers, you can access them from a Windows PC. There are a lot of versions of Windows out there, and many variations and details related to networking for each. This section describes a fairly common configuration on a Windows 7 computer accessing a network through a Time Capsule. If you have a different configuration, the details might be a bit different, but the overall process should be similar. Also, these steps assume that the Windows computer is already connected to the local network through a wireless or wired connection.

Something to consider first is that Windows networking relies on the concept of workgroups. The Macs you want to connect to Windows machines must be in the same workgroup. By default, the workgroup on both the Macs and Windows machines is called Workgroup. If you haven't changed the workgroup on the Windows machine, you don't need to do anything on the Mac. If you have changed the Windows workgroup, go to the Network pane of the System Preferences application, select the active network connection, click Advanced, click the WINS tab, enter the new workgroup name in the Workgroup field, click OK, and then click Apply.

Perform the following steps to access shared files from a Windows PC:

1. **On the PC, choose Windows ⇨ All Programs ⇨ Accessories ⇨ Run.** The Run tool opens.

2. **Type the DHCP address to the Mac on which file sharing permissions have been set up.** Include \\ before the address, as shown in Figure 4.12.

3. **Click OK.** You're prompted to log in to the MacBook Pro.

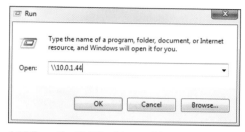

4.12 Type the DHCP address of the Mac with the files you want to share on the PC.

Note The DHCP address for a Mac is shown under the File Sharing status on the Sharing pane of the Systems Preferences application.

4. **In the User name field, type the username for an account on the MacBook Pro that has Windows sharing permissions enabled.**

5. **Type the account password in the Password field.**

6. **Click OK.** The Windows PC connects to the Mac, and you see all of the volumes and folders to which you have access based on the Mac's sharing configuration, as shown in Figure 4.13.

After the Mac's shared resources are mounted on the Windows Desktop, you can open them according to the permissions associated with the user account and resources you are using.

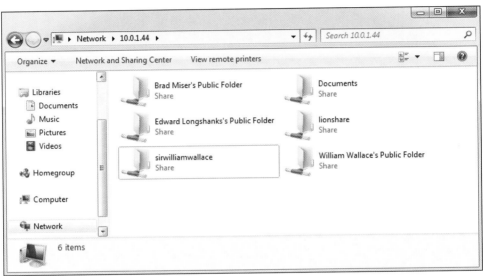

4.13 These shares are on Mac computers; however, they can be used on the Windows 7 machine according to their sharing permissions.

Sharing files from a Windows PC

Perform the following steps to share a folder and its files from a Windows PC:

1. **Right-click the folder that you want to share.**

2. **Choose Share with.**

3. **Choose Specific people.** The File Sharing dialog opens.

4. **On the drop-down list, choose the person with whom you want to share the item you selected.** The options include all of the user accounts on the Windows computer along with Everyone and Homegroup.

5. **Select which permission from the following list you want to provide for the item:**

   - **Read.** The user can only see the contents of the folder.

   - **Read/Write.** The user account can open and change the contents of the folder.

   - **Remove.** The user can delete items from the shared item.

6. **Click Share.** Windows begins sharing the items and you see information about them, as shown in Figure 4.14.

7. **Click Done.** You're ready to access the shared folder from another computer on the network.

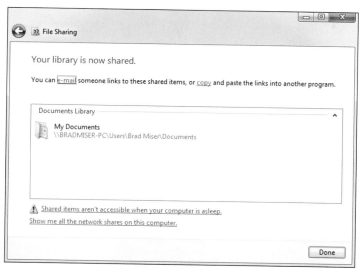

4.14 The My Documents folder is now being shared on the network.

Accessing shared files from a Windows PC using a Mac

To access shared files from a Windows PC, you need to know its address on the network (unless it is running Bonjour, in which case it should appear on the sidebar, the same as a Mac that is sharing files). You also must have a username and password. Perform the following steps to log in:

1. **From the Desktop, choose Go ⇨ Connect to Server.** The Connect to Server dialog appears.

2. **Type the address of the computer you want to access in the Server Address field.** The address should start with *smb://*, followed by the computer's IP address followed by /. For example, if the computer's IP address is *10.0.1.42*, the address you would type would be *smb://10.0.1.42/*, as shown in Figure 4.15.

4.15 Use the Connect to Server command to log in to a Windows PC that is sharing files.

3. **Click Connect.** The Login dialog appears.

4. **In the Name field, type the name of the user account you want to use to log in.** If your user account is part of a domain on the Windows PC, you must add the domain and \ as a prefix to the user account, as in *xyz\useraccount* (where *xyz* is the domain with which *useraccount* is associated).

5. **Type that account password in the Password field.**

6. **Select the Remember this password in my keychain check box.** This enables you to log in automatically. A dialog appears showing you the folders being shared.

7. **Click the shared resource you want to use on the Mac.** The shared folder is mounted on your Desktop and you can access it according to your permissions (see Figure 4.16).

4.16 Here, I've connected to a Windows PC to access files stored there.

Note   To determine the address of a Windows PC, open Network Connections. Right-click the active network connection, choose Status, and then click Details. You see the IPv4 address—use it in the Connect to Server dialog.

Sharing Screens

With screen sharing, you can control a Mac over the local network just as if you were sitting in front of it. This is very useful when helping other users on your network. Instead of physically moving to their locations, you can simply log in to their computers to provide help. Like file sharing, you can configure screen-sharing permissions on your MacBook Pro. You can also share the screens of other Macs that have screen-sharing permissions configured.

Sharing your MacBook Pro screen with other Macs

To share your MacBook Pro screen with other Macs on your network, follow these steps to configure screen-sharing permissions:

1. **Open the Sharing pane of the System Preferences application.**

2. **Choose the Screen Sharing service on the service list.** The controls for screen sharing appear. (If you select the On check box in this step, you don't need to perform step 8. However, it's usually better to select and configure a service before you turn it on.)

3. **Click Computer Settings.** The Computer Settings sheet appears.

4. **Select the Anyone may request permission to control screen check box if you want to allow anyone who can access your MacBook Pro to request to share your screen.** If you leave this deselected, only user accounts for whom you provide screen-sharing permissions are able to control your MacBook Pro.

5. **Select the VNC viewers may control screen with password check box, and type a password if you want people using Virtual Network Computing connections to be able to control your MacBook Pro.** For a local network, you don't really need to allow this, so, in most cases, you can leave this deselected.

6. **Click OK.** The sheet closes.

7. **Choose one of the following options in the Allow access for section:**

   - **All users.** Click this to allow anyone who has an account on your MacBook Pro to share its screen.

   - **Only these users.** Click this to create a list of user accounts that can share your screen. To add to the list, click the Add (+) button at the bottom of the user list. The User Account sheet appears. Select the user accounts with which you want to share your screen, and then click Select (you can also create a sharing account based on anyone in your Address Book). You return to the Sharing pane and the user accounts you selected are shown on the user list.

8. **Select the On check box for Screen Sharing (if you selected this in step 2, don't select again because you'll deselect it to turn Screen Sharing off).** Screen sharing services start and your MacBook Pro is available to users on your local network according to the access permissions you set. The Screen Sharing status becomes On, and under that status you see the screen-sharing address of your MacBook Pro on the network, as shown in Figure 4.17.

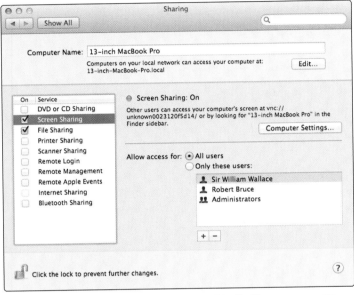

4.17 This MacBook Pro can share its screen with all of its user accounts.

When someone wants to share your MacBook Pro, you may see a permission dialog on your screen if the user requests permission to share your screen. To allow your screen to be shared, click Share Screen. The other person will see and be able to control your MacBook Pro.

Sharing another Mac's screen on a local network

You can access other Macs being shared with you by browsing the network for available computers or by moving to a specific address. The following steps allow you to connect to another Mac and share its screen:

1. **Open a Finder window in Columns view.** You can share screens starting from any Finder window view, but the Columns view will make it easier to follow the rest of these steps.

2. **In the Shared section of the sidebar, select the Mac with the screen you want to share.**

3. **Click Share Screen.** This command appears only if the Mac you selected has granted screen-sharing permission. The Share Screen Permission dialog appears, as shown in Figure 4.18.

Enter your name and password to share the screen of "Brad's MacBook Pro Next Gen".

Connect: ○ By asking for permission
⦿ As a registered user
○ Using an Apple ID

Name: bradm

Password: ••••••••

☐ Remember this password in my keychain

Cancel   Connect

4.18 Use the Share Screen Permission dialog to access another Mac on your network.

4. **Use one of the following options to share the other Mac's screen:**

   ● To request permission to share the screen, click the By asking for permission radio button, click Connect, and wait for the person using the other Mac to grant permission. On the Mac with the screen you are trying to share, a permission dialog appears. If the user allows you to share the screen, the other person's Desktop appears within the Screen Sharing window on your MacBook Pro Desktop. You can now work with the shared Mac as you would your own.

   ● To log in using a user account with screen-sharing permissions, click the As a registered user radio button, type the username in the Name field and the password in the Password field. Select the Remember this password in my keychain check box, and then click Connect.

   ● To share screens via an Apple ID, select Using an Apple ID, and then select the ID you want to use on the Apple ID pop-up menu.

Genius

If you request screen sharing from an account that isn't currently logged in on the computer screen you want to share, you see a dialog that enables you to either request to share the screen of the current user or to access the computer using the account under which you are logging in virtually. If you choose the latter option, you can use the account's folders and files even though it isn't active on the machine sharing its screen.

When you share a Mac's screen, you use the Screen Sharing application. Its window (which has the name of the shared Mac screen as its title) contains the Desktop of the shared Mac screen, including open Finder windows, applications, and documents, as shown in Figure 4.19. When your cursor is inside the Screen Sharing application window, any action you take is also done on the shared Mac screen. When you move outside the window, the cursor for your MacBook Pro separates from the shared Mac's cursor and the shared Mac's cursor freezes (unless, of course, the user at that Mac is doing something, in which case you see the results of his actions).

4.19 This Screen Sharing window shows a MacBook Air being controlled from a MacBook Pro.

When you access a shared Mac, its screen is automatically scaled to fit into the Screen Sharing application window. The Desktop you see in the Screen Sharing window depends on the resolution of the Mac Desktop you are sharing. If it is very large, such as a 24-inch iMac that also has an external display connected to it, the information in the shared window is quite small so that it all fits on your MacBook Pro screen. If the shared Mac's screen is larger than yours, you have to scroll to see all of it. You can access the Display pane of the System Preferences application on the shared Mac to decrease its resolution so that the image appears larger on your Desktop. You can also choose View ⇨ Turn Scaling Off to make the screen its actual size.

Caution

When you use screen sharing, you have the permissions granted by the user account you use. Be careful that you don't accidentally do something you didn't intend to on a shared computer. For example, don't use the shortcut ⌘+Q to quit applications when using the Screen Sharing application because that closes the active application on the shared Mac, not the Screen Sharing application itself. Use the Quit command on the Screen Sharing menu instead.

To move information from the shared computer to your own, copy it from the shared computer, and then choose Edit ⇨ Get Clipboard. This copies what you pasted to the Clipboard on your MacBook Pro where you can then paste it into your applications. To move information in the other direction, copy it on your MacBook Pro, and then choose Edit ⇨ Send Clipboard. This moves the data from your Clipboard to the Clipboard on the shared Mac, where it can be pasted into open documents.

You can also access the following menus at the top of the Screen Sharing window:

- **Control Mode.** Choose Control to take control of the other Mac. Select Observe if you only want to watch what is happening on that computer.

- **Scaling Mode.** Use these commands to determine how the screen you are sharing is scaled to fit inside the Screen Sharing window. Fit in Window shrinks the shared screen down so that you see all of it within the window. Show Full Size shows the screen at its actual size. If that is larger than the size of the Screen Sharing window, you have to scroll to see the entire screen.

- **Capture Screen.** Choose this to capture a screenshot of the contents of the screen you are sharing.

- **Clipboard.** Use these commands to work with the contents of your computer or the one with the screen you are sharing. To be able to use a shared Clipboard, choose Edit ⇨ Enable Shared Clipboard. When this command is enabled, click Shared Clipboard to work with it. Choose Get Clipboard to copy the contents of the Clipboard on the shared computer. Choose Send Clipboard to send the contents of your computer to the shared computer.

● **Display Selection.** If the shared computer has more than one display, choose the display you want to see. If you don't make a selection here, all of the displays will be shown in the Screen Sharing window.

Sharing Printers

Printers are a great resource to share on a network because you seldom need one printer for each computer. Typically, one or two printers per network are more than sufficient for everyone's printing needs. There are two basic ways to use printer sharing to make printers available on a network. You can connect a USB printer to an AirPort Extreme Base Station or Time Capsule and share it from there, or you can connect a USB or Ethernet printer directly to your MacBook Pro and share it with the network.

Note If a printer is networkable, you don't need to share it. Instead, connect the printer to the network through an Ethernet or wireless connection. This is better than printer sharing because no computer or base station resources are required for the networked printers.

Sharing USB printers connected to a base station

To share a USB printer from a base station, simply connect the printer to the USB port on the base station. Other computers will be able to add the printer using the Print & Scan pane of the System Preferences application.

Note To be able to access a shared printer, each computer must have the printer's software installed. Fortunately, Mac OS X includes the software for most printers by default or will download it automatically.

Sharing printers connected to a Mac

If a Mac has a printer connected to it directly through Ethernet or USB, you can share that printer with the network. However, in order for other computers to use that printer, the Mac to which it is connected must be active (it can't be asleep) and currently connected to the network. Because you'll probably move your MacBook Pro around a lot, this isn't convenient. However, if your network includes a desktop Mac to which a printer is connected, the following steps will allow you to share it:

1. **Connect and configure the printer to the Mac from which it is being shared.**

2. **Open the Sharing pane of the System Preferences application.**

3. **Select the On check box for the Printer Sharing service.** The service starts up.

4. **Select the check box for the printer you want to share.** Other computers can use the printer by adding it. The printer's name is the current printer name with *@yourmacbookpro* (where *yourmacbookpro* is the name of the computer to which the printer is attached).

Sharing an Internet Connection

Any Mac can share its Internet connection with other computers, similar to a base station. I don't recommend this for a permanent network because, for one reason, the Mac has to be active all of the time for the network to be available. However, it can be very useful when you are traveling with your MacBook Pro. You can share an Internet connection that you get via Ethernet with other computers or devices (such as an iPad) using Wi-Fi. You can also share an Internet connection that you get through Wi-Fi over your MacBook Pro's Ethernet port.

Note
You can't share an Internet connection using the same network connection from which the computer is getting its own Internet connection. For example, if your computer is using Wi-Fi to get its Internet connection, you need to use some other connection type, such as Ethernet, to share that Internet connection.

The following steps enable you to share an Internet connection:

1. **Connect and configure your MacBook Pro to access the Internet.**

2. **Open the Sharing pane of the System Preferences application.**

3. **Select the Internet Sharing service.** Its controls appear in the right part of the pane.

4. **On the Share your connection from pop-up menu, choose Ethernet if you get your connection through Ethernet, or Wi-Fi if you get your connection through Wi-Fi.**

Note
You can also share a connection you are getting via Bluetooth or FireWire, but those are much less common. The process to configure sharing those connections is similar to sharing an Ethernet connection.

5. **Select the On check box for the connection that other computers use to get their Internet connection from your MacBook Pro.** For example, if your MacBook Pro is using Ethernet for Internet access, select the On check box for Wi-Fi.

6. **If you selected Wi-Fi in step 5, click Wi-Fi Options; if not, skip to step 12.** The Wi-Fi Options sheet appears, as shown in Figure 4.20.

4.20 Use the Wi-Fi Options sheet to create a Wi-Fi network over which you can share an Internet connection.

7. **Type a name for the network you are creating in the Network Name field.** This is how others identify the network you provide.

8. **Choose the channel for the network on the Channel pop-up menu.** The default channel usually works, but you can choose a specific channel if your network has problems. If there are already other Wi-Fi networks in the same area, it is more likely that you will have to use a different channel.

9. **Choose WPA2 Personal on the Security pop-up menu.** I recommend that you always create a secure network.

10. **Type a password for the network in the Password and Confirm Password fields.**

11. **Click OK.** The sheet closes, and you return to the Sharing pane.

12. **Select the On check box for the Internet Sharing service.**

13. **Click Start in the resulting confirmation sheet.** Your MacBook Pro starts sharing its Internet connection. Other computers can connect to the Internet by joining the MacBook Pro's wireless network if you are sharing via Wi-Fi, as shown in Figure 4.21. They can also connect if they are connected to your MacBook Pro's Ethernet or FireWire ports directly or through a hub.

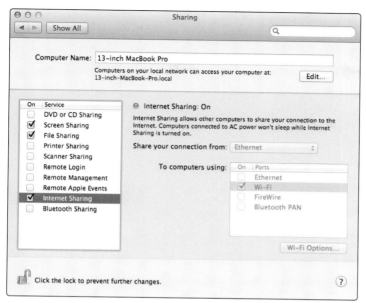

4.21 This MacBook Pro is sharing its Ethernet Internet connection through a Wi-Fi network.

Sharing with Applications

A number of applications also provide sharing on a local network. For example, iTunes enables you to share your library with the network so that other people can listen to and view its contents. You can also share your iPhoto libraries on the network so that people can access the photos in your database. Of course, you can access iTunes and iPhoto libraries that are being shared by others on the network, as well.

To set up sharing in those applications, open the Sharing tabs of their Preferences dialogs. Select the Look for shared libraries/photos check boxes to access resources that are being shared with you. Select the Share my library/photos check boxes to share your libraries on the network. Use the controls on the tab to define what you share, the name others must choose to access the shared content, and whether a password is required.

How Can I Control My MacBook Pro and Maintain Battery Power?

To get the most from your MacBook Pro, you can customize the keyboard and trackpad so that they work according to your preferences. You might want to add a mouse or external keyboard to your toolkit, especially for those times when you are using the computer at a desk. Bluetooth mice and keyboards enable you to do this without being tethered by cables. You can also use Bluetooth to share files. And, of course, you can't control your MacBook Pro if it is out of power, so you need to know how best to manage the MacBook Pro battery.

Using the Trackpad Effectively

A trackpad is an ideal input device for a mobile computer because it provides as much control as a mouse, but doesn't require anything external to be connected to the computer. The MacBook Pro trackpad provides all of the basic capabilities you need to point and click, but it doesn't stop there—it also supports gestures. Using combinations of your fingers and motion, you can manipulate objects in applications, scroll windows, zoom in and out, and so on. You can use the trackpad much more effectively by taking advantage of its gestures and tweaking all of its options to suit your preferences.

Note

If you've used an iPhone, iPod touch, or iPad, you've experienced Apple Multi-touch technology. You can control these devices using the normal motions of your fingers on the screen (such as a pinching motion to zoom in and out). The MacBook Pro incorporates a similar interface on its trackpad.

Configuring the trackpad

You can configure the trackpad to work according to your preferences with the Trackpad pane in the System Preferences application. The trackpad's configuration options are comprised of three tabs, as shown in Figure 5.1: Point & Click, Scroll & Zoom, and More Gestures.

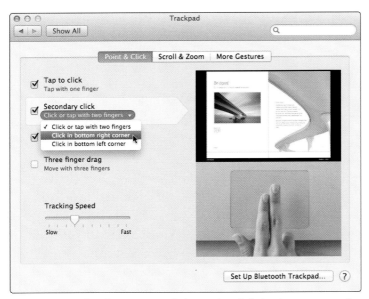

5.1 Use the Trackpad pane to tweak the trackpad's behavior to your preferences.

Use these tabs to configure the gestures you want to use for each of these general tasks. Follow these steps to configure each tab (the process is similar for each one):

1. **Click the tab for the type of gestures you want to configure.**

2. **Point to a gesture.** A video plays showing you how to move your fingers to form the gesture and its impact.

3. **If you want to use the gesture, select its check box.**

4. **If a gesture has a pop-up menu for further configuration, open the menu and choose an option for the gesture.** For example, you can set the number of fingers (three or four) you use to gesture for Mission Control.

5. **Repeat these steps until you configure all of the gestures you want to use.**

Consider the notes that follow as you configure and work with gestures:

- **There are three possible gestures for a secondary click (also known as a right-click on a two-button mouse): Tap with two fingers, click on the bottom-right corner of the trackpad, or click on the bottom-left corner.** The difference between a click and a tap is that when you tap, you don't depress the trackpad button, whereas when you click, you do depress the button.

- **The three-finger drag enables you to move objects on the screen by touching three fingers to the trackpad and moving your hand until the object is where you want it to be.** When you lift up your fingers, the object drops into its new location. If you used previous versions of Mac OS X, you may find this a big improvement over the somewhat difficult drag-and-lock feature.

- **Use the Tracking Speed slider on the Point & Click tab to set how far the pointer moves for the same movement of your finger on the trackpad.** The faster you set the tracking speed, the farther the pointer moves on the screen for the same motion of your fingers on the trackpad.

- **The scroll direction natural gesture may be a bit confusing at first.** In previous versions of the Mac OS, when you drag your fingers, the scroll bars move in the same direction as your fingers. For example, when you drag your fingers toward you, you scroll down the screen. With the scroll direction: natural option enabled, the movement is the opposite; dragging your fingers toward you results in the content moving down the screen (the scroll bar moves up the screen). This is the same movement that happens on an iPhone, iPod touch, or iPad. While it seems perfectly natural when you use your fingers on a screen, it may be counterintuitive on a trackpad, especially if you've used previous versions of Mac OS X. I recommend you try this option for a while to see if it does, indeed, seem natural to you.

- **Take extra time to explore the options on the More Gestures tab.** This is where you set gestures for the Mac OS X features that really benefit from them, including navigation between pages, moving between applications in full screen, Mission Control, and so on. Most of these gestures have options that you should check out, too.

Using gestures to control your MacBook Pro

Some gestures may immediately seem very natural to you, such as a one-finger tap to click the mouse button, while others might take some getting used to. I recommend that you at least watch the videos for all of the gestures and enable any that you think might be useful to you. Some take a little practice. For example, when you configure a four-finger swipe to get to Mission Control, you drag four fingers up the trackpad. Then, you move the pointer and tap a window to move into an application, or move the pointer and tap a space to move into it. This gesture makes accessing Mission Control quick and easy, but does a take a few repetitions until it becomes a normal part of your Mac use.

Genius

To make getting used to gestures faster and easier, leave the Trackpad pane of the System Preferences application open in the background where you can see it as you work. This can remind you of the gestures available and, if you forget how one works, you can quickly switch to the System Preferences application for a demo (maybe even using the Mission Control gestures to move there).

You may have to intentionally use some of the gestures for a little while, but they'll soon become second nature, and you'll be able to control things on the Desktop quickly and easily. If you find some unexpected actions happening, check the gestures you have configured again. Some of them might cause you a problem if they mimic a natural motion of your fingers. Disable the gesture, set its options to be more to your liking (such as the number of fingers used), or simply be aware of it until you get used to it.

Note

All Apple applications support gestures, but not all third-party applications (or even all versions of the same application) do. Trackpad gestures are a relatively recent innovation, so older versions of some applications might not support them even if the current one does. You just have to try the enabled gestures in the specific applications you use to find out if they are supported. If not, update the application, if possible.

Using the Keyboard Effectively

The MacBook Pro keyboard is used not only for typing but also for controlling your computer, particularly through keyboard shortcuts. In this section, I cover how to configure the basic functions of the keyboard and how to use it to efficiently control your MacBook Pro, and then how to control the language it uses.

Configuring the keyboard

Follow these steps to configure your keyboard:

1. **Open the Keyboard tab on the Keyboard pane of the System Preferences application, as shown in Figure 5.2.**

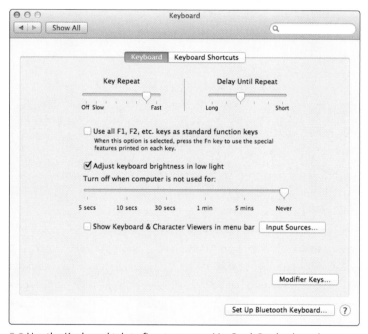

5.2 Use the Keyboard tab to fine-tune your MacBook Pro keyboard.

2. **Click and drag the sliders at the top of the pane to configure how keys repeat when you hold them down.** The Key Repeat slider controls how fast the corresponding character repeats, while the Delay Until Repeat slider controls how long you hold the key down to start repeating.

3. **If you want the function keys to behave as standard function keys instead of the default actions they are programmed to perform (such as F2 to brighten the display), select the Use all F1, F2, etc. keys as standard function keys check box.** If you select this option, you must hold down the Fn key and press the appropriate key to perform its action (such as F10 to mute your MacBook Pro).

4. **To enable the keyboard's backlighting, select the Adjust keyboard brightness in low light conditions check box and use the slider to set the amount of time backlighting remains on when the computer is not being used.** To conserve battery power, you want this time to be short, but not so short that the illumination turns off too fast for it to be of any use to you.

5. **If you want the Keyboard and Character viewers to be available on the menu bar, select the Show Keyboard & Character Viewers in menu bar check box.**

6. **To configure the input sources available to you, click Input Sources.** You move to the Input Sources tab on the Language & Text pane, which I cover later in this chapter.

7. **Back on the Keyboard tab, click Modifier Keys.** The Modifier Keys sheet appears, as shown in Figure 5.3.

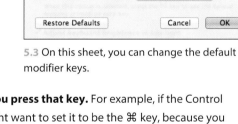

8. **For each of the four modifier keys, use the pop-up menu to select the action that you want to occur when you press that key.** For example, if the Control key is more convenient for you, you might want to set it to be the ⌘ key, because you use it more frequently. You can select No Action to disable a key, in which case it is grayed out on the sheet.

5.3 On this sheet, you can change the default modifier keys.

9. **Click OK to set your preferences and close the sheet.**

Genius

I have never discovered a real use for the Caps Lock key, but I have accidentally turned it on lots of times and found myself TYPING IN ALL CAPS, which is very annoying. You can disable this key by choosing No Action on its pop-up menu. Ah, now you don't have to yell as you type just because you accidentally hit this key.

Configuring language settings and the Input menu

You can configure the languages you use for the keyboard, along with other input preferences, using the Language & Text pane of the System Preferences application. The following steps walk you through configuring languages:

1. **Open the Language tab on the Language & Text pane of the System Preferences application, as shown in Figure 5.4.**

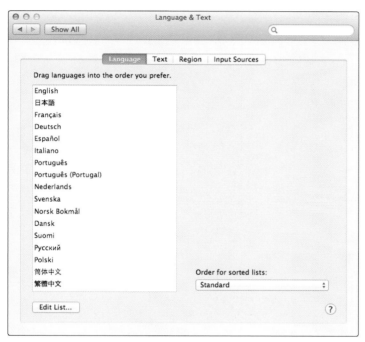

5.4 You can configure the MacBook Pro keyboard to use any (or all) of these languages.

2. **Click Edit List.**

3. **On the resulting sheet, deselect the check box for any language you don't want to be available, and then click OK.** The sheet closes and the language check boxes that were not selected are removed from the list. On the tab, you see a warning that you have to log out, and then log in again for the changes to take effect in applications.

4. **Drag the languages up or down the list to change their order, keeping the one you want to be the default at the top of the list.**

5. **On the Order for sorted lists pop-up menu, choose the language that should be used to sort lists.** This is used regardless of the language you happen to be using at any point in time. For example, if you choose English on the list and have Italian as the current keyboard language, lists are still sorted according to English. If you choose Standard, the sort will be according to the current language.

Follow these steps to configure global symbol and text substitution:

1. **Open the Text tab of the Language & Text pane of the System Preferences application, as shown in Figure 5.5.**

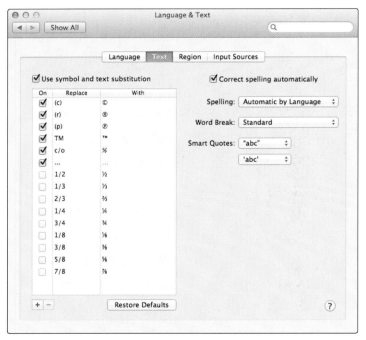

5.5 On the Text tab, you can configure global substitutions and other text settings.

Note

The settings on the Text tab are global, meaning that your MacBook Pro uses them unless overridden by an application. For example, if you use Word and have autocorrect set to change *(c)* to the word *copyright*, that setting overrides the global text substitution setting (which is the copyright symbol, ©, by default).

2. **Select or deselect the On check box for any text substitutions you want to enable or disable, respectively.**

Genius

To create custom substitutions, click the Add (+) button at the bottom of the substitution list. A new entry appears and is enabled by default. Type the characters to be replaced, press Tab, and then type with what those characters will be replaced. The substitution is added to the list and can be used just like the defaults. To remove a substitution, select it and click the Remove (–) button. To disable it, deselect its On check box.

3. **To disable the Mac OS X Spell Checker, deselect the Correct spelling automatically check box.**

4. **If you leave the spell-checker enabled, choose how you want it to function on the Spelling pop-up menu.** The default is Automatic by Language, which means your current language is used. You can open the menu to choose a specific language or choose Setup to do an advanced configuration of the spell-checker.

5. **On the Word Break pop-up menu, choose how you want word breaks to be applied.** You can choose Standard (the default) or a specific language from the pop-up menu.

6. **Use the Smart Quotes pop-up menu to determine what is substituted when you press either single or double quotes.**

Follow these steps to configure format options:

1. **Open the Region tab of the Language & Text pane of the System Preferences application, shown in Figure 5.6.**

2. **Choose the region format you want to use on the Region pop-up menu.**

3. **Use the pop-up menus to configure options for the various formats, such as the calendar and currency.**

4. **To specifically configure a format, click its Customize button.** Use the controls on the resulting sheet to customize the format, and then click OK to use the new settings.

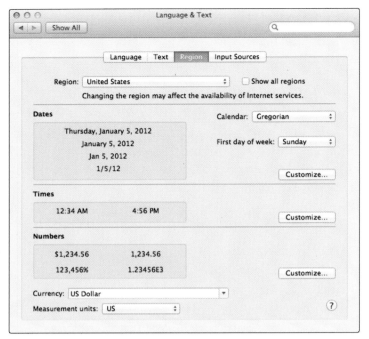

5.6 On the Region tab, you configure the date, time, number, and currency formats.

You can also configure the Input menu, which enables you to quickly choose among languages and select some other handy keyboard tools. Follow these steps to set it up:

1. **Open the Input Sources tab of the Language & Text pane of the System Preferences application.**

2. **If you want the Keyboard & Character Viewer to be available, select its On check box.** The menu appears on the Finder menu bar.

3. **Select the check box next to each input source you want to make available.**

4. **If you selected at least two input sources, select the Use the same one in all documents radio button to use that same input source in every application.** Select the Allow a different one for each document radio button to choose whether more than one input source can be available at the same time.

5. **Select the Show input menu in menu bar check box.** The Input menu appears on the menu bar. Its icon is the flag for the currently selected input source if you have at least two sources enabled, along with the Keyboard & Character viewer. If you have only one language and the Keyboard & Character viewer enabled, the menu's icon is the viewer instead of a flag.

Using keyboard tricks

It's worth your time to learn some of the ways you can control your MacBook Pro via the keyboard; there's a lot of power hidden behind those mild-mannered keys.

Controlling the keyboard backlight

If you've ever tried to use a computer in a dark environment (such as on an airplane at night), you'll really appreciate the MacBook Pro's backlit keyboard. When enabled, backlighting works automatically. When your MacBook Pro senses that the environment is dark, the backlight comes on. (As covered earlier, you can set how long the keyboard remains illuminated after you press a key.) When things brighten up, backlighting shuts off.

When backlighting is on, you can use the following function keys to manually control its brightness:

- **F5.** Press this key to decrease the brightness of the backlighting.

- **F6.** Press this key to increase the brightness of the backlighting.

Controlling your MacBook Pro with function keys

As shown in Table 5.1, the MacBook Pro includes a number of built-in functions on the function keys that are quite useful.

Table 5.1 MacBook Pro Default Function Keys

Function Key	What It Does
F1	Decreases display brightness.
F2	Increases display brightness.
F3	Opens Mission Control.
F4	Opens or closes the Launchpad.
F5	Decreases the brightness of keyboard backlighting.
F6	Increases the brightness of keyboard backlighting.
F7	Rewind/Previous in various applications, such as iTunes.
F8	Play/Pause in various applications, such as iTunes.
F9	Fast-forward/Next in various applications, such as iTunes.
F10	Mutes sound.
F11	Decreases volume.
F12	Increases volume.
Eject (non-Retina models)	Ejects the selected ejectable device or disc (if one is inserted).
Power (Retina models)	Turns the MacBook Pro on or off

By default, you can perform these functions by simply pressing the appropriate function key. As I cover later in this chapter, you can also remap these keys to different functions if you so choose. Remember, you can select the Use all F1, F2, etc. keys as standard function keys check box on the Keyboard tab of the Keyboard pane to make the standard function keys available. If you do this, hold the Fn key down and press the function keys shown in Table 5.1 to perform their default functions.

Controlling your MacBook Pro with default keyboard shortcuts

Mac OS X includes support for many keyboard shortcuts by default. For example, you've probably used ⌘+Q to quit applications. There are many more keyboard shortcuts available to you. The only challenge to using keyboard shortcuts is learning (and remembering) which ones are available to you. Fortunately, as described in the following list, there are a number of ways to discover keyboard shortcuts:

- **The Keyboard Shortcuts tab on the Keyboard pane of the System Preferences application**. If you click this tab, you see a list of Mac OS X keyboard shortcuts. Select the type of shortcuts in which you are interested on the left pane of the window and the current shortcuts appear in the right pane, as shown in Figure 5.7. You can also use this pane to change the current shortcuts and create new ones.

5.7 You should become familiar with the keyboard shortcuts for the commands you use most frequently.

- **Menus.** When you open menus, keyboard shortcuts are shown next to the commands for which they are available.

- **Mac Help.** Open the Help menu and search for shortcuts for the Finder and your favorite applications.

Configuring keyboard shortcuts

Using the Keyboard Shortcuts tab of the Keyboard pane, you can configure keyboard shortcuts. You can enable or disable the default keyboard shortcuts, change them, or add your own. Perform the following steps to configure default keyboard shortcuts:

1. **Open the Keyboard Shortcuts tab on the Keyboard pane of the System Preferences application (see Figure 5.7).** You see a list of standard OS keyboard shortcuts in various categories, such as Launchpad & Dock, Mission Control, Keyboard & Text Input, and Screen Shots.

2. **Select the category containing the shortcuts you want to change.** The current commands and associated shortcuts are shown in the right pane.

3. **Disable or enable any of the listed shortcuts by deselecting or selecting its check box.**

4. **To change the key combination for a shortcut, double-click it and, when it is highlighted, press the new key combination you want to use for that command.**

Creating your own keyboard shortcuts

You can follow the steps below to create your own keyboard shortcut for any menu command in any application:

1. **Identify the specific command for which you want to create a keyboard shortcut.** If it is a command specific to an application, note the exact name of the command (including whether it includes an ellipsis). You can find commands on application menus or by accessing an application's Help system.

2. **Open the Keyboard Shortcuts tab on the Keyboard pane of the System Preferences application.**

3. **Click Application Shortcuts in the left pane of the window.**

4. **Click the Add (+) button at the bottom of the list of shortcuts.** The Add Shortcut sheet appears, as shown in Figure 5.8.

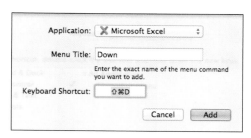

5.8 You can use this sheet to create your own keyboard shortcuts in any application.

5. **On the Application pop-up menu, choose All Applications if you want the shortcut to be available for all applications, or choose a specific application to create the shortcut only within it.**

Genius

The applications shown on the Application pop-up menu are only those at the root of the Applications folder. To access an application not shown, choose Other and use the resulting Open dialog to select the application for which you want to create a shortcut.

6. **In the Menu Title box, type the name of the command for which you want to create a shortcut exactly as it appears on its menu.** If the command contains an ellipsis, you must also include it.

Genius

You can type the name of any command on any menu in an application, even if it is nested within other commands. For example, Word has a Page Break command that you use to manually insert a page break in a document. To choose the command, you open the Insert menu, choose Break, and then choose Page Break. To create a shortcut for this command, type Page Break in the Menu Title field.

7. **In the Keyboard Shortcut field, press the key combination for the shortcut that you want to use to access the command (see Figure 5.8).**

8. **Click Add.** The sheet closes and you return to the Keyboard Shortcuts tab. The shortcut you just added is shown either under the related application in the Application Shortcuts category, or under All Applications if you configured it that way in step 5.

9. **Open the application in which you created the shortcut.** The keyboard command you created appears next to the command on the application's menu.

10. **Test the shortcut.** Sometimes, applications already have a shortcut mapped to the one you create, which can cause a conflict. You can resolve these either by disabling the application's shortcut or choosing a different keyboard shortcut.

Navigating with the keyboard

One of the least used (but most useful) aspects of keyboard shortcuts is keyboard navigation. You can use the keyboard to access almost any area on your MacBook Pro in any application, including the Finder. For example, you can open any menu item by using only keys, even if that item does not have a keyboard shortcut assigned to it.

To see what the default keyboard navigation tools are, open the Keyboard Shortcuts tab on the Keyboard pane in the System Preferences application. Next, select Keyboard & Text Input. The commands and how they work are explained in Table 5.2.

Table 5.2 Keyboard Navigation

Default Shortcut (hold the Fn key down if the standard function key preference is not enabled)	Action	What It Does
Control+F7	Change the way Tab moves focus	By default, pressing the Tab key in windows and dialogs moves you only between text boxes and lists. This command toggles between that mode and having the Tab key take you to every element in a dialog or window.
Control+F1	Turn keyboard access on or off	Enables or disables the following five shortcuts.
Control+F2	Move focus to the menu bar	Highlights the Apple menu; use the Tab or arrow keys to move to other menus and commands on the menu bar.
Control+F3	Move focus to the Dock	Makes the Finder icon on the Dock active. Use the Tab or arrow keys to move to icons on the Dock.
Control+F4	Move focus to the active window or next window	Moves into the currently active window or takes you to the next if you are already in a window.
Control+F5	Move focus to the window toolbar	If you are using an application with a toolbar, this makes the toolbar active. Use the Tab or arrow keys to select a button on the toolbar.
Control+F6	Move focus to the floating window	If you are using an application that has a floating window, this takes you into that window.
⌘+'	Move focus to the next window	Moves you among the open windows in the current application.
Option+⌘+'	Move focus to the window drawer	Some applications use a drawer that appears on the side of the application's window. It contains tools, much like a toolbar. This shortcut moves you into the drawer of the current window.
Control+F8	Move focus to the status menus	If you have enabled additional menus (such as the Displays menu) in the Mac OS X menu bar, this command highlights the first one. Use the arrow or Tab keys to move to, or select, menus and their commands.

continued

Table 5.2 Keyboard Navigation (continued)

Default Shortcut (hold the Fn key down if the standard function key preference is not enabled)	Action	What It Does
⌘+spacebar	Select the previous input source	When you have multiple input sources configured, this returns you to the one you used most recently.
Option+⌘+spacebar	Select next source in Input menu	When you have multiple input sources configured, this moves you to the previous one on the menu.

Note At the bottom of the Keyboard Shortcuts tab, there are two radio buttons: Text boxes and lists only, and All controls. Like the Control+F7 keyboard shortcut, these change what the Tab key does within windows and dialogs, either moving to only text boxes and lists, or moving to all of the controls.

When something, such as a menu, is ready for your action (in other words, when it is selected), Mac OS X calls that being in focus. For example, the shortcut for putting the menu bar in focus is Control+F2. If you haven't set your keyboard to use the standard function keys, hold down the Fn key and press Control+F2. The apple marking the Apple menu is highlighted to show it is in focus. Once it is in focus, you can move to any menu or command by pressing the right- and left-arrow keys until the menu you want to use is highlighted. Then, use the down-arrow key to open the menu. Once open, use the down-, up-, left-, and right-arrow keys to select the command you want. When that is selected, press Return to activate it. It takes a little effort to get the hang of this, but once you do, you can quickly move to any menu command.

Using the Input menu

The Input menu enables you to change the current language you are using or activate specific tools, such as the Character Viewer. A flag representing the default language appears at the top of this menu on the menu bar (unless you have only one language, and the Character and Keyboard Viewers enabled, in which case the Input menu icon is the Viewer icon). When you open it, you see the items you configured there, as shown in Figure 5.9.

5.9 The Input menu enables you to change input sources and open other tools, such as the Keyboard Viewer.

You can change the current input source (indicated by the check mark) to a different one by selecting a different source on the menu. When you do this, the keyboard is converted to the layout appropriate to the source you selected.

Using the Character Viewer

The Character Viewer is a tool to help you find special characters in various languages and quickly apply them to your documents. You can open the Character Viewer in either of the following ways:

- **Open the Input menu and select Show Character Viewer.**

- **In the Finder, choose Edit ⇨ Special Characters.**

Genius

If you select the Show Keyboard & Character Viewers in menu bar check box on the Keyboard tab, the Input menu appears on the menu bar.

When the viewer opens, you see that it has three panes, as shown in Figure 5.10. The far-left pane shows the categories of available characters. When you select a category, the characters within it appear in the center pane. When you select a character, details about it appear in the far-right pane.

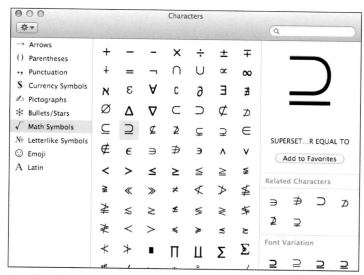

5.10 The Character Viewer enables you to configure and select special characters.

Perform the following steps to find and use a special character:

1. **In a document, put the cursor where you want to insert a special character.**

2. **Open the Character Viewer.**

3. **Select the category of the character you want to view in the left pane.** For example, select Math Symbols to view mathematical symbols. The characters in the category you select appear in the center pane.

Genius To display additional categories of characters, open the Action menu and choose Customize List. Select or deselect the check boxes for the categories of characters you want, or do not want, to see.

4. **Select the character you want to insert.** Details about it appear in the far-right pane.

5. **View the Font Variation section to see different versions of the character by font.** When you select a character in the Font Variation section, it appears in the preview area at the top of the window.

6. **To insert the character, double-click it.** It is inserted into the document in the font variation on which you clicked.

The following list includes a few more pointers about using the Character Viewer:

- **Favorites.** If you click Add to Favorites, the current character is added to your character favorites category, which appears after you add at least one favorite. You can return to your favorites by clicking the Favorites category.

- **Recents.** If you click the Recently Used item on the category list, the characters you've used recently appear, and you can use them again.

- **Search.** You can search for characters by typing text in the Search bar. Characters meeting your search criterion are shown in the right pane. You also see the Search category in the left pane.

- **Character size.** To change the size of the characters displayed in the Character Viewer, open the Action menu and choose Small, Medium, or Large.

Using the Keyboard Viewer

The Keyboard Viewer is a simple tool that shows you the layout of the keyboard in specific situations. To use it, select Show Keyboard Viewer on the Input menu. The Keyboard Viewer appears, as shown in Figure 5.11. You see what each key on the keyboard represents for the current input source. Hold down the modifier keys to see their impact.

5.11 If you want to see what pressing a key or a combination of keys does, check out the Keyboard Viewer.

Configuring Bluetooth

Bluetooth support is built in to your MacBook Pro, so you can wirelessly connect to and use any Bluetooth device. Bluetooth communication is set up between two devices through a process called *pairing*, in which each device recognizes and can then communicate with the other. A single device can communicate with more than one other Bluetooth device simultaneously. Each device with which your MacBook Pro communicates over Bluetooth must be paired separately.

To pair two devices together, you must make sure they can find one another. To accomplish this automatically, the devices must be *discoverable*, meaning that they are broadcasting their Bluetooth signals to other devices in the area. This is so that those devices can find and pair with the discoverable device. If you don't want your MacBook Pro to be discoverable by other devices, you can turn this off, but that makes pairing devices a bit more difficult.

Bluetooth communication requires hardware (transmitter/receiver) and software. Both of these are part of your MacBook Pro, but you need to configure Bluetooth services on your MacBook Pro before you try to connect Bluetooth devices to it. The following steps will help you configure Bluetooth services:

1. **Open the Bluetooth pane of the System Preferences application.** As shown in Figure 5.12, in the center part of the Bluetooth pane, you see the devices with which your MacBook Pro is currently communicating or the No Devices message if you haven't yet paired it with anything.

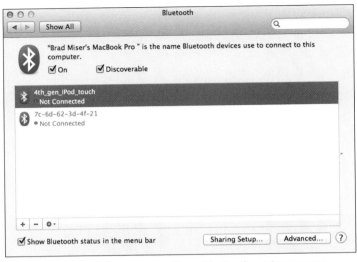

5.12 Use the Bluetooth pane to configure Bluetooth services on your MacBook Pro.

2. **Select the On check box.** Bluetooth services start.

3. **Select the Discoverable check box.** This makes your MacBook Pro discoverable by other devices because your MacBook Pro transmits signals that they can detect. You can still connect to your configured Bluetooth devices when this box is not selected, but your MacBook Pro won't be automatically detected by other devices.

4. **Select the Show Bluetooth status in the menu bar check box.**

5. **Click Advanced.** The Advanced sheet appears.

6. **Ignore the Open Bluetooth Setup Assistant at startup if no keyboard is detected and the Open Bluetooth Setup Assistant at startup if no mouse or trackpad is detected check boxes.** These are for desktop computers that might only have Bluetooth input devices. Because your MacBook Pro has a built-in keyboard and track-pad, it always has input devices.

7. **Select the Allow Bluetooth devices to wake this computer check box.** When you use a Bluetooth mouse or keyboard, you can wake your MacBook Pro with one of those devices.

8. **If you don't want audio devices to be able to connect to your MacBook via Bluetooth, select the Reject incoming audio requests check box.** If this is checked, some devices won't function correctly, such as a device that controls music playback in iTunes via Bluetooth.

9. **Click OK.** The sheet closes. Your MacBook Pro is ready to connect to Bluetooth devices.

Adding a Bluetooth Mouse

Using Bluetooth, you can easily connect a mouse to your MacBook Pro. Follow these steps to set up a new Bluetooth mouse by pairing it with your MacBook Pro using the Bluetooth Setup Assistant:

1. **Power up the mouse and if it is not auto-discoverable, press its discoverable button.** These are usually located on the bottom of the mouse. When you press this button, the mouse goes into Discoverable mode, which causes the device to start broadcasting a Bluetooth signal that your MacBook Pro can detect. Apple's wireless mouse becomes discoverable as soon as you turn it on.

2. **Open the Bluetooth menu and choose Set Up Bluetooth Device.** The Bluetooth Setup Assistant opens and searches for Bluetooth devices.

3. **Click Mouse to select it.**

4. **Click Continue.** Your MacBook Pro attempts to pair with the device. When the process is complete, you see the Conclusion screen. The Bluetooth mouse is ready to configure.

5. **Click Quit.**

The follow steps are for configuring an Apple Magic Mouse (mice that have other features are configured specifically for those, but the general process of setting them up is similar):

1. **Open the Mouse pane of the System Preferences application.**

2. **Use the Point & Click tab to set the point-and-click options for the mouse.** These are similar to those for the MacBook Pro trackpad.

3. **Use the More Gestures tab to configure the additional gestures you want to be able to use.** Again, these are similar to the trackpad options.

Adding a Bluetooth Keyboard

There may be times when you prefer to use an external keyboard instead of the built-in MacBook Pro keyboard. The process, like the one for setting up a mouse, is easy and convenient. The following steps walk you through the process of adding a Bluetooth keyboard:

1. **Turn on the keyboard and, if it is not auto-discoverable, press its discoverable button.** These are usually located on the bottom of the keyboard. When you press this button, the keyboard goes into Discoverable mode, which causes it to start broadcasting a Bluetooth signal that your MacBook Pro can detect. The Apple Wireless Keyboard becomes discoverable when you turn it on.

2. **Open the Bluetooth menu and choose Set Up Bluetooth Device.** The Bluetooth Setup Assistant opens. Your MacBook Pro searches for available Bluetooth keyboards and presents all of those it finds on the list.

3. **Select the keyboard you want to pair.**

4. **Click Continue.** The pairing process starts and you see the passcode screen. Here, you see the passkey that you need to type on the keyboard to complete the pairing process.

5. **On the Bluetooth keyboard, type the passkey shown in the Assistant's window.** If the pairing is successful, you see the Conclusion screen.

6. **Click Quit.**

After you pair a Bluetooth keyboard with your MacBook Pro, configure it by opening the Keyboard pane in the System Preferences application and clicking Set Up Bluetooth Keyboard. You see controls for the specific keyboard you are using. Configure the keyboard to suit your preferences.

Sharing Files with Bluetooth

There are a lot of other ways to use Bluetooth, too. For example, you can use it to network with other computers and share files. This is really useful because you can easily create temporary networks between the devices so they can share files without requiring detailed network configurations (however, if the computers among which you want to share files are all Macs running Mac OS X Lion or later, AirDrop is a much easier and better way to share files). First, configure each computer to share files via Bluetooth. Next, follow these steps to configure your MacBook Pro:

1. **Open the Sharing pane of the System Preferences application.**

2. **Select the Bluetooth Sharing check box.** The Bluetooth Sharing tools appear on the right side of the pane, as shown in Figure 5.13.

3. **Set the following preferences using the pop-up menus:**

   - **When receiving items.** Ask What to Do prompts you when someone tries to send a file via Bluetooth. Accept and Save, and Accept and Open accept the items being sent, and either saves them to your computer, or saves and opens them. Never Allow prevents your MacBook Pro from receiving items via Bluetooth. I recommend that you choose Ask What to Do so you have to allow files to be moved onto your computer via Bluetooth instead of them being accepted automatically.

   - **Folder for accepted items.** Use this menu to choose the location where files you receive via Bluetooth are stored.

- **When other devices browse.** This setting determines how your MacBook Pro responds when another device browses it. I recommend you choose Ask What to Do, which presents a prompt when another device tries to connect to your MacBook Pro. The other options are Always Allow and Never Allow. I recommend that you never use the Always Allow option because someone could browse your computer without your knowledge.

- **Folder others can browse.** Use this menu to choose a folder that computers connecting to your MacBook Pro can browse. You want to choose the folder where you store files that you want other people to be able to copy. Don't select a folder that contains files you don't want others to view.

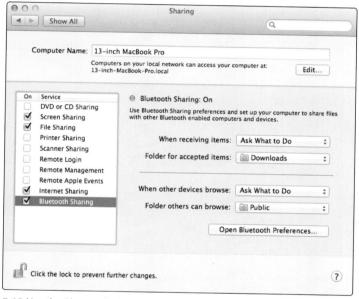

5.13 Use the Bluetooth Sharing controls to determine how your MacBook Pro manages files via Bluetooth.

Next, you need to pair your MacBook Pro to the computer with which you are going to share files. This process works similarly to pairing your MacBook Pro with mice or keyboards. Open the Bluetooth Assistant and click the Add (+) button. Your MacBook Pro scans for available devices. Select the computer with which you want to exchange files and click Continue. You see the attempting to pair screen. A passcode is sent from your computer to the one you selected. If the passcodes match, the user of the other computer accepts the connection request and the two computers are paired.

Genius   If you click the Passcode Options button on the Bluetooth Setup Assistant screen, you can configure the passcode. For example, you can set a specific passcode for a device with which you are trying to pair if it has a fixed passcode.

Follow these steps to send a file to the paired computer:

1. **Open the Bluetooth menu and choose Send File.**

2. **In the resulting dialog, move to the file you want to send and click Send.**

Genius   You can also send a file by opening the Bluetooth menu, choosing the computer to which you want to send a file, and selecting Send File. You can choose Browse Device to access a folder for which browsing is allowed. If allowed, you see the contents of that folder and can drag files onto your computer.

3. **Select the computer to which you want to send the file and click Send.** Your MacBook Pro attempts to send the file to the selected computer. If the person to whom you are sending the file accepts it, it is copied there.

When someone attempts to send a file to you, a dialog appears (assuming that you set the preference to be prompted). In the dialog, you see basic information about the file, as shown in Figure 5.14. Click Accept to copy the file from the other computer and store it in the location you selected. After the process is complete, click Close to close the dialog, or Show to show the transferred file in a Finder window.

5.14 Click Accept to accept a file being sent to your MacBook Pro via Bluetooth.

Caution   Never accept files you aren't expecting and make sure that you know the source of any files you accept. Accepting a file of unknown origin or type can be very dangerous. You should leave the prompt preferences selected so that you are aware of any activity occurring on your computer via Bluetooth.

Maintaining the Battery

To be able to use your MacBook Pro efficiently, it (obviously) must be running. Like all devices with batteries, a MacBook Pro can operate only as long as its battery continues to provide power. Fortunately, with the current models, this is quite a long time. Still, once your battery runs out, your trusty MacBook Pro becomes so much dead weight. To get the most working time while you're mobile, you should practice good energy-management habits. These include a combination of using the Mac OS X battery management tools, conserving battery power, and being prepared to connect to an external power source whenever you have the opportunity.

Monitoring battery status

You can use the Battery menu to keep an eye on your MacBook Pro power level. This way, you know how much working time you have left and can take action if you are going to run out of power soon. Perform the following steps to configure the Battery menu on your MacBook Pro:

1. **Open the Energy Saver pane of the System Preferences application.**

2. **Select the Show battery status in the menu bar check box.**

3. **Open the Battery menu.**

4. **To include a percentage along with the icon, open the menu and choose Show Percentage, as shown in Figure 5.15.**

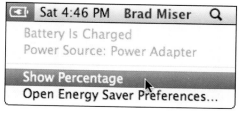

5.15 The Battery status helps you know the power state of your MacBook Pro.

As you work with your MacBook Pro, keep an eye on the Battery menu, shown in Figure 5.16. At the top of the menu, you see the parameter you configured (such as time remaining). When you open the Battery status menu, the first item shown is the percentage of power remaining if you selected the Time view, or the time remaining if you selected the Icon or Percentage view. You also see the current source of power (Battery or Power Adapter).

5.16 Monitor the Battery menu as you work so that your MacBook Pro doesn't suddenly come to a grinding halt.

When the battery gets close to being discharged, warnings appear that provide an estimate of the remaining time and recommend that you save your work. If you keep going, the MacBook Pro eventually goes into Sleep mode and you won't be able to wake it until you connect it to a power source.

While it can remain in Sleep mode for a long time, a MacBook Pro eventually runs out of even the low level of power required to keep it going and shuts off. The MacBook Pro goes into a hibernation mode and any open documents are usually saved (there is a slight chance that any unsaved changes may be lost when this happens). In most cases, you can recover your open documents as soon as you power your MacBook Pro again. Beyond the very minor possibility of losing unsaved changes, there really isn't any risk if you let the MacBook Pro run completely out of power.

When you connect the MacBook Pro to a power source, the Battery menu displays information about the charging process instead of time remaining. The battery icon contains the lightning bolt symbol to indicate that it's currently being charged. The time displayed on the menu is the time remaining until the battery is fully charged. When it is fully (or close to fully) charged (mid-90 percent or higher), the battery icon contains the electrical plug symbol to show that you are operating from the power adapter.

Note When you connect the adapter to the MacBook Pro, its status light is amber while the battery is charging. When fully charged, the status light turns green.

Extending battery life

You can use the Energy Saver to minimize power use while operating on battery power. You can also adopt simple practices to minimize the amount of power your MacBook Pro uses so that you get the most time possible from the battery.

Using the Energy Saver

On the Energy Saver pane of the System Preferences application, you can tailor how the computer uses power and extend the working life of the battery for as long as possible. There are two basic ways to configure power usage on a MacBook Pro: You can use the default settings or customize them. You configure settings for operating on battery power and for operating on the power adapter. Once they are configured, the MacBook Pro automatically uses the settings for the power source you are using. Follow these steps to set up your MacBook Pro for minimum energy use and maximum working time:

1. **Open the Energy Saver pane of the System Preferences application.**

2. **Click the Battery tab, as shown in Figure 5.17, to configure energy use while operating on battery power.**

5.17 These options apply when your MacBook Pro is operating on battery power.

3. **Use the top slider to control the amount of inactive time before the entire system goes to sleep.** The MacBook Pro uses the least amount of power (only slightly more than when it is shut off) when it is asleep. Of course, it wakes up a lot faster than it starts up, so sleep is a good thing. You want to set a time that conserves power but doesn't occur so frequently that it interrupts what you are doing.

4. **Use the lower slider to set the amount of inactive time before the display goes dark.** The display is one of the highest drains on battery power, so you can extend its life by having it sleep after shorter periods of activity. Of course, if it goes to sleep too quickly, it can be intrusive and annoying, so you need to find a good balance between saving power and having your screen go dark.

5. **In most cases, you should leave the Put hard disks to sleep when possible check box selected.** If you notice that you have to pause frequently during tasks so the MacBook Pro can save data to the hard drive, try deselecting this check box.

6. **Select the Slightly dim the display while on battery power check box if you want your display to have a lower brightness when operating on the battery.** Dimming causes the screen to go to a lower brightness setting so it uses less power. In my experimentation, it appears that this function reduces screen brightness by about two ticks on the brightness indicator.

7. **Click the Power Adapter tab.** You see slightly different options in the pane, as shown in Figure 5.18.

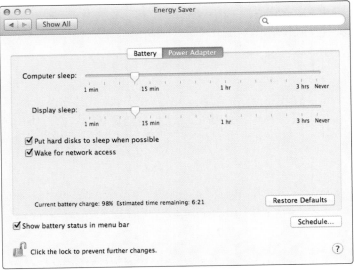

○ ○ ○　　　　　　　　　　Energy Saver

◀ ▶　Show All　　　　　　　　　　　　　　　　　　　　　　Q

Battery　Power Adapter

Computer sleep:　───────⎯⎯⎯───────────────────
　　　　　　　　　1 min　　　15 min　　　　　　　1 hr　　　　　3 hrs　Never

Display sleep:　───⎯⎯⎯───────────────────────
　　　　　　　　　1 min　　　15 min　　　　　　　1 hr　　　　　3 hrs　Never

☑ Put hard disks to sleep when possible
☑ Wake for network access

Current battery charge: 98%　Estimated time remaining: 6:21　　　Restore Defaults

☑ Show battery status in menu bar　　　　　　　　　　　Schedule...

🔓 Click the lock to prevent further changes.　　　　　　　　　　ⓘ

5.18 These options apply when your MacBook Pro is connected to the power adapter.

Automatically Starting or Stopping MacBook Pro

You can configure MacBook Pro to automatically start, sleep, restart, or shut down according to a schedule. Perform the following steps to do so:

1. **Open the Energy Saver pane of the System Preferences application (See Figure 5.18).**

2. **Click Schedule.** The Schedule sheet appears.

3. **To set an automatic start-up or wake time, select the Start up or wake check box.** Next, set the time you want this event to occur using the pop-up menu and time box.

4. **To set an automatic sleep, restart, or shutdown time, select the lower check box on the sheet.** Select Sleep, Restart, or Shut Down on the pop-up menu, and then set the time you want the selected event to occur using the pop-up menu and time box.

5. **Click OK.** The sheet closes and the schedules you set take effect.

If the lid of the MacBook Pro is shut, the schedule has no effect.

8. **Configure these settings the same as you did for operating on the battery.** Usually, saving energy is less of a concern when operating on the power adapter, so you can extend sleep times to prevent interruptions.

9. **Select the Wake for network access check box if you want the MacBook Pro to wake up when network activity is detected.** This setting replaces the Slightly dim the display setting on the battery power tab.

Note

To return the energy configuration to what Apple considers optimal for most users, click Restore Defaults.

Adopting low-energy habits

Although configuring the energy use of your MacBook Pro has some impact on how long you can operate on battery power, you can also adopt low-energy habits to further maximize battery life. The following tips can help you do this:

- **Lower the brightness of your display.** Because it makes high demands on battery power, you want to set the brightness of the display at the lowest possible level to maximize battery life. To dim your screen, use the Brightness slider on the Displays pane of the System Preferences application. You can also press F1 to decrease or F2 to increase the brightness.

- **Set the brightness level so that it adjusts automatically.** Open the Displays pane of the System Preferences application and ensure that Automatically adjust brightness is enabled. This automatically dims the display in low light conditions and increases it in brighter environments. If you use the MacBook Pro in bright conditions for extended periods, you might want to disable this and manually set the brightness level to the dimmest possible.

- **Avoid applications that constantly read from the hard drive.** While you probably won't have much choice on this, some applications have settings that affect hard drive use, such as autosave features. You can increase the amount of time between automatic saves to reduce hard drive use and, thereby, save energy.

- **Avoid applications that constantly read from a CD or DVD.** If you can copy the files that you need onto your hard drive, you use power at a lower rate than if your MacBook Pro is constantly accessing its removable media drive. For example, when you want to listen to music or watch movies, add the content to your iTunes library so you don't need to use the CD or DVD drive.

- **Use an iPod, iPhone, or iPad.** Playing content in iTunes requires a lot of hard drive activity and iTunes is a heavy battery power user. If you can use another device for these tasks, it saves your MacBook Pro for those you can only do (or do best) on it.

- **Configure keyboard backlighting.** When you are in low light conditions, the backlit keys make your MacBook pro much easier to use. However, backlighting also uses more power. Try to reduce the amount of time for which, and the level of brightness at which, the keys are backlit. You can also disable backlighting to save the most energy. These settings are on the Keyboard subtab of the Keyboard pane in the System Preferences application. You can also press F5 to decrease or F6 to increase the brightness of the backlighting.

- **Put your MacBook Pro to sleep whenever you aren't actively using it by closing the lid.** When you open the lid or press a key, the MacBook Pro wakes up quickly, so putting it to sleep frequently doesn't waste a lot of time.

Genius

You can also set a hot corner for display sleep by clicking the Hot Corners button on the Mission Control pane of the System Preferences application. If you aren't going to be using your MacBook Pro for a little while, move the pointer to the hot corner to put the display to sleep.

Powering your MacBook Pro while traveling

If you are traveling for a long time, the odds are good that you're going to run out of battery power, even if you tweaked your MacBook Pro for maximum operating time and practice low-energy habits. You can reduce the chances of running out of power by being ready to power your MacBook Pro while you are on the move.

Note

Most airports have power outlets available in the gate areas, but they aren't always obvious to see and can be hidden by chairs or other obstacles. Some airports have charging stations, which provide a handy way to top off your MacBook Pro's battery.

The following are some recommended items that can help you manage your power on the move:

- **Standard power adapter.** Whenever there's a power outlet available, you can use the included adapter to run the MacBook Pro and charge its battery.

- **MagSafe Airline Adapter.** With this adapter, you can connect your MacBook Pro to the power outlet available in some airline seats. The seat must have an EmPower or 20mm power port.

- **International adapters.** If you travel internationally, get a set of power adapters so that you can connect the MacBook Pro power adapter to power outlets in a variety of countries.

Caution

While the airline adapter looks like it might be compatible with the DC power port in automobiles, it isn't.

Maintaining Battery Life

Over time, the accuracy of the battery charge indicator decreases, along with the battery's ability to hold a charge. However, you can follow these steps to calibrate the battery and improve its capability:

1. **Charge the battery so it's full.**

2. **Leave the battery in the fully charged state for at least two hours by leaving the power adapter connected.**

3. **Disconnect the power adapter.**

4. **Use the MacBook Pro on battery power until you see the second or third low power warning.**

5. **Save all of your open documents and quit all applications.**
   Eventually, your MacBook Pro goes to sleep.

6. **Let the MacBook Pro sleep or shut it down for five hours.**

7. **Reconnect the power adapter and fully recharge the battery.**

Advantage of iCloud?

iCloud is a suite of web-based services that puts your data on the Internet. From there, it can be accessed by multiple devices, including your MacBook Pro, iPhones, iPads, and iPod touches. This keeps e-mail, contacts, calendars, and so on in sync on all of your devices, so that the same information is available to you regardless of the device you're using. You can store documents on iCloud and work on the same version of them on each device. An iCloud account includes a website with applications so you can work with your information from any computer.

Getting Started with iCloud

To use iCloud, you need an iCloud account. The good news is that obtaining an iCloud account is fast, easy, and free. A free account includes access to almost all of the services described in this chapter, along with 5GB of online storage space. After you obtain an account, you configure it on your MacBook Pro and iOS devices so that iCloud services are available on each of them. Then, access your iCloud website to become familiar with the valuable functions it provides.

You may already have an iCloud account and just don't realize it. For example, if you have shopped at the iTunes Store, you created an Apple ID. You use this same Apple ID for your iCloud account. If you don't have an Apple ID, creating one takes only a few minutes.

Note If you used the previous rendition of Apple online services, called MobileMe, you can convert your MobileMe account into an iCloud account. Visit me.com/move and you're prompted to convert your account to iCloud. After you work through the online instructions, you'll be ready to start using iCloud.

Follow these steps to create a new iCloud account:

1. **Open the System Preferences application.**

2. **Click the iCloud icon.** The iCloud pane opens.

3. **Click Create an Apple ID (see Figure 6.1).**

6.1 Creating an iCloud account is simple and quick.

4. **Follow the on-screen instructions to complete the process.** When finished, you are logged in to your new iCloud account and can configure the services you want to use.

5. **On the iCloud pane, leave the default selections selected and click Next.**

6. **Click Allow and the Allow Guest Login at the prompts.** You're ready to configure iCloud services, which I explain later in this chapter.

Note   When you create an iCloud account, you have the option of also creating a new iCloud e-mail address or using an existing one. If you choose to use an existing e-mail address, it becomes your Apple ID. This chapter assumes you are working with an iCloud e-mail address.

If you already have an Apple ID or iCloud account, you can follow these steps to configure your MacBook Pro to use it:

1. **Open the System Preferences application.**

2. **Click the iCloud icon.** The iCloud pane opens.

3. **Type your Apple ID and password (see Figure 6.1).**

4. **Click Sign In.**

5. **On the iCloud pane, leave the default selections selected and click Next.**

6. **Click Allow and the Allow Guest Login at the prompts.** You're ready to configure iCloud services, which I explain next.

Synchronizing Data on Multiple Devices

One of the most useful features of iCloud is that you can make the same information available to you on your MacBook Pro, other Macs, iPhones, iPads, and iPod touches. This information includes e-mail, contacts, calendars, and so on. To use data synchronization, you configure the specific data you want to keep synchronized on each device.

Configuring iCloud on a MacBook Pro

Use the following steps to determine which information on your MacBook Pro (or any other Mac, for that matter) is synced on iCloud:

1. **Open the iCloud pane of the System Preferences application, shown in Figure 6.2.**

6.2 Use the iCloud pane to determine the types of information you want to sync on your MacBook Pro.

2. **Select the check boxes for the information you want to sync.**

3. **Deselect the check boxes for information you don't want to sync.**

You can configure the following types of information to sync between your MacBook Pro and iCloud:

- **Mail.** This causes your iCloud e-mail to be enabled in the Mail application when selected, or disabled when deselected.

- **Contacts.** When you enable this setting, the contact information stored in the Contacts application is copied to iCloud. It can then be accessed there via the Contacts web application and any other device that is set up to sync contact information. When changes are made to contacts on any synced device, they are also made on your MacBook Pro.

- **Calendars & Reminders.** Use this check box to sync your calendars from the Calendar application and reminders from the Reminders application on iCloud so you can access them on any synced device.

- **Notes.** With this enabled, notes you manage in the Notes application are copied to iCloud. Likewise, any notes synced from other devices are copied to your MacBook Pro.

- **Safari.** This setting causes your Safari bookmarks to be copied to and from iCloud. This is a great way to easily access your favorite websites from any iCloud-enabled device.

- **Photo Stream.** With Photo Stream enabled, your MacBook Pro can access the photo storage that is included as part of your iCloud account. After you enable Photo Stream on the iCloud pane, configure the photo application you want to use to work with your synced photos on your MacBook Pro. As of this writing, the two applications that support Photo Stream are iPhoto (which is installed on MacBook Pro) and Aperture (which can be purchased and downloaded from the App Store). To enable Photo Stream in iPhoto, open Preferences and click the Photo Stream tab, as shown in Figure 6.3. Select all three check boxes to ensure that photos are synced to and from your MacBook Pro. When new photos are added to your Photo Stream, they are automatically added to your photo library. Likewise, when you add new photos to the library, such as by importing them from a digital camera, they are added to the Photo Stream, and thus, moved onto the other devices on which Photo Stream is enabled.

6.3 Photo Stream, which is being enabled in iPhoto in this figure, is a great way to protect photos you take with an iOS device because they are automatically downloaded to your MacBook Pro.

Caution If you use an iOS device (such as an iPhone) to take photos, you should definitely use Photo Stream because it temporarily backs up your photos on iCloud and permanently stores them on your MacBook Pro. If something happens to the iOS device, it is unlikely that you will lose any photos. (Note that the iOS device must be connected to Wi-Fi for photos to be copied to and from iCloud.)

- **Documents & Data.** This setting allows iCloud-enabled applications to store documents on iCloud so that you can work with them from any iCloud-enabled Mac or iOS device. This topic is covered in detail later in this chapter.

- **Back to My Mac.** This enables you to use your iCloud account to access services on one Mac from a different Mac. These services can include file and screen sharing, and so on. For example, suppose you are traveling with your MacBook Pro and want to access files stored on your iMac in a different location. With Back to My Mac, you can connect to the iMac and use file sharing to get to the files you want just as if you were sitting at that computer.

Note

How Back to My Mac performs is tied to the specific settings of the network to which the Macs are connected. To get help in configuring your network for best performance, click the More button for the Back to My Mac service.

- **Find My Mac.** You can use this to locate or secure a Mac that is no longer in your control. It is explained in detail later in this chapter.

On the iCloud pane, you see the Account Details button. If you click it, you can use the resulting sheet to change the name or description associated with the iCloud account. At the bottom of the iCloud pane, you see the iCloud Storage gauge (see Figure 6.2). Here, you see the amount of iCloud storage available to you and how much of that space you are currently using, which is represented by the green portion of the bar. By default, your iCloud account includes 5GB of storage space. This is usually fine if you primarily use iCloud to sync information. If you use iCloud to sync documents, you may want to add storage to your account.

You can mange your iCloud storage space by clicking Manage. The Manage sheet appears, as shown in Figure 6.4. On the left side of this sheet, you see the various types of information currently stored on iCloud, such as backups, e-mail, and so on. You also see applications configured to store documents on iCloud, such as Pages or Numbers. When you select a type of information, details about it are displayed in the right pane. For example, when you select an application, you see the documents from it that are currently being stored on iCloud.

You can manage how information is being stored in various ways. For example, you can select a document and click Delete to remove it from iCloud. You can also click Delete All to remove all of the selected type of information from iCloud. If you click Buy More Storage, a sheet appears, as shown in Figure 6.5. Here, you can manage the amount of storage space available to you. You can add storage space or downgrade if you don't need the space you have.

If you click View Account on the Manage Storage sheet (see Figure 6.4), you can view all of, and change certain information about, your account, such as your Apple ID, your storage plan, payment information, and the country/region associated with your account.

6.4 Use this Manage sheet to work with your iCloud storage space.

6.5 If you store a lot of documents on iCloud, you may want to upgrade the storage space.

Note
As explained later in this chapter, you can also use your iCloud website to manage your iCloud account.

Configuring iCloud syncing on an iOS device

iCloud is a perfect match for iOS devices, which are iPhones, iPads, and iPod touches. If you have any of these, you can take advantage of iCloud by following these steps and configuring its services on the device:

1. **On the Home screen, tap Settings.** The Settings app opens.

2. **Tap iCloud.** You move to the iCloud Settings screen and are prompted to enter your iCloud account information, as shown in Figure 6.6.

3. **Enter your Apple ID and password.**

4. **Tap Sign In.** Your iCloud account is configured on the device.

5. **If you're prompted about merging information already on your iCloud account, tap Don't Merge if you don't want the information on your device to be moved to your iCloud account.** Tap Merge if you do.

6. **If prompted about location, tap Allow to allow iCloud to access your device's location or Don't Allow if you don't want this to happen.** You need to allow this for some features (such as Find My iPhone) to work. Next, you are prompted to choose the type of information you want to sync on your device.

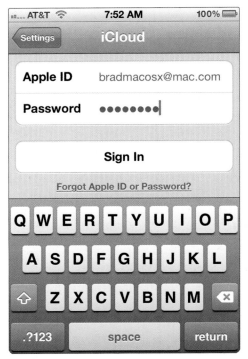

6.6 When you move to the iCloud Settings screen, you're prompted to enter your iCloud account information.

7. **Set the slider to the On position next to each kind of information you want to sync on your device, as shown in Figure 6.7**. For example, if Mail is set to On, e-mail syncs between your iCloud account and the device. If you set a slider to the Off position, that information won't sync between your iCloud account and the device. The options you have on an iOS device are the same as those on a MacBook Pro (which are described earlier in this chapter), except that the settings for Calendars and Reminders are separate on an iOS device.

6.7 You can configure the information you want to sync on an iOS device by setting these status switches to On if you want the info included or Off if you don't.

Working with Your iCloud Website

You iCloud website has applications you can use for e-mail, contacts, and calendars. You can also use the Find My iPhone feature to locate your MacBook Pro and secure it if it is out of your control. You can store and access documents there, too. To access these features, just follow the steps below to log in to your iCloud website:

1. **Navigate to www.icloud.com.**

2. **Enter your Apple ID and password.** To save your information on the computer so you can move directly into your website when you come back to this address, select the Keep me signed in check box.

3. **Click the right-facing arrow or press Return.** You log in to your website and can work with the iCloud web applications or manage your account on the iCloud Home screen, as shown in Figure 6.8.

6.8 Once logged in, you see the applications available on your iCloud website.

Managing your iCloud account

One of the functions available on your iCloud website is the ability to manage your account. To access this functionality, move to your iCloud website and log in. Click the account link (which shows your name) at the top of the iCloud window. You then see the Account dialog, as shown in Figure 6.9.

6.9 Use the Account dialog to change various aspects of your iCloud account.

You can do all of the following things in the Account dialog:

- **Change the image associated with your account by hovering over it and clicking Edit.** On the resulting sheet, you can change the zoom level of the image or click Choose to replace it with a different one.

- **Change the language or time zone associated with your account by clicking the related links.**

- **Reset your Photo Stream (that is, delete all of the photos stored there) by clicking Advanced, and then clicking Reset Photo Stream.**

- **Clicking Help takes you to the iCloud Help website.**

- **Click your Apple ID to move to the My Apple ID website.**

After you finish making changes, click Done. Your changes are saved and the dialog closes.

Note If you ever forget your password or want to reset it, go to http://appleid.apple.com. Here, you can reset your password or manage your account. You can also create another iCloud account.

Working with iCloud web applications

Your iCloud website includes three web applications designed to help you work with key information. These are Mail for e-mail, Contacts for working with contact information, and Calendar, which provides web access to your calendars. If you configured your MacBook to sync this information with your iCloud account, these applications enable you to access, change, and add to the synced information. If you don't allow syncing, you can still use these applications, but the information they contain is only available on the website.

Working with the iCloud web applications is similar to working with their Desktop counterparts: Mail, Contacts, and Calendar. To use an application, click its icon and you move into it. Figure 6.10 shows the Calendar application, which looks and works very much like the Desktop Calendar application covered in Chapter 9.

The web applications have two buttons that aren't as obvious as most of the other commands that you see. The iCloud button, located in the upper-left corner of the window, takes you back to the iCloud Home screen. From there, you can choose a different application or function. The other button, indicated by the gear icon, opens a menu of commands that are specific to each application; explore this menu in each application so that you are aware of the commands available to you. One command you should definitely access is Preferences. This enables you to configure the application's preferences, just as you would with a Desktop application.

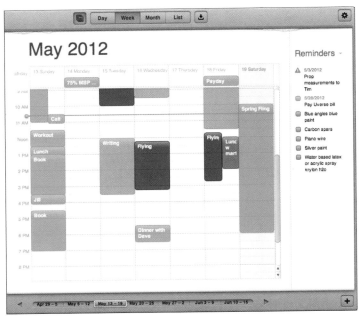

6.10 If you've used the Calendar Desktop application, its counterpart iCloud web application will be familiar to you.

Using Find My Mac

Your iCloud website includes the Find My iPhone module, which enables you (despite its somewhat misleading name) to also find your MacBook Pro in the event that you lose control of it. Because MacBook Pros are easy to move, they are also easy to lose or steal. Find My Mac provides tools for locating your MacBook Pro and limiting the damage to you should it fall into unfriendly hands.

Perform the following steps to enable Find My Mac:

1. **Open the iCloud pane of the System Preferences application.**

2. **Select the Find My Mac check box.**

3. **Click Allow at the prompt.** You can locate your MacBook Pro via the Find My iPhone application on your iCloud website or by using the Find My iPhone app on an iOS device.

Perform the following steps to locate a Mac:

1. **Log in to your iCloud website.**

2. **Move to the Home screen.**

3. **Click Find My iPhone and provide your Apple ID password, if prompted.** All of the devices for which you have enabled the Find My Device feature under your iCloud account are shown on the My Devices list. If a device is online and has been located, it is marked with a green dot.

4. **Select the MacBook Pro you want to locate.** Its current location is shown on the map.

5. **Click the Info (*i*) button.** You see the Info dialog shown in Figure 6.11.

6.11 The MacBook Pro has been located.

You can perform any of the following actions after you locate a MacBook Pro (or other Mac or iOS device):

- **Play a sound or send a message.** This does just what it says. A sound, message, or both is played on the MacBook Pro. This provides information to the person who has the Mac. The sound can also help you locate the device if it is in your general vicinity.

- **Remote lock.** Perform this action to lock the MacBook Pro so it can't be used. This can protect your computer without changing its data.

- **Remote wipe.** This action is a last resort to protect your data. It erases the MacBook Pro storage space. You should only do this in a worst-case scenario.

Follow these steps to send a sound or message to your MacBook Pro:

1. **Locate the MacBook Pro and open the Info dialog.**

2. **Click Play Sound or Send Message.**

3. **Type the message you want to display.**

4. **If you want a sound to play, set the Sound status to On.** Note that the sound always plays at full volume regardless of the sound settings, even if the MacBook Pro is muted.

5. **Click Send.** The message is sent to your MacBook Pro, as shown in Figure 6.12, and the sound is played if you enabled that option. You also receive a confirmation e-mail to the e-mail address associated with your Apple ID that displays the message.

Important Message
Hey, where's my MacBook Pro?

OK

6.12 If this book had a soundtrack, you'd hear a somewhat annoying alert tone while this message is displayed.

To stop the sound from playing and clear the message, unlock it and tap OK on the message prompt. If you don't require a password to stop the screen saver or wake your MacBook Pro, anyone who has it can perform this action, which is why requiring a password is a good idea.

The following steps walk you through the process of remotely locking your MacBook Pro to prevent someone from using it:

1. **Locate your MacBook Pro and open the Info dialog.**

2. **Click Remote Lock.** You're prompted to create a passcode by entering it.

3. **Type the passcode you want to use.**

4. **Retype the passcode at the prompt.**

5. **Type a message you want to be displayed on the MacBook Pro while it is locked.**

6. **Click Lock.**

7. **Click Lock Mac at the prompt.** The Lock command is sent to the MacBook Pro, it restarts, and the screen shows that it is locked and requires the passcode to be unlocked.

To use the MacBook Pro, the proper passcode must be entered. When it is, the MacBook Pro restarts and operates normally. If you've lost control of your MacBook Pro, follow these steps to try to protect your data:

1. **Locate the MacBook Pro and open the Info dialog.**

2. **Click Remote Wipe.**

3. **Create and confirm a passcode.**

4. **Create the message you want to be displayed (such as your name and phone number) on the MacBook Pro screen after it has been wiped.**

5. **Click Wipe.**

6. **Confirm the action at the prompts.** All of the data on your MacBook Pro is erased.

To update the location of your device, click the Refresh (curved arrow) button in the upper-right corner of the My Devices list.

The following are some more pointers that might help you find your Mac:

- **If you lose control of your MacBook Pro, use an escalation of steps to try to regain control.** Immediately play a sound, send a message to it, and then lock it. This will hopefully prevent someone else from using it while you locate it. If the device is near you and you've just forgotten where it is, the sound might help you find it again. If you don't get results, you can wipe the MacBook Pro to delete the data it contains. This is a severe action, so you don't want to do it prematurely.

- **Remote wiping is a bit of a two-edged sword.** It protects your data by erasing your MacBook Pro, which also means you can't use Find My Mac to locate it anymore. You should only use this if you're pretty sure that someone has your computer because after you wipe it, there's no longer any way to track its location. How fast you move to a wipe also depends on whether you required a password to unlock it. If you did, you know that your MacBook's data can't be accessed without that password. It will take some time for a miscreant to crack it, so you might be slower on the Wipe trigger. If your MacBook Pro doesn't have a password, you might want to pull the trigger faster.

- **If you do recover your MacBook Pro after a wipe, you'll have to restore all of its software and data (from your backups, of course).**

- **As you use Find My Mac, you receive e-mail notifications about various events, such as when a device is locked, when a message you sent is displayed, and so on.** These are an excellent way to track what is happening with your device, even though you can't see it.

- **If Find My Mac can't find your computer, select it on the list of devices.** The device is shown in the right part of the window. You can initiate the same actions as when the device is found, although they won't actually happen until the device becomes visible again. To be notified when this happens, select the Email me when this Mac is found check box. When the device becomes visible to Find My Mac, you receive an e-mail, and can then take the appropriate action to locate and secure it.

- **The circle around a device's dot indicates how precise its location is; the larger the circle is, the less precise the device's location.**

Caution For security, you should require a password to stop the screen saver or wake your MacBook Pro. You can set this on the General tab of the Security & Privacy pane in the System Preferences application. You can also configure a message to appear on the screen when it's locked, such as your name and contact information. This way, if your MacBook Pro is found by someone who wants to return it to you, he can get in touch with you.

Using iCloud with Documents

If you have multiple devices (and who doesn't these days?) you probably want to share documents on all of them so that you need not be concerned whether you are using the most current version. iCloud enables you to store documents on your iCloud website. Applications that support iCloud document storage can then access those documents from any device that you use.

For this functionality to be available, an application must have iCloud support enabled. As of this writing, Apple's Pages, Numbers, Preview, TextEdit, and Keynote support this functionality. As time passes, other applications will likely add this support. To use iCloud with your documents, make sure that the Documents & Data check box on the iCloud pane of the System Preferences application is selected as described earlier.

Genius iOS apps, such as Pages, Numbers, and Keynote, can also store and work with documents on iCloud. They work similar to Desktop applications. When iCloud support is enabled in an App, you see all of the available documents on iCloud. Simply tap a document to work with it. Like MacBook Pro applications, changes to documents are stored on the cloud automatically.

When an application is iCloud-enabled, you can choose to store documents with which you work on the cloud. As you make changes to those documents, the revised versions are stored on the cloud automatically. This ensures that you have access to the current version of the document, regardless of the device you happen to be using at any time.

Working with documents stored on the cloud is straightforward. Follow the steps below (which use Pages as an example) to work with documents on the cloud:

1. **Launch Pages.**
2. **Choose File ➪ Open.** The Open dialog appears.

3. **Click the iCloud button, as shown in Figure 6.13.** You see the documents with which Pages can work and that are stored on the cloud.

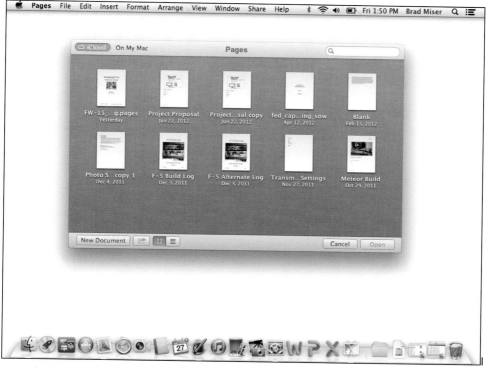

6.13 iCloud-enabled applications, such as Pages, enable you to work with documents stored on the cloud.

4. **Select the document with which you want to work and click Open.** The document opens and you can work with it just like a document that is stored on your computer. The application saves changes and when you close the document, those changes are pushed to the cloud so the cloud version is the most current.

Genius

In iCloud-enabled dialogs, you can preview documents by selecting their thumbnails, and then clicking the left and right arrows.

The following are some pointers for working with iCloud-enabled applications:

- **To create a new document on the cloud, click the New Document button in the iCloud document dialog.** You move back into the application and a new document is created. When you save the document, it is saved on the cloud.

- **To store any new document on the cloud, choose iCloud on the Where menu in save dialogs.**

- **To create a new folder on the cloud, drag one document onto another that you want to be in the same new folder.** You are prompted to name the new folder, as shown in Figure 6.14. Type the name of the new folder, and then press Return.

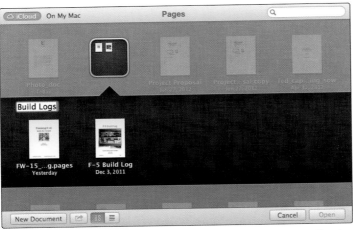

6.14 You are prompted to name a new folder after it's created on iCloud.

- **To add documents to an existing folder, simply drop them onto the folder.**

Genius You can also work with your documents through your iCloud website. Log into your website and navigate to the documents. You can download documents to your computer, or upload revised and new documents. This is useful when you want to access documents, but are not able to use a device that offers integrated iCloud access.

- **To delete a folder, remove the documents from it by dragging and dropping them outside the folder**. After the last document is removed, the folder is deleted.

- **To work with documents stored on your MacBook Pro, click the On My Mac button.**

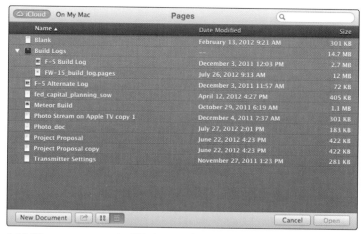

6.15 When you access the iWork area of your iCloud website, you see the documents associated with specific applications.

Genius

iTunes Match is an iCloud service that puts all of the music content in your iTunes library on iCloud so that you can access it from any computer (Mac or Windows) or iOS device connected to the Internet. This is particularly useful for iOS devices because you don't have to sync them to listen to your music. iTunes Match costs about $25 per year for U.S. residents.

How Do I Manage Contacts and E-mail?

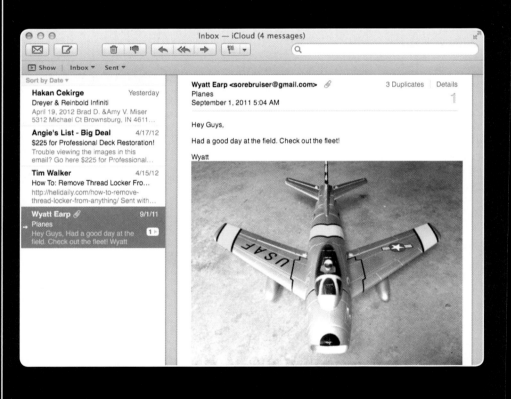

Your MacBook Pro comes equipped to help you keep in touch. The Contacts application enables you to store contact information that you can use in many applications, including Mail, Safari, and Messages. You'll also want to be able to access your contacts from your iPhone, iPod, or iPad and, for this reason, synchronizing contacts is a snap. E-mail is a great way to communicate and there are a number of ways you can configure the Mail application. Once you've used e-mail for a while, you'll want to work with file attachments to keep your e-mail organized.

Adding Contact Information to Contacts

Contacts uses an address card model, which I suppose originated with the Rolodex way back in the analog era. Each contact, be it a person or an organization, is represented by a card containing contact information. Contacts cards are virtual (vCards), making them flexible because you can store a variety of information on each one. You can also store different information for various contacts.

Note

In previous releases of Mac OS X, the Contacts application was called Address Book.

In fact, each card in Contacts can hold an unlimited number of physical or e-mail addresses, phone numbers, dates, notes, and URLs. Because vCards are flexible, you don't have to include each piece of information for every contact—you can include only the info that you have. Contacts (with a few exceptions) only displays fields that have data in them so your cards don't have a lot of empty fields.

Configuring the card template

When you create a new card, it is based on the Contacts card template, which determines the data fields that are on the card initially. You can change what information is included on the template and, thereby, on the cards you create. You should configure the template before you start creating cards so that they include the specific information you want them to. Follow these steps to configure the Contacts card template:

1. **Open the Contacts Preferences dialog.**

2. **Click Template.**

3. **You can modify the template in any of the following ways:**

   - **Remove fields you don't want by clicking the Delete (–) button.**

   - **Add more fields of an existing type by clicking the Add (+) button next to that type.** Choose the label for the new field on the pop-up menu to the left of it.

   - **Rename any field currently on the template by choosing a different label on the pop-up menu to the left of each one.**

- **Add types of fields that don't appear on the template by opening the Add Field pop-up menu at the top of the dialog and choosing the type you want to add, as shown in Figure 7.1.** Fields that are already on the template are marked with a check mark and grayed out. After you make a selection, the new field appears on the template in the appropriate location based on the type of field you added (for example, the Nickname field appears at the top of the card, just below the first and last names).

4. **Close the Preferences dialog.** New cards that you create will include these fields on the template.

7.1 Configure the Contacts template so it contains the fields you want on the cards you create.

Creating a contact manually

Follow these steps to manually create address cards for contacts you want to add to Contacts:

1. **Open the Contacts application.** It uses an address book model with the following three views:

   - **Groups view.** This shows your address groups on the left side of the left page and a list of the contacts in the selected group on the right side of the left page. On the right page, you see the card for the contact you selected on the left page, as shown in Figure 7.2.

7.2 The Groups view provides the most information.

Genius

You can override the template fields on any card by adding new ones. However, when you add a field to a card, it is added only to that card, not the template. To add a new field to all cards you create in the future, add it to the template instead.

- **List and Card view.** In this view, the list of contacts is shown on the left page for the selected group and the card for the selected contact is shown on the right.

- **Card Only view.** This view shows one page containing the card of the selected contact. You can create a contact in any view.

Genius

To quickly change views in Contacts, press ⌘+1 for Groups, ⌘+2 for List and Card, or ⌘+3 for Card Only. You can also choose a view on the View menu, or click one of the buttons in the lower-right corner of the left page or the bottom-left corner of the Card view.

2. **Choose File ➪ New Card or click the Add (+) button.** A new, empty card based on the template appears in the Card pane. The name of the card when you create it is *No Name* and the first name is ready to be edited.

3. **Type the contact's first name, last name, and company (if applicable).**

Note

If the card is for a company, select the Company check box, and then type the company name (first and last name information is optional for companies).

4. **Click the pop-up menu next to a field (such as work), select the type of contact information you want to enter, and then type the information for that field.** For example, select mobile on the pop-up menu next to a Phone field, and then type the mobile phone number.

5. **To remove a field from the card, click its Delete button (–).** The Delete button appears only after you have entered information for a field.

Genius

If the information you want to enter isn't available on the pop-up menu, open it and choose Custom. Type the label for the field you want to add and click OK. You return to the card and the custom label appears on it. Type the information for that field to add it to the card.

6. **To add another field of the same type to a card, click the Add (+) button next to a field of the type you want to add.** This appears after you fill in all of the empty fields of a specific type, such as e-mail addresses. A new field appears, and you can select its type and enter the appropriate information.

Note When you select a data type, Contacts automatically creates a field in the appropriate format, such as for phone numbers when you select mobile.

7. **Use one of the following options to add an image to the card:**

   - **Drag an image file from the Desktop and drop it onto the Image well, located immediately to the left of the name fields.** The image sheet appears and you are ready to go on to step 8.

   - **Double-click the Image well and the Image sheet appears.** Click Defaults, choose one of the Mac OS X default images, and then move on to step 8.

   - **Double-click the Image well and the Image sheet appears.** Click Recents, choose an image that you've used before, and then move on to step 8.

   - **Double-click the Image well and the Image sheet appears.** Click Faces, choose a face from your iPhoto or Aperture image library, and then go on to step 8.

   - **Double-click the Image well and the Image sheet appears.** Click Camera, take a picture with the MacBook Pro camera, and then move on to step 8.

8. **Drag the slider to the left to make the image smaller or to the right to make it larger.**

9. **Drag the image around within the image box until the part that you want to be displayed is contained within the box, as shown in Figure 7.3.**

7.3 You can configure images for contacts and they appear when you receive an e-mail or a call from that contact on an iPhone.

10. **Click Done.** You return to the card and the image is stored on it.

11. **Click Done.** The card is saved, as shown in Figure 7.4.

7.4 After you complete the information on a card, it's available for you to refer to or use (such as when sending an e-mail).

Genius

To apply special effects to a contact's image, click the Effects button located just above the Done button on the Image sheet. The Effects dialog appears and you can page through it to preview effects. Click the one that you want to apply to the image.

Importing vCards

Creating vCards manually is fun, but it's a lot easier to import a vCard that you receive from someone else. One of the most common ways to receive vCards is as an e-mail attachment. A vCard file has .vcf as its extension. Just drag the vCard from the e-mail onto your Desktop.

To add a vCard to Contacts, drag the vCard file from the Desktop and drop it onto the list of contacts in the Contacts window. Click Import in the sheet that appears, and the card is then added to your Contacts. You can edit and use cards created from vCards the same as you do those created manually.

Adding contact information from e-mail

Many applications that involve contact information allow you to add that information to your Contacts. For example, when you receive e-mail in Mail, you can follow these steps to add the sender's name and e-mail address to Contacts:

1. **Move the pointer over the name or address shown in the From, Cc, or Bcc fields.**

2. **When the address is highlighted to indicate it has become a menu, point to the downward arrow at the right end of the address, and then click the trackpad button to open the Action menu.**

3. **Choose Add to Contacts.** A new card is created with as much information as Contacts can extract (usually the first and last name, along with the e-mail address).

4. **Use Contacts to edit the card (such as to add more information to it).**

Editing cards

As time passes, contact information changes, and you might want to edit or add more information to existing cards. With Contacts, editing your cards is very similar to creating them. Follow these steps to edit an existing card:

1. **Select the card you want to edit on the contact list.**

2. **Click Edit.** All of the current fields become editable. The empty fields that were on the template when the card was created also appear.

3. **Use the edit tools to make changes to the card.**

4. **Click Done.** Your changes are saved.

Your Address Card

One of the most important cards in Contacts is your own. When you first started your MacBook Pro and worked through the registration process, the information you entered was added to a card in Contacts. This card identifies your contact information in various places, including the Safari AutoFill feature that enables you to quickly complete web forms. You should review and update your card as needed so that its information is always current.

To jump to your card, choose Card ⇨ Go To My Card. Your card is selected on the list and appears in the Card pane. Notice that your card is the only one in the Name list with the Silhouette icon and the text label *me* in the card image. Review the information on your card and make any necessary changes by following the steps for editing contact cards covered previously.

You can make any card yours by selecting it, and then choosing Card ⇨ Make This My Card. You can also send your card to others as a vCard by viewing it and clicking the Share button at the bottom. You can choose to share your card via a message in Messages, an e-mail, or AirDrop.

Working with Cards in Contacts

After Contacts has the contact information with which you want to work, you start to get a lot of benefits from the work you've done. You can browse your contact information or search for specific information. You can also change the way you see contact information.

Browsing contact information

Unless you have many, many cards in Contacts, browsing can often be the fastest way to find one that you want to use. When you browse for contact information, you can usually get to specific cards without typing any information, which makes the process fast and easy.

Setting format and sort preferences

Make sure that Contacts displays names and sorts cards according to your preferences. Follow these steps to get it set up:

1. **Choose Contacts ⇨ Preferences.**

2. **Click the General tab, shown in Figure 7.5.**

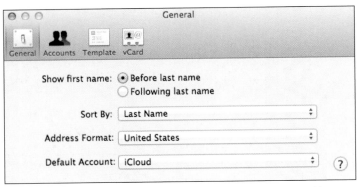

7.5 Configure the order in which Contacts should display a first and last name.

3. **In the Show first name section, click Before last name if you want names to be shown with the first name followed by the last.** Click Following last name if you prefer last names to appear first.

4. **On the Sort By pop-up menu, choose Last Name to have cards sorted by last name or First Name to sort by first name.**

5. **On the Address Format menu, choose the country with the formatting you want to be used for physical addresses.**

You can copy the URL to a map for an address so that you can e-mail it to someone or add it to a document. Find the card containing the address you want to map out. Perform a secondary click on the address's label, and then choose Copy Map URL. The URL for the map is created and copied to the Clipboard. Move to a document (such as an e-mail message) and paste the URL into it.

6. **On the Default Account pop-up menu, choose under which account you want contact information to be stored by default.** For example, if you have an iCloud account, you can choose it so that whenever you create a new contact, it is available from any device that can access your iCloud account.

7. **Close the Preferences dialog.**

Browsing for cards

Follow these steps to browse for cards:

1. **Move into the Groups view and select the group that you want to browse from the list of groups on the left page.** To browse all of your contacts, click All Contacts. The contacts in the selected group appear on the Contacts list.

Genius Just like your own, you can share any contact's card by viewing it, clicking the Share button, and then choosing the option you want to use to share the information.

2. **Scroll the list of contacts.**

3. **Select the contact whose card you want to use**. The card you selected is displayed on the right page.

Browsing for cards in Card Only view

When you are using the Card Only view, you see only address cards. You can still browse your contacts by choosing View ➪ Card Only. You see only cards, as shown in Figure 7.6. Next, click the right arrow at the bottom of the window to browse forward by one card. Click the left arrow to browse back one card, until you see the one with which you want to work.

7.6 You can make the Contacts window more compact by choosing the Card Only view.

195

Searching for cards

When you search for cards in Contacts, it searches all fields on all of your cards simultaneously. Perform the following steps to search for cards in the Groups view:

1. **Select the group for which you want to search.** To search all of your contacts, click All Contacts. All cards in the selected group appear on the Contacts list.

Genius To search in the currently selected group, move into List and Card view, and then type the search term in the Search bar above the Contacts list. When you select a card on the results list, it appears in the Card pane.

2. **Type the text for which you want to search in the Search box.** As you type, Contacts starts searching all of the fields in the cards. As it finds matching cards, it shows them in the Name list. The more you type, the more specific the search becomes.

Genius You can search in the Card view by typing a search term in the Search bar at the top of the window. As you type, the cards available are limited to those that meet your search term. You can browse through the resulting cards until you find the one you want.

3. **Click the card that you want to use when it appears in the Name list.** The card opens on the right page, as shown in Figure 7.7.

To end a search, click the Clear button, which is the x within the gray circle in the Search bar. All of the cards within the selected group appear again.

Genius To see multiple cards at the same time, move to the first card you want to see, and then choose Card ⇨ Open in Separate Window (or press ⌘+I). The card opens in its own window. Move to the next card and do the same thing. You can open as many cards as you want in an independent window.

7.7 When you search, Contacts highlights the search term on each card that it finds.

Organizing Cards with Groups in Contacts

Groups are useful because you can do one action and it affects all of the cards in that group. For example, you can create a group containing family members whom you regularly e-mail. Then, you can address a message to the one group instead of addressing each person individually. There are two kinds of groups in Contacts. Manual groups are those you create, and then manually place cards into. Smart Groups are a collection of criteria and Contacts automatically places cards into Smart Groups based on these criteria.

Genius

The information you see on cards is active, meaning that you can click on its label to start a task. For example, when you click an e-mail address's label, an action menu appears containing useful commands. You can choose Send Email to create a new message addressed to that contact in your default e-mail application. You can also start a FaceTime chat, send a message via Messages, and so on.

Creating groups manually

Follow these steps to create a group:

1. **Choose File ⇨ New Group.** A new group appears on the Group list with its name ready to be edited.

Note You won't be able to add duplicate contacts to a group. If a contact is already in a group, the group is not highlighted when you drag over it.

Genius To add multiple cards to a group at the same time, hold down the ⌘ key while you click each card that you want to add.

2. **Type the name of the group and press Return.** You can name a group anything you want.

3. **Select the group containing the cards you want to add to the new group (select All Contacts to browse all of your contacts).** Browse or search for the first card you want to add to the group.

4. **Drag the card from the Name list and drop it onto the group to which you want to add it, as shown in Figure 7.8.**

7.8 Drag cards from the Name list onto a group to add them to that group.

Creating Smart Groups

Smart Groups are also collections of cards. However, unlike regular groups, you don't have to manually add each card to the group. Instead, you define criteria for the cards you want included in the Smart Group, and then Contacts automatically adds the appropriate cards. For example, suppose you want a group for everyone with the same last name. Simply create a Smart Group with that criterion and Contacts automatically adds all of the people with that last name to the group. The following steps walk you through creating a Smart Group, which is quite different from creating a regular group:

1. **Choose File ⇨ New Smart Group.** The New Smart Group sheet appears, as shown in Figure 7.9.

2. **Type the name of the group.**

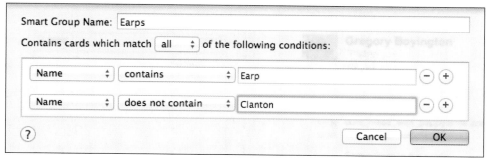

7.9 This Smart Group includes all of my contacts named *Earp*, but not *Clanton*.

3. **Choose the first field you want to include in the criteria on the first pop-up menu (which is Card by default).** For example, to base a criterion on name, choose Name.

4. **Choose how you want the information you enter to be included on the center pop-up menu.** Going back to the Name example, the options on the center menu include the following: Contains, does not contain, is, and is not.

5. **Type the information that you want to be part of the criterion in the empty fields.** If you selected Name and contains on the pop-up menus, type the name you want the criterion to find.

6. **Click the Add (+) button at the end of the criterion to add another to the group.**

7. **If the group has at least two criteria, choose all on the top pop-up menu if all criteria must be met for a card to be included in the group.** Choose any if only one criterion must be met.

8. **Click OK.** The Smart Group is created and all of the cards that meet the criteria you defined are automatically added to it.

Genius

Another way to create a group is to select the cards you want placed into it. Choose File ⇨ New Group From Selection. A new group is created and the cards you selected are placed into it. To complete the group, type its name, and then press Return.

Changing groups

The following tips will be helpful if you ever decide to change or delete a group:

● **To add cards to a manual group, drag them onto its name on the Groups list.**

● **To remove cards from a manual group, select the group and the card you want to remove, and then press Delete. Click Remove from Group.** The card is removed from the group, but continues to be in Contacts.

- **To change a Smart Group, select it, and then choose Edit ⇨ Edit Smart Group.** Change the criteria it uses and the cards contained in the group are automatically changed.

- **To delete a group, select it, press Delete, and then confirm it at the prompt.**

Genius

You can easily search for information on your MacBook Pro related to any card. Select the card for which you want to search. Hold down the Control key and click the card. Choose Spotlight *cardname*, (where *cardname* is the name of the card you selected). A search is performed and a Finder window appears showing the results. Double-click any of the results to see the details of the found item.

Synchronizing Contact Information with iPhones, iPod touches, or iPads

If you have an iPhone, iPad, or iPod touch, you'll want to keep your contact information on your device in sync with your Contacts on your computer. You can do this using iTunes or iCloud, Exchange, or other accounts that can be accessed wirelessly and support contact information. One of the advantages of using iTunes is that you don't have to deal with any type of account. You can also synchronize your contact information when you sync your audio, video, applications, and other content. The benefit of using iCloud (or other similar accounts) is that your contact information can be synced wirelessly and automatically.

Synchronizing via iTunes

The following steps will help you easily move your contact information from Contacts onto your Apple mobile device by synchronizing it:

1. **Connect the device to your MacBook Pro.** iTunes opens if isn't open already.

Note

If you've set up the device for wireless syncing, you can skip step 1.

2. **Select the device on the iTunes source list.**

3. **Click the Info tab, as shown in Figure 7.10.**

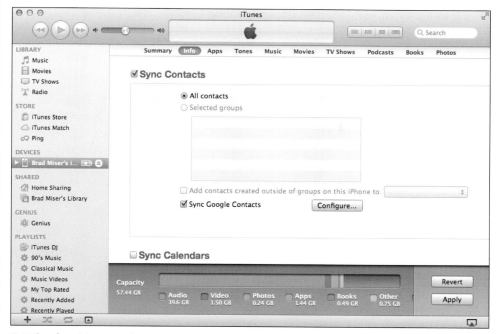

7.10 Synchronizing your Contacts with an iPhone is a great way to ensure that your contact information is always available to you.

4. **Select the Sync Contacts check box.**

5. **Select either All contacts or Selected groups to determine which contacts are synced.**

6. **If you choose Selected groups, select the check box for each group with information you want included in the sync.**

7. **If you want contacts you create on the device to be placed within a specific group in Contacts, select the Add contacts created outside of groups on this *device* to check box, (where *device* is the kind of device you are syncing).** Choose the group from the pop-up menu.

8. **If you use Google Contacts and want to sync those contacts, select the related Sync check box and log in to your account at the prompt.**

9. **Scroll down the screen until you see the Advanced section.**

10. **If you want the contact information on the device to be replaced by your contacts in Contacts the next time it is synced, select the Contacts check box.** If you don't select this check box, the contact information on the device is merged with your Contacts information.

11. **Click Apply.** The changes you made are saved and the contact information on the device is synced. The next time you sync the device, updated contact information is copied from the MacBook Pro to the device, or vice versa.

Synchronizing via iCloud

Syncing your contact information with iCloud is wireless and you can set how frequently information is updated. Changes you make on the mobile device are moved back to iCloud. If your MacBook Pro is also set to synchronize through iCloud, it receives those changes during the next sync (see Chapter 6 for more information).

Note You must already have an iCloud account to be able to use it to sync; see Chapter 6 for more information.

Follow these steps to configure an iPhone, iPad, or iPod touch for iCloud syncing:

1. **On the device, tap Settings to open the Settings application.**

2. **Tap iCloud.**

3. **Enter your Apple ID and password, as shown in Figure 7.11.**

4. **Tap Sign In.**

5. **Tap Off next to Contacts if required (if the status is On already, skip this step).** Contact syncing starts and the Contacts status changes to On.

6. **Configure the other syncing options in the same way.**

7. **Tap Settings.**

8. **Tap Mail, Contacts, Calendars.**

9. **Fetch New Data.**

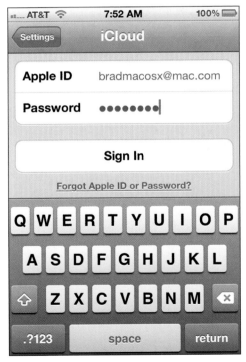

7.11 You can configure your iCloud on an iPhone to have access to your contacts.

Note If you already have information on the device, you're prompted to merge that information with iCloud. If you choose Merge, the information on the device is uploaded to your iCloud account.

10. **If you want changes to data on the iCloud cloud or device to be transferred immediately, enable Push by setting its status to On.**

11. **Set the time interval at which the device should check for new data or transfer its changed data by fetching.** Tap Manually if you only want to get information on your command.

Genius You can configure different iCloud sync options for e-mail, calendars, and contacts by moving to the Fetch New Data screen and tapping Advanced. Then, tap the Mail part of your account and tap Push, Fetch, or Manual. Do the same for the Contacts, Calendars part of your account. For example, you might want to set Push for your e-mail because it changes more quickly, and have calendar and contact updates moved through Fetch.

Configuring E-mail Accounts in Mail

One of the benefits of Mail is that you can configure many e-mail accounts in it, and easily work with all (or just one) of them at any point in time.

Genius You can also create and manage e-mail, contact, and calendar accounts using the Mail, Contacts & Calendars pane of the System Preferences application (which is covered in Chapter 2). The benefit of configuring accounts there instead of within individual applications is that many applications can access those accounts once you've configured them on that pane. For example, if you've configured a Mail-compatible account on that pane, you don't need to add it to Mail because that happens automatically.

Mail works with the following kinds of e-mail accounts:

- **iCloud.** If you have an iCloud account, you also have an iCloud e-mail account. This is convenient because you can use Mail to access your e-mail, or you can use the iCloud website to work with it almost as easily.

- **POP.** Post Office Protocol e-mail accounts are one of the most common types provided by many Internet service providers and other organizations that provide e-mail services. POP is a client-based protocol, meaning that e-mail is typically downloaded to the computer on which it is read and removed from the e-mail server (most include an option to leave e-mail on the server). Under POP, the client is the authoritative source of e-mail for an account.

- **IMAP.** Internet Message Access Protocol is a newer e-mail protocol. It is primarily a server-based protocol, meaning that e-mail is usually left on the server while it is read. The server itself is the authoritative source of e-mail for an account. iCloud e-mail is based on IMAP.

Note

Gmail uses IMAP as do most other similar accounts. You are only likely to use a POP account for specific Internet access providers.

- **Exchange.** Microsoft Exchange Server technology is dominant in the business world for managing e-mail.

While there are technical differences among these kinds of accounts, they are seldom important when it comes to performing e-mail activities. The differences show up primarily in how you configure Mail to work with the various types of accounts. There are a number of attributes that you need to know to configure an e-mail account in Mail. The following are the most common attributes; however these vary from type to type:

- **E-mail address.** You can often create the initial part of the address, but the domain (everything after the @) comes from the provider.

- **Incoming mail server address.** Mail that you receive is delivered through an incoming mail server.

- **Username.** This is usually everything before the @ in your e-mail address.

- **Password.** Sometimes, you have two: one for both the incoming and outgoing mail servers.

- **Outgoing mail server address.** To send e-mail, you need to configure the outgoing mail server through which it is to be sent.

- **User authentication.** To configure an authenticated account, you need a username and password. Accounts use different kinds of authentication. You don't need to understand the technical details, you just need to know which specific kinds of authentication your accounts use so you can configure them correctly.

When you obtain an e-mail account, you receive information for each of the attributes that need to be configured.

Configuring iCloud accounts

One of the benefits of an iCloud e-mail account is that it is automatically configured when you register your account in the Mail, Contacts & Calendars pane of the System Preferences application. However, just in case you ever need to reconfigure it, the following steps walk you through how to set up iCloud e-mail in Mail:

1. **Launch Mail and open Preferences.**

Note If you've never used Mail before and you don't have an iCloud (or any other) e-mail account set up in the System Preferences application, Mail guides you through the set up process the first time you open it.

2. **Click the Accounts tab.** The list on the left side of the Accounts pane contains currently configured accounts. When you select an account on this list, the tools you use to work with it are shown in the right part of the pane.

3. **Click the Add (+) button located at the bottom of the list.** The Add Account sheet appears.

4. **Type your name in the Full Name field.** This is the name that is shown as the From name on any e-mail that you send. It defaults to the name you entered when you first started your MacBook Pro, but you can change it to something else if you want.

5. **Type the e-mail address for the account in the Email Address field.**

6. **Type the password for the account in the Password field.**

7. **Click Create.** Mail logs in to your iCloud account. If successful, the sheet closes and you see the account on the Account Summary sheet. This sheet confirms the information about your account and presents it to you.

8. **To enable other applications to access the account, select the Notes, Contacts, or Calendars & Reminders check boxes.**

9. **Click Create.** You see the new account on the Accounts list.

10. **Select the account you created.** You see its configuration information in the right pane of the window, as shown in Figure 7.12. You can use the account as is, or you can more fully configure it by continuing through the remaining steps.

7.12 The basic configuration of an iCloud account requires only that you type your name, member name, and password.

Note

One of the best features of an iCloud account is that you can configure and use aliases (see Chapter 6 for more information). If you click the Edit Email Aliases button, you move to the iCloud website where you can configure these.

11. **Change the default description (which is iCloud) to something more meaningful, such as your e-mail address or other text that enables you to more easily recognize the account.** This is especially useful if you have multiple accounts of the same type because the description identifies the account in several places within Mail.

12. **Click the Mailbox Behaviors tab, shown in Figure 7.13.**

13. **Select the Store check boxes to store e-mail on the iCloud server or deselect them to store it on your MacBook Pro.** For example, if you select the Store draft messages on the server check box, messages saved in the Draft state are stored online where you can access them from any device using the e-mail account. If this is not selected, these messages are stored only on your MacBook Pro. This is significant because you are only allotted a specific amount of online space, so you want to make sure you use it most efficiently.

7.13 Mailbox Behaviors determines where your iCloud e-mail is stored.

14. **Use the pop-up menus to determine when Mail deletes or permanently erases sent, junk, or trash messages.** The longer the time set is, the longer the messages are available to you, but the more storage space they require.

15. **Use the Trash check boxes to determine what Mail does with messages you delete.**

16. **Click the Advanced tab.**

Genius

To temporarily stop working with an account, move to the Account Information tab and deselect the Enable this account check box. Select it to resume using the account. When you disable an account, it disappears from the Mailboxes section of the Mail window, but remains configured in the application so you can easily start using it again.

17. **If you don't want the account to automatically be checked for new messages, deselect the Include when automatically check for new messages check box.** To retrieve information for the account, use Mail's Get New Mail command.

18. **Use the Keep copies of messages for offline viewing pop-up menu to determine where messages and attachments are stored.** The default keeps copies of all messages and attachments on your MacBook Pro. However, you can choose other actions, such as storing messages only and ignoring attachments, to save some hard drive space.

19. **Close the Preferences window and save your changes.**

Genius

If you use iCloud e-mail aliases, you only need to configure your primary iCloud e-mail address in Mail. That's because e-mail sent to one of your aliases is actually delivered to the primary address. However, it can be helpful to set the colors associated with each alias so you can easily tell to which a message was sent (see Chapter 6 for more information).

Configuring POP accounts

Many e-mail accounts use POP. Follow these steps to add and configure a POP account in Mail:

1. **Launch Mail and open Preferences.**

2. **Click the Accounts tab.**

3. **Click the Add (+) button located at the bottom of the list.** The Add Account sheet appears.

4. **Type your name in the Full Name field.** This is the name that is shown as the From name on e-mail that you send.

5. **Type the e-mail address and password for the account in the respective fields, and then click Continue.** At the prompt, click Setup Manually or, if you see an error message, click Continue. You see the Incoming Mail Server window.

Note

The easiest way to tell what kind of account you are working with is to look at the included documentation. It will identify the account type as part of the configuration information you need to set up the account in an e-mail application. You can also look at the addresses associated with the account. For example, a POP account's incoming and outgoing servers typically include *pop*.

6. **On the Account Type pop-up menu, choose POP.** Type a description of the account in the Description field. If necessary, edit the server address *popserveraddress* (where *popserveraddress* is the name of your incoming mail server) in the Incoming Mail Server field. This is usually something like pop-server.*provider*.com (where *provider* is the domain

name of your e-mail account provider), but it can take other forms, as well. The important part is to use the address included in the account information provided to you.

Note

Mail tries to configure information, such as server addresses, based on information you enter. Sometimes it's right and sometimes it's not. Make sure you carefully review this information and change it as needed before you move on to the next step.

7. **If necessary, edit your account's username and password.** Mail takes this from the information you entered, but you need to make sure this is for the incoming server, which can sometimes be different from the outgoing one.

8. **Click Continue.** You see the Incoming Mail Security window. If the account uses Secure Sockets Layer (SSL) security, select that check box.

9. **Choose the type of authentication the account uses for incoming e-mail on the Authentication pop-up menu, and then click Continue.** Again, make sure this is for incoming e-mail as the security settings may be different than for outgoing. You see the Outgoing Mail Server window.

10. **Edit the description of the outgoing server in the Description field.** If necessary, edit the address, which is usually something like smtp-server.*provider*.com (where provider is the name of the account provider), in the Outgoing Mail Server field. Make sure this matches the information you received from your provider.

11. **If the provider uses authentication, select the Use Authentication check box.** If necessary, edit your account's authentication username and password (this can be the same as that for incoming mail, but it may be different.), and then click Continue.

12. **At the prompt, click Setup Manually.** You see the Outgoing Mail Server window.

13. **If the account uses Secure Sockets Layer (SSL) security, select that check box.**

14. **Choose the type of authentication the account uses for outgoing e-mail on the Authentication pop-up menu.** You see the Outgoing Mail Server window.

15. **Click Continue.** You see the Account Summary window.

16. **Click Create.** The account is created, and its mailboxes are added to the Accounts window.

17. **Select the account on the Accounts list and use the Account Information, Mailbox Behaviors, and Advanced tabs to more fully configure it.** This is similar to using these tabs for an iCloud account, although the options you see are different because the account types are, as well.

18. **Close the Preferences window and save your changes.**

Configuring IMAP accounts

If you've configured an iCloud account (the details are covered earlier in this chapter), then you've already learned how to configure an IMAP account because iCloud accounts *are* IMAP accounts. In most cases, you only have to select IMAP as the account type, and then type your name, and the account username and password for Mail to be able to access it. Once the account is created, you can configure specific actions for it, such as where certain kinds of mail are stored.

Configuring Exchange accounts

How or if you can configure Mail to access an Exchange e-mail account depends on how the organization providing the account allows it to be accessed. The only way to know which path you need to take is to contact your IT organization and find out which version of Exchange is being used, and if IMAP access to your Exchange account is allowed. If IMAP access to your Exchange e-mail is provided, configuring your Exchange account in Mail is similar (albeit, with a few differences) to other IMAP accounts. When you reach the Incoming Mail Server screen, you should select either Exchange 2007 or Exchange IMAP. Each of these requires slightly different details for you to provide to configure the account.

If your account is provided through Exchange 2007, all you need is your e-mail address and password. You can also add your contacts from the Contacts application and calendars from the Calendars application to your Exchange account by selecting the related check boxes, as shown in Figure 7.14. This is the ideal situation because Mail automatically discovers all of the required elements to access your Exchange account for you (which is similar to how it works with an iCloud account). Also, you have access to your Contacts and Calendar information within any application you use to access Exchange, such as Outlook on a Windows PC.

If your account is provided through an older version of Exchange, things get a bit more complicated. If the account is provided via IMAP, configure it in the following way using an incoming mail server (similar to other IMAP accounts):

1. **Move to the Add Account sheet and configure it with your name, e-mail address, and password.**

2. **Click Continue.**

3. **On the Account Type pop-up menu, choose Exchange IMAP.**

4. **Type a description of the account.**

5. **Type the incoming mail server address.**

Account Summary

Mail found a server account for the email address you provided. The following account will be set up on your computer:

Account type: Exchange

Full name: Brad Miser

Email address:

Server address:

Also set up: ☑ Contacts
☑ Calendars

Cancel   Go Back   Create

7.14 Configuring an Exchange account with Exchange 2007 is quite simple.

6. **Type your username as domain\username.** You need to get your domain from your IT organization.

7. **In the Outlook Web Access field, type the address of your OWA server without a prefix (as in: owa.company.com).** Like the domain, there's no way to figure out this address; you must get it from your IT organization. In some cases, the address has / exchange at the end. When you configure this address, Mail filters out all non–e-mail items from your account before downloading them to Mail.

8. **Complete the account setup the same as you would with other kinds of accounts.**

Many organizations don't allow IMAP access to an Exchange account, in which case you won't be able to access the account in Mail. If you can access your Exchange account via an Outlook Web Access (OWA) server, you can get to your e-mail, contacts, and other Exchange information via a web browser. Move to your organization's OWA server, type your username and password, and log in. In most cases, you have to include a domain in front of your username, such as in xyz\username.

If the organization doesn't provide IMAP or OWA access to your Exchange e-mail, you have to run Windows on your MacBook Pro so that you can use Outlook to access it (see Chapter 12 for more information). You can do this using Boot Camp or one of the available virtualization applications, such as VMware Fusion or Parallels Desktop for Mac.

Testing e-mail accounts

After you configure your e-mail accounts, expand the Inbox by clicking the right-facing triangle next to it. Under the Inbox, you see an Inbox for each e-mail account that you configured, as shown in Figure 7.15. If you don't see an icon containing an exclamation point, the accounts are properly configured and ready to use. If you do see this icon, you need to correct the account configuration.

7.15 No caution icon means that these three e-mail accounts have been successfully configured in Mail.

As a final test, send e-mail to and from each address to make sure that it is configured as you want it to be. If you find any problems or want to make any changes, open the Accounts pane of the Preferences dialog. Select the account you want to change, and then use the three tabs to make any necessary changes.

Working with File Attachments in Mail

E-mail is one of the easiest and fastest ways to exchange files with other people. Using Mail, you can attach files of any type to e-mails that you send.

Genius

Sending compressed files through e-mail

I'm going to recommend something here that many people don't do as standard practice, which is to compress files before attaching them to e-mail messages, even if you are sending only one file with a message. There are three reasons why this a good idea: Sending a compressed file requires less bandwidth; compressed files are less likely to be screened out by spam or virus filters on the recipient's e-mail (although some e-mail systems are configured to screen compressed attachments); a compressed file gives the user a single file to deal with instead of an attachment for each file.

So, before moving into Mail, follow these steps to compress the files you want to send:

1. **Move to a Finder window showing the files you want to send.**

2. **Select the files you want to send.** Remember, to select multiple files, you can hold the ⌘ key down while clicking files.

3. **Choose File ⇨ Compress # items (where # is the number of files you selected).** The files you selected are then compressed into a Zip file. Mac OS X uses Zip as its default compression scheme, which is a very good thing because it is also the dominant compression standard on Windows computers.

4. **Rename the Zip file.** The default name for Zip files is always Archive.zip when you compress more than one file. If you compress a single file, it takes the name of the file you compressed.

After you prepare the compressed file, you can use any of the following techniques to attach it to an e-mail message:

- **Drag the file onto the New Message window.**
- **While the message to which you want to attach files is active, choose File ⇨ Attach Files.** Then, use the Choose File sheet to select the file you want to attach.

- **While the message to which you want to attach files is active, press Shift+⌘+A.** Use the Choose File sheet to select the file you want to attach.

- **Click the Attach button on the New Message window's toolbar.** The Choose File sheet appears; use it to select the file you want to attach to a message.

Caution

The way that Mail embeds file attachments into messages can cause problems for some e-mail applications. In that case, you have to find another way to transfer the file, such as an FTP site or a service, such as Dropbox.

Of course, many times people attach files that haven't been compressed to e-mail (I do it more than occasionally). When you place a file that hasn't been compressed in a new message window, you see a thumbnail preview of the file with its icon, the filename, and its size in parentheses. If the file type is one that can be displayed in the message, such as a TIFF image or a PDF file, you actually see the contents of the file embedded within the body of the message.

Preparing attachments for Windows users

Because Mac and Windows operating systems use different file format structures, Windows users sometimes end up with two files when you e-mail them attachments. One is the useable file and the other is unusable (the names of the files are filename and _filename). Recipients can safely ignore the second one, however, it is still confusing. You can choose to attach individual attachments as Windows-friendly by selecting the Send Windows-Friendly Attachments check box in the Attach File dialog. If you always want to send files in the Windows-friendly format, choose Edit ⇨ Attachments ⇨ Send Windows-Friendly Attachments.

Genius

You can use the Photo Browser button (the one with the icon of a picture) in the New Message toolbar to easily find photos in your iPhoto library. Drag them into a new message window to attach them to an e-mail.

Working with received files

When you receive a message that has files attached to it, you see the files in the body of the message. The same as when you send files in a message, you see the file icon, name, and size. If Mail can display the content of the attached files, that content appears in the message body. If the details of the header are hidden, click the Details button, and the Save and Quick Look buttons appear.

The following list includes various ways in which you can work with file attachments:

- **Download and use the attachment.** If a file is not yet downloaded to your MacBook Pro, click its icon (the downward-facing arrow) in the message body to download it. When the attachment has been downloaded, the download icon is replaced by an icon representing the file type. Once the file has been downloaded, click its icon to open the document in the associated application.

- **Click the Quick Look button.** The Quick Look window opens and you can preview the contents of the files, as shown in Figure 7.16. If you have an application that can open the file, click the Open with button to open the file in that application.

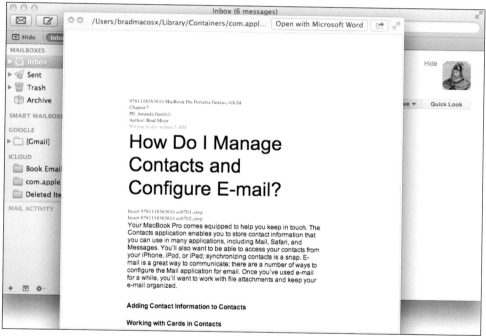

7.16 Use the Quick Look function to preview files attached to a message.

Genius

If the details are hidden, perform a secondary click on the file icon and choose Quick Look Attachment.

- **Choose File ⇨ Save Attachments.** Use the resulting sheet to choose the location in which you want to save the files.

- **Click the Save menu button next to the attachment information at the top of the message.** The file is saved to your Downloads folder.

- **If multiple files are attached, open the Save pop-up menu.** Choose Save All to save the files to the location of your choice or choose a specific file that you want to save.

- **Drag the file icon from the message onto a folder on your Desktop to save it there.**

- **Open the attachment's contextual menu and select one of the listed actions.** The actions include: Open Attachment, which opens the file in its native application; Open With, which enables you to select the application in which you want the file to open; Save Attachment, which prompts you to choose a location in which to save the file; or Save to Downloads folder, which saves the attachment in your designated Downloads folder.

Genius If the contents of the file are being displayed and you would rather see just an icon, open the file's contextual menu and select View as icon. To view the file's content again, open the menu and select View in Place.

Organizing E-mail in Mail

As you send and receive e-mail, you end up with a lot of messages that you need to manage. Fortunately, Mail provides a number of ways to organize your e-mail, including mailboxes, Smart Mailboxes, and Smart Mailbox folders.

Using mailboxes

You can create your own mailboxes to organize your messages. These are much like folders on your Desktop. The mailboxes you create are shown in the Mailbox pane below the Inbox and other special mailboxes. You can also create nested mailboxes to create a hierarchy of mailboxes in which to store your messages. Follow the steps below to create a nested mailbox:

1. **Click the Add (+) button at the bottom of the Mailbox pane.**

2. **On the resulting pop-up menu, select New Mailbox.** The New Mailbox sheet appears, as shown in Figure 7.17.

3. **On the Location pop-up menu, select the location where you want the mailbox to be stored.** If you select On My

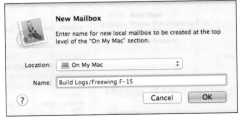

7.17 Creating a nested mailbox.

Mac, the folder is created on your computer. If you use an IMAP, Exchange, or iCloud account, you can select that account to create a folder on its server.

4. **Type the name of the mailbox you want to create in the Name field.** To create a nested mailbox, separate the name of each mailbox by a slash (/). For example, to create a mailbox called Fan Mail within a mailbox called Mail to Keep, you would type Mail to Keep/Fan Mail. To create a separate mailbox, just type the mailbox name.

5. **Click OK.** The mailbox is created and appears in the Mailbox pane in the location you selected. If you created a nested folder, the top-level folder has a triangle next to it; click this to expand the folder so you can see the folders it contains.

Genius

After you create folders, you can nest them by placing them within one another. Simply drag the folder you want to nest onto the folder in which you want it placed.

To use the mailboxes you create, you move messages between them, just like you move folders and files between folders on your Desktop. You can move messages from one mailbox to another in any of the following ways:

- **Drag and drop a message from the Message List pane onto a mailbox.** This moves the message from the Inbox into the folder. If the Inbox is stored on a server (such as an IMAP account), the messages that you move to folders stored on your MacBook Pro no longer count against your storage space allocation.

- **Drag messages from the Message List pane in one Viewer to the Message List pane in another.** This copies the messages to the mailbox shown in the second Viewer window.

- **Select messages, and then choose Message ➪ Move To.** On the menu, select the mailbox to which you want to transfer the messages.

- **Select messages and then choose Message ➪ Copy To.** On the menu, select the mailbox in which you want to create copies of the selected messages.

- **Select messages and then choose Message ➪ Move Again to move the selected messages to the same mailbox into which you most recently transferred mail.**

- **Select messages and press Option+⌘+T to move the selected messages to the same mailbox into which you most recently transferred mail.**

- **Open a message's contextual menu and select the Move To, Copy To, Move Again, or Apply Rules command.**

- **Select messages and then choose Message ➪ Apply Rules.** Select a rule that transfers the messages.

Genius

You can create and use rules to have Mail handle your e-mail automatically. For example, you can have e-mail from a specific person stored in a designated location and color-coded. To create and manage rules, open Preferences and click the Rules tab.

Using Smart Mailboxes

You can use Smart Mailboxes to organize your e-mail automatically based on criteria you define. For example, you might want to collect all of the e-mail you receive from a group of people with whom you are working on a project in a specific folder. Rather than having to place these messages in the folder by dragging them out of your Inbox individually, you can create a Smart Mailbox so that mail you receive from these people is automatically placed in the appropriate folder.

However, when mail is shown under a Smart Mailbox, it isn't actually stored there. Because a Smart Mailbox is a set of conditions rather than a place, it shows messages stored in other locations, rather than being a place where those messages are actually stored. So, if a message in an IMAP Inbox matches a Smart Mailbox's conditions, it is shown under that mailbox, but it also appears in the Inbox for the IMAP account. You should use mailboxes to store and organize e-mail on your MacBook Pro and use Smart Mailboxes to show messages stored in various folders in one place. The following steps walk you through the process of creating a Smart Mailbox:

1. **Click the Add (+) button at the bottom of the Mailbox pane.**

2. **On the resulting pop-up menu, select New Smart Mailbox.** The Smart Mailbox sheet appears, as shown in Figure 7.18.

3. **Type the name of the mailbox into the Smart Mailbox Name field.**

4. **Select the first condition for the mailbox on the first pop-up menu in the conditions box.** For example, select From, which bases the condition on the name or e-mail address in the From field.

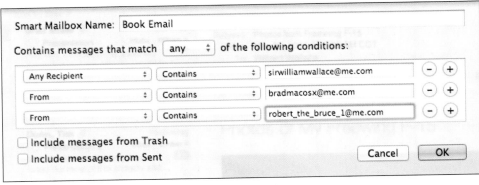

7.18 This Smart Mailbox collects e-mail from specific people.

5. **Select the operation for the condition on the second pop-up menu.** What you see on this menu depends on the condition you selected. For example, to create a Smart Mailbox for mail from a specific person, you would select Contains or Is equal to.

6. **Type the condition text or date in the box.** For example, type a person's name if you are creating a Smart Mailbox to collect mail from that specific person.

7. **To add another condition, click the Add (+) button on the right side of the sheet and configure it with steps 4 to 6.**

8. **If you have configured more than one condition, select all on the matching pop-up menu above the condition list if all conditions must be true for mail to be stored in the Smart Mailbox.** Select any if only one of the conditions must be true.

9. **If you want messages that are in the Trash folders to be included in the Smart Mailbox, select the Include messages from Trash check box.**

10. **If you want messages that are in the Sent folders to be included in the Smart Mailbox, select the Include messages from Sent check box.**

11. **To remove a condition you no longer want to use, click the Remove (–) button next to it.**

12. **Click OK.** The Smart Mailbox is created in the Smart Mailboxes section of the Mailbox pane. Any e-mail that meets its conditions is organized under that mailbox.

Genius

To change the conditions for an existing Smart Mailbox, open its contextual menu and select Edit Smart Mailbox or double-click its icon. Use the resulting Smart Mailbox sheet to make changes to it. When you click OK, e-mail that meets the new conditions is shown when you select the Smart Mailbox.

If you want to organize your Smart Mailboxes, you can create a Smart Mailbox folder, and then place your Smart Mailboxes within it. Follow these steps to set this up:

1. **Choose Mailbox ➪ New Smart Mailbox Folder.** The Smart Mailbox Folder sheet appears.

2. **Name the new Smart Mailbox folder.**

3. **Click OK.** The Smart Mailbox folder appears in the Smart Mailboxes section.

4. **Drag Smart Mailboxes into the Smart Mailbox folder that you created to place them there.** When you do this, an expansion triangle appears so that you can expand the Smart Mailbox folder to see its contents.

How Do I Communicate and Share in Real Time?

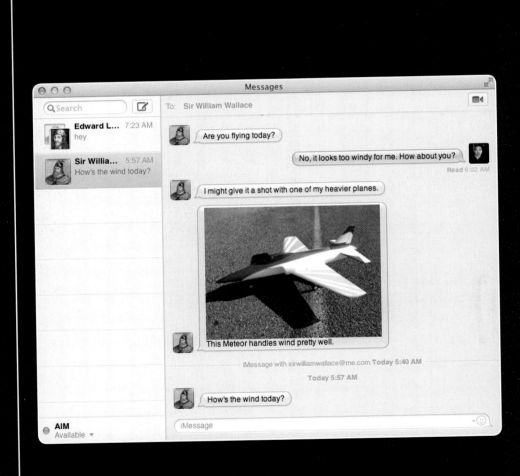

With your MacBook Pro, you can take advantage of the Mac OS X real-time communication applications, which are FaceTime and Messages. FaceTime enables you to have visual and audio communication with other Mac, iPhone, iPod touch, and iPad users. Messages enables you to conduct text, audio, and video chats, and share Desktops while you chat. You can use Messages to communicate with just about anyone who has a chat application on a computer or iOS device. You'll also want to take advantage of the built-in sharing capabilities offered by many applications.

Conversing with FaceTime

FaceTime is a great way to communicate because you can both see and hear the person with whom you are chatting. You can use FaceTime to video chat with anyone who uses a Mac, iPhone, iPod touch, or iPad. Using FaceTime is simple, fun, and free (all you need is an Apple ID, which you can get at no cost if you don't already have one).

To be able to chat on FaceTime with someone, both people need to be running the FaceTime application. It is currently available only for Macs, iPhones, iPod touches, and iPads. Also, the devices involved in a FaceTime chat must be connected to the Internet. (iPhones may support FaceTime over a cell connection in the future.) Only two devices can be involved in a FaceTime chat (unless you're using Messages—in that case, more than two devices can be involved in chats). You also must know the person's e-mail address or iPhone number. Before you can start chatting on FaceTime, you need to configure some basic settings. Once these are in place, conducting FaceTime chats is easy.

Configuring FaceTime

To start using FaceTime, perform the following steps to sign in to your Apple account and confirm your e-mail address:

1. **Launch FaceTime.** The first time you launch FaceTime, it prompts you to type your Apple ID.

2. **Type your Apple ID (if necessary) and password.**

3. **Click Sign In.**

4. **Confirm or update your e-mail address.** People will use your e-mail address to request a FaceTime session, so it is important that the application is configured with the correct e-mail address.

Note iPhones can use e-mail addresses to message over a Wi-Fi network, or phone numbers to message over a cellular network. Only iPhones can use phone numbers to message, as they are the only iOS devices capable of using a cellular network.

5. **Click Next.** Your information is verified, and the contacts section is added to the FaceTime window, as shown in Figure 8.1. You can use this section to access the contacts stored in Contacts and place FaceTime calls to them. You are now ready to start using FaceTime.

8.1 After your account is verified, you see the Contacts pane on the right side of the FaceTime window.

Genius

You can designate contacts with whom you frequently chat on FaceTime as favorites and they appear on the Favorites tab. Click the Favorites tab, click the Add button (+) at the top of the window, browse to the contact you want to add, and then click it. Click the contact information you want to use for FaceTime, such as the person's iPhone number or e-mail address (if only one type of contact information is available, it is selected automatically).

Starting a call

To request a FaceTime call, choose one of the following options to select the person with whom you want to communicate:

- Click the Favorites tab, and then click the person you want to call.

- Click the Recents tab, and then click on a contact with whom you've recently communicated.

223

● Click the Contacts tab, browse your contacts, and then click the contact information you want to use to place the call. This can be an e-mail address or a phone number (if the person has an iPhone).

A FaceTime request is sent to the person you select. While the call is being placed, you see the name of the person you are calling at the top of the FaceTime window. You also hear the ringer indicating a call is being placed. If the person accepts your request, the FaceTime session starts, and you can hear and see the other party while conducting the call. If the person declines or is not available, you see a *not available* message.

Receiving a call

When someone wants to chat on FaceTime with you, a window appears, as shown in Figure 8.2. In the top-right corner of the window, you see the person who is trying to contact you. At the bottom of the window, you see the Decline and Accept buttons. To start the conversation, click Accept and conduct the call as described in the next section. To decline the call, click Decline. The person who sent the request then receives the *not available for FaceTime* message.

8.2 A FaceTime conversation is just a click away.

Note

On a Mac, the FaceTime application doesn't have to be running to receive calls. If someone tries to call you and your FaceTime application isn't running, it opens and you can accept or decline the FaceTime session.

Note After a few moments, the title bar and buttons on the FaceTime screen disappear. Move the pointer over the window and the buttons reappear.

Conducting a call

The following controls are available while you conduct a FaceTime call, as shown in Figure 8.3:

- **Drag the preview window (which is the view of you that the other person is seeing) to change its location.**

- **If you hover over the preview window, the Rotate button appears; click it to rotate the window.**

- **Mute the audio and darken the video in the preview window (the other person can still see you) by clicking the Mute button (the microphone).**

- **Click End to end the FaceTime session.**

- **Click the Full Screen button (the diagonal arrows) to enlarge to a full-screen FaceTime window.**

8.3 FaceTime is a great way to keep in touch with people, be they close or far away.

Note Like other applications, FaceTime can be moved into the background. However, if the conversation continues, the other person can still hear and see you, even if you can't see the preview in the FaceTime window.

Messaging with Messages

With Messages, you can have text, audio, and video chats. You can also share Desktops, photos, and other documents with people. Messages enables you to chat with multiple people at the same time and conduct multiple chats simultaneously.

Configuring Messages

Before you can start chatting, you need to do some basic configuration to prepare Messages. Most importantly, you must configure the accounts you want to use to chat. There are two basic paths to this end: You can allow the Assistant to walk you through the account setup steps the first time you start Messages, or you can manually configure the accounts (you can do this at any time). You'll also want to use various Messages Preferences to tweak it and make it work as well as possible for you.

Creating and configuring chat accounts

To chat, you need to configure Messages with at least one chat account. You can use the following types of accounts with Messages:

- **Apple ID/iCloud**
- **AOL Instant Messenger (AIM)**
- **Google Talk**
- **Jabber**
- **Yahoo!**

You can also use Bonjour to use Messages on a local network. While this isn't really a type of account, it behaves in a similar way. The various devices that use Bonjour can automatically detect and connect to each other for many reasons, including chatting. While it is a good thing to be able to use these types of accounts in Messages, the capabilities available to you in Messages chats are dependent on the type of account you use, and the types of accounts and applications the people with whom you chat are using.

Trying to figure out which capabilities you can use for which types of accounts can be a bit confusing. The easiest way to determine whether you can chat with someone is to simply try it. If an option (such as audio chat) is available to you, you can use it. If not, either you or the other person (or both) will have to try to use a different account. There are many potential combinations of account types and applications that you may encounter. You can use almost all of the Messages features if you have an Apple ID/iCloud and AIM account, and enable Bonjour. The good news is that when you have an Apple ID/iCloud account, you also have an AIM account.

For the purposes of this chapter, I assume that you are using an Apple ID/iCloud account, and want it set up as an AIM account, as well. I also assume that the people with whom you are chatting have similar configurations. If not, you may not be able to take advantage of all that Messages offers.

Note If you use your Apple ID/iCloud account in Messages on an iOS device (such as an iPhone), you always have your chats available on your MacBook Pro and those devices. For example, you can start a chat on your MacBook Pro, and then move over to your iPhone without missing a beat.

To get started, launch Messages and use the following steps to configure it through the Assistant, which starts with the Welcome screen:

1. **Review the information in the Welcome screen.**

2. **Click Continue.** The Enter Apple ID window appears.

3. **Type your Apple ID and password and click Sign In.**

4. **Select the Send Read Receipts check box if you want to know when people receive and read your messages.**

5. **If you want to receive messages at other accounts, too, click the Add (+) button, type the e-mail address, and then click Continue.** You see the Conclusion screen.

6. **Click Done.** You've completed the basic Messages configuration and move to the Messages application.

Genius You can also create and manage accounts using the Mail, Contacts & Calendars pane of the System Preferences application, which is covered in Chapter 2. If you've configured a Messages-compatible account on that pane, you don't need to add it to Messages—that happens automatically.

Messages offers a number of preferences so that you can configure the way it works. You don't have to set all these preferences at once; you can adjust them at any time to tweak the way in which Messages works. To access Messages preferences, choose Messages ➪ Preferences. The Preferences window has a number of tabs that I summarize throughout the rest of the chapter. As you explore all of the preferences Messages offers, watch for others not mentioned here that might be useful to you.

You can use the Accounts tab to add new chat accounts, as shown in Figure 8.4, or to make changes to your existing ones. You can create and use multiple kinds of accounts within Messages, but you should definitely use your Apple ID/iCloud and AIM accounts.

To configure a new Messages account of any type, click the Accounts tab, and then click the Add (+) button at the bottom of the Accounts list. The Account Setup sheet appears. Use this to create a new account just as when you first launched Messages and the Assistant led you through the process (see the steps covered earlier in this chapter). To add an AIM account using your Apple ID, choose AIM on the Account Type menu, type your Apple ID and password, and then click Done.

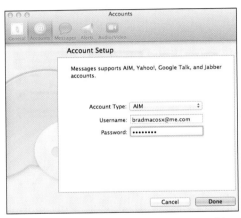

8.4 If you use an Apple ID/iCloud account, add an AIM account to increase the functionality of Messages.

To configure existing Messages user accounts, click the Accounts tab of the Preferences window. Next, select the chat account you want to configure from the list in the left side of the window. Then, use the tools and settings in the right side of the window to configure the account details. Because some configuration options are different for certain types of accounts, you might not see all of the useful options summarized in the following lists.

Note
You have to be logged out of an account before you can make some changes on the Account Information or Server Settings subtabs. To log out, deselect the account's Enable this account check box. You have to be logged in to make changes on the Privacy subtab. To log in, select the Enable this account check box.

The following are some of the more useful settings on the Account Information subtab:

- **Enable this account.** Deselect this check box to temporarily disable an account. You won't be able to open the account's buddy list or use it to chat until you select this check box again.

- **Allow multiple logins for this account.** Select this check box if you have multiple logins in Messages for the same account, such as when using the same account on multiple computers simultaneously.

- **Description.** This is the name of the account shown on the accounts list and, more importantly, at the top of buddy lists. For some accounts, it defaults to the e-mail address, which can be long. Consider creating a shorter, more easily identifiable description.

- **Add new buddies I chat with to "Recent Buddies."** When you select this check box, anyone with whom you chat is added to your recent list, making it easier to chat with him again.

Note To delete an account, select it, and then click the Remove (–) button. (In most cases, you can just disable an account by deselecting the Enable this account check box instead.)

With an AIM account, the following options on the Privacy subtab enable you to configure some security-related aspects of your chats:

- **Block others from seeing my status as idle.** If you select this check box, your status never appears as Idle (which usually indicates you are logged in, but nothing is happening on your computer). If you're concerned that people might interpret this status inappropriately, you might want to hide it.

- **Allow AOL's servers to relay video chats.** AIM is huge in the chat world. With this option enabled, AOL servers can relay video chats in Messages. With it disabled, your video chats won't be relayed.

- **Privacy levels.** The radio buttons determine the people who can see your status when your account is available for chatting. For example, if you select Allow people in my Buddy List, only those whom you have configured as chat buddies can see your status. You also choose to allow or block specific people from accessing your status. The tighter your privacy settings are, the lower the number of people who can chat with you.

You only need to use the Server Settings subtab if you are having trouble chatting with the standard configuration. This isn't likely unless you are using your MacBook Pro behind a firewall of some kind. In that case, you need to get some help from the system administrator to chat (some organizations frown on chatting and block attempts to do so).

Genius

You can use Bonjour to chat on a local network. Select Bonjour on the Accounts list. Because it doesn't cross outside of your local network, you see only the Account Information subtab. Select the Enable Bonjour instant messaging check box and use the other options to configure the way it works. This is particularly useful if you want to enable chatting within your network, but not over the Internet (such as if you have young children).

Setting General preferences

The aptly named General tab of the Messages Preferences dialog, shown in Figure 8.5, enables you to configure some general behaviors.

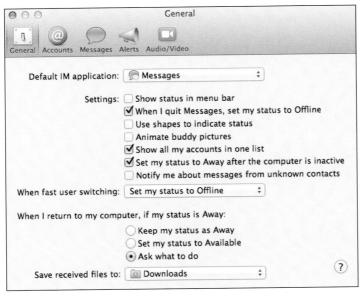

8.5 Use the General settings to change overall behaviors of Messages.

The following are some of the more useful settings:

- **Show status in menu bar.** This places a Messages menu on your menu bar. From there, you can easily change your chat status, see which of your buddies is available, and move to your buddy lists.

● **When I quit Messages, set my status to Offline.** If you enable this, Messages sets your account status to Offline when you quit Messages.

● **Set my status to Away after the computer is inactive.** This is useful because it auto-matically lets people know you aren't actively using your computer and that they shouldn't expect a response from you.

● **When fast user switching.** Use this pop-up menu to automatically set your status when someone else logs in to your MacBook Pro.

● **When I return to my computer, if my status is Away.** Use these radio buttons to set a Messages status when you return to your user account.

● **Save received files to.** Use this pop-up menu to select the folder into which files are stored when you receive them through Messages.

Setting Messages preferences

The Messages pane enables you to set various formatting options for your messages, as shown in Figure 8.6.

8.6 Use the Messages preferences to format how your text chats appear and to set options, such as saving transcripts.

The following are some useful controls:

- **Pop-up menus.** Use these menus to set the colors for your text balloons and the text that appears within them. If you choose a color on the background menus, you can also choose a text color; with Automatic selected, Messages applies colors automatically.

- **Set Font buttons.** Use these buttons to select the font for your chats (sending and receiving). These are enabled only when you have selected something on the color menus.

- **Use a keyboard shortcut to bring Messages to the front.** Select this check box and choose the keyboard shortcut on the pop-up menu to bring Messages quickly to the front.

- **Watch for my name in incoming messsages.** When you select this check box, if your name appears in an incoming message, you are alerted to it.

Setting Alerts preferences

Use the Alerts pane to set the alerts and notifications that Messages uses to get your attention. Select the event for which you want to configure an alert on the Event pop-up menu, and then select the specific alert on the check boxes and pop-up menus to configure it. You can choose a sound, bouncing the Messages icon on the Dock, running an AppleScript, or an announcement. You can be alerted about many different events, including when you log in and out. You want to strike a balance between being notified appropriately and being annoyed, so I recommend that you set alerts for only a couple of key events, especially if you use Messages frequently.

Setting Audio/Video preferences

You can use these preferences to prepare for audio and video chats. The following are the important settings:

- **Image preview.** At the top of the pane, you see the current image that is being received from the MacBook Pro camera. If you can see yourself well, then people with whom you chat will also be able to.

- **Audio meter.** Just under the image preview is an audio meter that provides a graphic representation of the volume level being received. You can use the built-in microphone or another audio input device, such as a Bluetooth headset.

- **Camera and microphone menus.** You use these to determine which camera and microphone you use for chatting. In most cases, you'll use the built-in MacBook Pro camera and microphone. However, if you have external or Bluetooth devices, you can use those instead.

Using Messages to text chat

For many people, instant or text messaging is the preferred method of communication. Text chats are easy to do, fast, and convenient. Using Messages, start your own text chats or answer someone's request to text chat with you. You can also chat with more than one person simultaneously.

Follow these steps to text chat with others:

1. **Click the new message button located just to the right of the Search bar at the top of the Messages window.**

2. **Type the e-mail address or phone number of the person with whom you want to chat in the To field or click the Add Contact (+) button.** Use the resulting sheet to select a person from your contacts, and then choose the address or phone number to which you want to send a message. If the address you are typing is recognized, options are presented to you, and you can click one to select it. In some cases, you can choose the type of account you want to use, such as iMessage or AIM. You should choose the type of account that supports the features you want to use. For example, if you might want to have an audio chat, choose the AIM account.

Note When you type valid information, the contact's name is highlighted in blue. If you choose or enter a type of address that isn't available for the contact, the contact's name is highlighted in red.

3. **Repeat step 2 to send the message to more than one person.**

Genius You can use the pop-up menu (identified with a smiley) at the end of the text bar to add emoticons to what you type.

4. **Type the message you want to send in the message field at the bottom of the window, and then press Return.** The message is sent and you see it on the right side of the window along with a status, if available. When the person replies, you see it along the left side of the window, as shown in Figure 8.7. You also see the image associated with the person, if applicable.

5. **Type your reply to continue the conversation.**

6. **To send a file (such as a photo) to the person, drop it onto the conversation.** If you don't drop it into an existing message, a new one is created and the file is added to it, as shown in Figure 8.8. When you send the message, the person can use the file you sent.

8.7 This chat is underway.

7. **If a file is sent to you, double-click it to open a Quick Look, or click the downward-facing arrow to download the file to your MacBook Pro.** When you open a file via Quick Look, you can open it in an application (such as to save it on your MacBook Pro) using the Open with button that appears in the Quick Look window.

8.8 You can send photos during a chat by simply dragging an image file from the Desktop onto the message.

Your messages with the same person or people are all collected in one conversation. To move back to an existing conversation, select it on the list of conversations in the left pane of the Messages window, as shown in Figure 8.9. You see the messages, photos, and other elements of the conversation.

8.9 You can move among your conversations by selecting the one with which you want to work.

When someone starts a new conversation with you, it appears on the conversation list. If a new message is sent for an existing conversation, it is added to that conversation. In both cases, you experience the new message alerts you configured. Conversations with new messages are also marked with a blue dot.

Note iCloud messages support status information at the message level. When someone is composing a message to you, you see the bubble with an ellipsis in it. You can also get read receipts for iCloud messages.

You can delete a conversation by hovering over it and clicking the Delete button (x) that appears. If you click Delete at the prompt, the conversation is removed from Messages. If you have an AIM or similar account configured, a status menu appears in the lower-left corner of the Messages window. Open this menu to change your status to something else (such as Offline) if you don't want to chat with other people through that type of account.

Note iCloud messaging doesn't include the concept of account status, so you won't see any status information for it.

Using Messages to audio or video chat

Messages also supports audio and video chats. However, to use these options, you and the people with whom you want to chat must be using a type of account and application that supports audio or video chatting (such as an AIM account). iCloud accounts don't support video or audio chats, except via FaceTime, of course.

Genius If you are communicating with someone whose account is configured for FaceTime chats, you can switch to a FaceTime conversation by clicking the video camera icon at the top of the conversation window. Then, choose the person's FaceTime e-mail address or phone number. The FaceTime application becomes active and you can conduct the conversation as described earlier in this chapter.

Follow these steps to conduct an audio chat:

1. **If you already have a conversation with the person with whom you want to chat on the conversation list, select it.** If not, start a new conversation using an account that supports audio or video chatting.

2. **Click the Video camera icon.** The available options are presented on a pop-menu, as shown in Figure 8.10.

3. **Click Audio.** A chat request is sent to the person to whom you sent the request. If the person accepts your request, the chat starts and you see the audio chat window shown in Figure 8.11.

8.10 Messages presents the chat options available to you when you click the Video camera icon.

As you chat, use the following controls to manage your chat session:

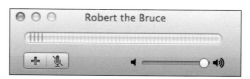

8.11 An audio chat is a great way to communicate with someone, no matter where they are located. And you don't have to worry about phone charges.

- **Audio meter.** Use the Audio meter to gauge your own volume. As you speak, the green part of the bar should move to at least the halfway point. If not, you can use the Input level control on the Sound pane of the System Preferences application.

- **Add.** Click the Add (+) button located in the lower-left corner of the window to add more people to the audio chat. Just like text chats, you can add multiple people to an audio chat.

- **Mute.** Click the Mute button (the microphone with a slash through it) to mute your end of the conversation. Click it again to unmute your sound so that people can hear you again.

- **Volume slider.** Drag this to the right to increase the volume or to the left to decrease it.

When someone wants to audio chat with you, you see a window with that person's name as its title and the Audio icon. Click the window and then click one of the following buttons:

- **Text Reply.** Click this button to decline the audio invitation and start a text chat.

- **Decline.** Click this button to decline the audio invitation. The person who sent it to you sees a status message stating that you declined.

- **Accept.** Click this button to accept the invitation and start the chat.

Note

If you are listening to iTunes when you start a FaceTime audio or video chat, it automatically pauses. It starts playing again when the chat ends.

Conducting a video chat is very similar to an audio chat. First, move into an existing conversation or create a new one using an account that supports video chats, and then click the video camera icon. On the resulting menu, choose Video. A video chat request is sent. When the person accepts your chat invitation, you see her image in the larger part of the chat window. The smaller, inset preview window shows you what the other person is seeing in her chat window. Start talking and watching. The same as with audio chats, you have controls available to you in the video chat window, as shown in Figure 8.12.

8.12 You can video chat with multiple people at the same time, which is something you can't do with FaceTime.

The following are some helpful video chat control tidbits:

- **Add.** Click the Add (+) button to add more people to the video chat. You can include up to three other people.

- **Mute.** To mute your end of the conversation, click the Mute button; click it again to unmute it.

- **Fill Screen.** To make the chat window fill the Desktop, click the Fill Screen button (the diagonal arrows). To see the toolbar while in Full Screen mode, move the pointer.

- **Effects.** When you click the Effects button, you see the Video Effects palette. You can browse the available effects and click one to apply it to your image. The preview updates, and the other participants see you as the effect changes.

● **Present documents.** Drag a document from your Desktop into the chat window. A prompt appears; choose the Share with Theater option. The larger part of the chat window is taken up by the document so all participants can see it. You can then present the document by using the on-screen controls.

Note If the audio or video is sporadic, or you can't hear or see the other participants, in most cases the cause is that one or more of the participants doesn't have sufficient bandwidth to engage in video chats.

Applying Backgrounds During a Video Chat

You can apply backgrounds to video chats that make it appear as if you are someplace else. A background can be a static image or a video. Messages includes some backgrounds by default or you can also use your own images.

Follow these steps to add a default background:

1. **Start a video chat.**
2. **Click the Effects button.**
3. **Scroll to the right in the Video Effects palette until you see the background images and video provided by default.**
4. **Click the image or video that you want to apply as a background.**
5. **Move out of the camera view at the prompt.**
6. **When the prompt disappears, move back into the picture.** It looks as if you are actually in front of the background. The effect isn't perfect, but it is pretty amazing.

Follow these steps if you would rather add your own images or video as backgrounds:

1. **Choose Video ⇨ Show Video Effects.** The Video Effects palette appears.
2. **Scroll in the palette until you see the User Backdrop categories.**
3. **Drag an image file or video clip into one of the User Backdrop wells.**
4. **Click the image or video that you want to apply as a background.**
5. **Start a video chat and apply the background you added.**

Sharing Desktops during a chat

You can share your Desktop with those with whom you chat. When you do this, the other person can also control your computer. He sees your Desktop on his screen and can manipulate your computer using his keyboard and mouse (or trackpad). Using a similar process, you can share someone else's Desktop to control that person's computer from afar. Just like audio and video chatting, you must use an account that supports screen sharing and the other participant must also be using a Mac.

Follow these steps to share someone else's Desktop and take control of her computer:

1. **Select an existing conversation or start a new one.**

2. **Click the video camera icon.**

3. **Choose Ask to Share** *name***'s screen (where** *name* **is the other person involved in the conversation).** A sharing request is sent to that participant. If accepted, you see the other person's Desktop on your display, as shown in Figure 8.13. In the small preview window (which is labeled My Computer), you see your own Desktop. You can now work with the other person's computer just as if you were sitting in front of it. For example, you can make changes to documents or use commands on menus. An audio chat is started automatically so you can communicate with the other person.

4. **To move back to your Desktop, click the My Computer window.** The two windows flip-flop so that your Desktop is now the larger window and you can control your MacBook Pro.

5. **Click back in the other computer's window to control it again.**

6. **When you finish sharing, click the Close button on the My Computer window.**

Note

Like video chats, screen sharing is very dependent on a high bandwidth Internet connection for the participants. If you try to use an insufficient connection, there may be a large time lag between when one person performs an action and its effect on the computer being shared.

To share your Desktop with someone else, perform steps 1 and 2, but instead of step 3, choose Share My Screen with *name* (where *name* is the name of the person with whom you are chatting). If the person accepts your request, you see a message that screen sharing has started. The other user can now control your computer as if he were sitting in front of it. He can also talk to you because when you share the Desktop, you also have an audio chat session going. Expect to see your MacBook Pro do things without any help from you. You can stop screen sharing by choosing Buddies ⇨ End Screen Sharing.

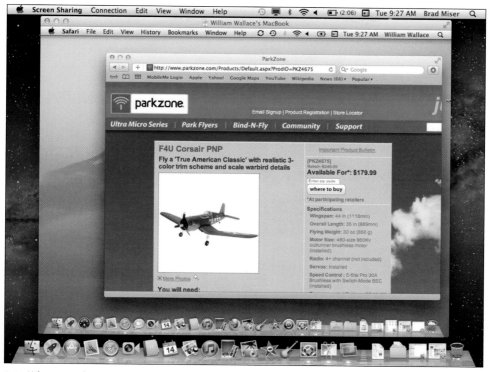

8.13 When you share someone else's Desktop, you can control her computer.

Caution

When you share your screen, you are sharing control of your MacBook Pro. Someone who shares your screen can do anything remotely that you can do directly.

Sharing Your Content

You may be surprised to discover that, in addition to sharing via FaceTime and Messages, there are many other applications that enable you to share content. You can use the Share menu in many different places to share files or other types of content. The Share menu is accessed through the Share button, an example of which is shown in a Finder window in Figure 8.14. The Share button is located in different places in the various applications, but its basic purpose is the same: to present you with options you can use to share the content with which you are working.

The options you see on this menu depend on the application and type of content with which you are working. The following are some of the options that may be available to you:

- **Email**
- **Message**
- **AirDrop**
- **Flickr**
- **Twitter**

When you choose an option, the appropriate application opens and you can use it to share the content with which you are working. For example, if you choose Message, the Messages application becomes active, and you can use it to send the content to someone else.

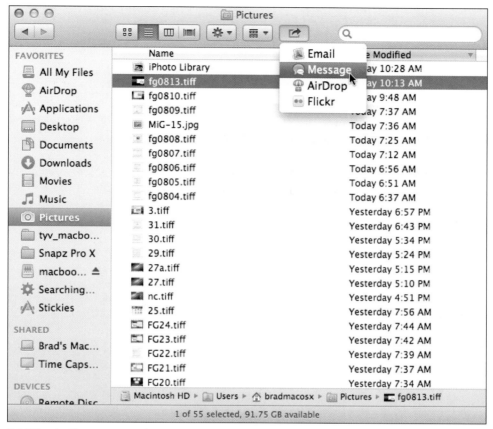

8.14 Use the Share menu to share content (in this case, image files selected in the Finder window) with others.

How Can I Manage My Calendars?

With Calendar, you can manage your time by creating calendars that help you be where you're supposed to be, when you're supposed to be there. Calendar is very useful as a personal calendar tool and, even if that's all it did, it would be worth using. However, Calendar is also designed for calendar collaboration. You can publish calendars so that others can view or share them on their Macs. Likewise, you can subscribe to other people's calendars so that you can see all upcoming events of interest to you in one place.

Managing Calendars

Calendar is a complete calendar tool that enables you to take control of your busy life and coordinate with other people. In this section, I cover how to get started with Calendar, from setting important preferences, to configuring your calendars, events, and reminders.

Configuring Calendar preferences

Before you jump into managing your calendars, take a few moments to configure some of Calendar's preferences (open the Calendar menu and choose Preferences) so that it works the way that you want. Calendar's Preferences window has four tabs: General, Accounts, Advanced, and Alerts. You can set the following preferences on the General tab, shown in Figure 9.1:

- **Days per week.** On this pop-up menu, choose 7 if you want your calendars to include all seven days of the week. Choose 5 if you want only five days (the workweek, for example) to be shown.

- **Start week on.** On this pop-up menu, choose the day that you want to be considered the first of your week.

- **Scroll in week view by.** This pop-up menu enables you to choose to scroll by weeks or days when you view Calendar in the Weeks view.

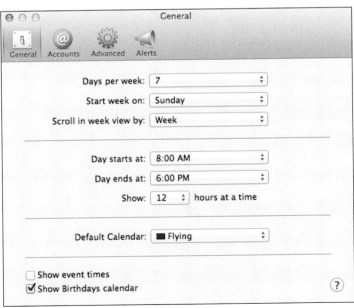

9.1 The Calendar General preferences enable you to configure how weeks and days are displayed.

- **Day starts at, Day ends at, Show.** Use these pop-up menus to show when your work-day starts and ends, as well as how many hours you want displayed on the calendar when you view it in Day or Week view. The start and end times for your days don't really matter—Calendar just shades hours outside of this period.

- **Default Calendar.** When you manage more than one calendar, this is where you choose which one you want to be the default when you create new events or reminders (you can always change the calendar with which any event is associated).

- **Show event times.** When this option is selected, the times associated with events are shown. While useful, this can really clutter the view if you have several events on the same days.

- **Show Birthdays calendar.** Select this if you want Calendar to display the birthdays of the contacts you're managing in Contacts. This can be a helpful way to remember the birthdays of important people because reminder events for them are automatically added to Calendar.

The Accounts pane enables you to add accounts (such as iCloud or Google) that support calendars so that you can view those events, along with those that you create in Calendar. Calendars from the following sources are also supported in Calendars:

- **CalDAV.** CalDAV is a set of standards for calendars to enable applications on different devices to share calendar information. Calendar supports these standards, so if you have access to accounts that include CalDAV calendar information, you can access that information in Calendar.

- **Exchange.** This is, perhaps, the most useful supported source because it is so widely used by businesses and other organizations. If you have a Microsoft Exchange 2007 account at work or another organization, you can add your Exchange calendars to Calendar. Calendar also supports various Exchange functions, such as the ability to view the availability of others when setting up meetings. If your organization is running an older version of Exchange that is not supported in Calendar, or if it doesn't allow external access to Exchange except through specialized network access, you won't be able to access your Exchange calendars in Calendar. To see if your organization supports Exchange 2007 and client access from outside its firewall, contact your IT department.

- **iCloud.** Of course, Calendar supports iCloud calendars.

- **Google.** You can set up and access Google calendars in Calendar.

- **Yahoo!** The same goes for Yahoo! calendars.

247

The steps to add calendar information from these sources are similar. The following is a quick example of how to add Google calendar information to Calendar:

1. **Click the Accounts tab of the Calendar Preferences window.**

2. **Click the Add (+) button at the bottom of the account list on the left side of the window.** The Add an Account sheet appears, as shown in Figure 9.2.

9.2 You can add calendars from other sources, such as Google, to Calendar.

3. **Choose Google on the Account Type menu.**

4. **Type your Gmail address and password.**

5. **Click Create.** You are logged in to the account you configured. If successful, you return to the Preferences window where you see the new account on the Accounts list.

6. **Configure the options for the account.** Options include using the Refresh Calendars pop-up menu to determine how often the calendar information from the account is updated.

Genius

For some types of accounts, you can allow others to access it by using the Delegation tab. To do so, the other person's account must be the same type as yours. Click the tab, click Edit, and then click the Add button (+). Type the account name for the person to whom you are providing access, select the Allow Write check box if that person can change your calendars, and then click Done.

The Advanced tab of the Calendar Preferences window is shown in Figure 9.3.

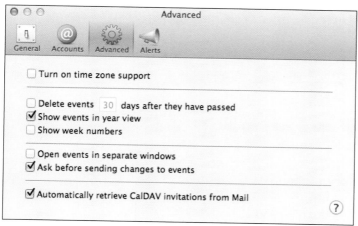

9.3 An important setting on the Advanced tab is the time zone support.

The following options are available on the Advanced tab:

- **Time zone support.** When you enable this, a time zone is associated with all of your calendars and each event you configure on them. Calendar automatically takes the time zone set for your MacBook Pro, but maintains the time zone associated with each event. This makes keeping events at the right time easier regardless of the time zone in which you happen to be. For example, if you travel to a different time zone, you can simply choose it in the Calendar window and all event times are adjusted according to the difference between Calendar's time zone and that of the event. You should enable this feature even if you don't travel outside of your current time zone because it can still help you coordinate with events outside your time zone.

- **Delete events.** Use this check box and number field to determine if and when events are deleted from your calendar. I don't recommend that you allow events to be deleted because you lose the historical information in Calendar, which can be a valuable resource.

- **Show events in year view.** Select this check box if you want to see indications of your events when you are viewing your calendar in the Year view.

- **Show week numbers.** When you enable this, you see numbers at the beginning of each week that indicate the number of the week relative to the 52 weeks in a year.

- **Open events in separate windows.** When this is selected and you open an event, it appears in a separate window instead of as a sheet attached to the event on the calendar. I find this setting makes events much easier to work with, so you might want to give it a try.

- **Ask before sending changes to events.** When you set up an event, you can invite others to it. This setting prompts you when you make a change to an event that has invitees. This prompt can help you prevent sending unnecessary or unintended messages to people you have invited, such as when you change the alert setting on the event about which others don't need to be notified.

- **Automatically retrieve CalDAV invitations from Mail.** If this is enabled, when you receive an e-mail message containing an invitation, Calendar automatically grabs it. You then use Calendar to manage it (such as to accept or reject it).

Alerts notify you when events are coming up. You can determine the alert for a specific event when you create it. You can configure the following list of default alerts on the Alerts tab:

- **Account.** Use this menu to choose the account for which you want to configure default alerts. When you create a new event on a calendar for this account, the default alert settings are used.

- **Events.** Choose the default alert time for events you create. Options range from at the time of the event to a number of minutes, hours, or days before the event.

- **All Day Events.** Choose the default alert time for all-day events you create. Options span from On day of event to 1 week before.

- **Birthdays.** Use this menu to select when you want to be alerted about upcoming birthdays.

- **Use these default alerts only on this computer.** When this is selected, your default alerts are only used when you create events on your MacBook Pro. If you use a different computer or a website to create events, default alerts from those sources apply instead.

- **Notification Center.** Select the Turn off shared calendar messages in Notification Center check box if you don't want alerts and messages originating from calendars you are sharing to appear in the center. Select the Turn off invitation messages in Notification Center check box if you don't want these alerts to appear in the center.

Creating calendars

There are two levels of calendars that you deal with when you use Calendar. The first level is the overall calendar, which is what you see inside the Calendar window. This calendar includes all of the information being managed or shown by the application. The second level is comprised of the individual calendars on which you create events and reminders, as well as those you share or to which you subscribe. There are many good reasons to create multiple calendars for your events and reminders.

The classic example is one calendar for work events and another for personal ones. When creating calendars, you should also consider publishing them. If there are some events you don't want shown in a published version, you can create one calendar for those events and another for those that you want to share. On the other hand, you don't want to create so many calendars that they become unwieldy.

Follow these steps to create a calendar:

1. **Choose File ⇨ New Calendar ⇨ *location* (where *location* is the account where you want the calendar to be created).** For example, if you choose an iCloud account, the new calendar is created on your iCloud website. You can then access it there or on any device that delivers iCloud calendar information. The Calendar list opens, a new calendar appears on the list, and its name is highlighted so that you know it is ready to edit. Your calendars are shown on the list in groups by where they are stored, such as iCloud, Google, Subscriptions, and so on.

Note

Not all account types support multiple calendars. When performing step 1, you see only those that do.

2. **Type the name of the calendar, as shown in Figure 9.4, and then press Return to save it.** You can name a calendar anything that you want.

3. **Perform a secondary click (such as by Control+clicking on it) on the new calendar.**

4. **Choose Get Info.** The calendar's Info sheet appears.

5. **Choose the color you want to associate with the calendar on the Color pop-up menu.**

6. **Type a description of the calendar in the Description field.**

9.4 Calendars you create are shown in the section of the Calendars list under the account on which they are created.

Caution

If you're not satisfied with the default colors, choose Other on the Color pop-up menu, and use the Color Picker to create or select others.

7. **If you want alerts on the calendar to be ignored, select the Ignore alerts check box.**

8. **If you want events on the calendar to determine your availability for others trying to schedule you, select the Events affect availability check box.** If this is not selected, when people check your calendar, any events are not reflected.

9. **Click OK.** The sheet closes and the new calendar is ready to use.

Genius

To see the account associated with a calendar, click Account Info. You then move to the Accounts pane of the Calendar Preferences dialog.

Managing calendars

To see the calendars you are managing in Calendar, click Calendars. The list of calendars appears in a pane on the left side of the Calendar window. To hide the list, click Calendars again. The list organizes the calendars by the location or account with which they are associated. If you have subscribed to calendars, they appear in the Subscriptions section. To include a calendar's events and reminders in the one being displayed in the Calendar window, select its check box. If you deselect a calendar's check box, its events and reminders are hidden, but the calendar's information remains in the application.

To remove a calendar, select it and choose Edit ➪ Delete. If you confirm the action at the prompt, the calendar, along with all of its events and reminders, is removed from Calendar. Most of the time, you're better off hiding a calendar because it won't appear in Calendar anymore, but you can access its information at any time. When you delete a calendar, all of its information goes with it.

Calendars have various icons to show their status. For example, when a calendar has been published, it is marked with the waves icon. If Calendar is currently unable to access the server on which a calendar is located, it is marked with the ~ icon. When a calendar's information is being refreshed, it is marked with the rotating circle icon. When a calendar needs your attention, such as to respond to an invitation, it is marked with an icon showing how many items there are to which you need to respond.

Adding events to calendars

You can use Calendar events to plan your time. For example, you can invite others to join a meeting by sending them an invitation. In addition to the time and date, you can include all sorts of useful information in Calendar events, such as file attachments, URLs, and notes. The following steps walk you through how to add an event to a calendar:

1. **Click the Add button (+) in the Calendar toolbar.** The Create Quick Event tool appears.

Genius

You can also create an event by dragging over the calendar to indicate the time you want to set for the event. You can then configure the rest of its details as described in this section. You can also choose File ➪ New Event.

2. **Type information about the event, such as its title, date, and time, as shown in Figure 9.5.** Calendar attempts to interpret what you type into a new event.

9.5 Use the Create Quick Event tool to enter basic information about an event.

3. **Press Return.** The event is created and its info window appears attached to the event (unless you enabled the separate window preference), as shown in Figure 9.6. You're now ready to add more details to the event.

4. **Edit the name, if necessary, and type the event's location in the Location text box.**

5. **Use the all-day check box, and the from, to, time zone, and repeat tools to set the time and date of the event, and whether it repeats or is a one-time occurrence.**

6. **Use the show as pop-up menu to set your availability during the event.** This lets other people who have access to your calendar information know whether you are available at this time.

7. **Use the calendar pop-up menu to associate the event with a calendar.**

8. **Use the alert tools to configure one or more alerts for the event.** There are a number of actions you can choose for an alert, such as a message with sound, e-mail, and sound only. The action you choose can present other tools to configure, such as to select an e-mail address for an e-mail alert. You can have as many alerts for an event as you want.

9.6 Events can contain a lot of useful information.

9. **To add other people to the event, click Add Invitees and type the names or e-mail addresses of those you want to invite.** If Calendar finds a match for what you type, click it to enter the associated e-mail address. Continue adding invitees by typing more e-mail addresses in the Invitees box.

10. **To associate a file with the event, click Add File.** Use the resulting Open dialog to browse and select the file you want to attach.

Genius

To determine whether the people you want to invite to an event are available to attend, click Available Meeting Times. The Availability window appears and the event time is represented by a colored bar. You see your availability, along with that of each person you invited. Use the Next Available Time button to look for the next time invitees are available. You can also move the event on the timeline to change it. When you are finished, click Done.

11. **If a URL is associated with the event, type or paste it in the URL field.**

12. **Type text about the event in the notes field.**

13. **If you added people to the attendees list, click Send; if not, click Done.** After you click Send, an e-mail is created in your default e-mail application. The event is attached to the e-mail and it is sent. After you click Done, any changes that you made to the event are saved.

Genius

To add people from the Contacts application to an event, choose Window ➪ Contacts. You can then drag people from the Contacts window onto the Invitees list.

The following tips can help you manage the events that you create:

- **You can change the calendar on which an event occurs by opening its contextual menu, choosing Calendar, and then selecting the event's new calendar.**

- **You can change the date on which an event occurs by dragging it from one date to another in the calendar.**

- **As you configure events, icons appear at the top of it on the calendar to indicate when an alert has been set, whether the event has attachments, whether it is a repeating event, whether people have been invited, and so on.**

- **When you change an aspect of a repeating event (such as an alert) you're prompted to make the change to all events or only the current one.** If you choose only the current one, the current event is detached from the series and is no longer connected to the other instances of the same event. This is indicated by (detached event) being appended to the frequency shown in the repeat section for the event.

- **You can e-mail an event to others by opening its contextual menu and selecting Mail Event.** This is the same action that happens when you click Send for an event. The difference is that you can address the e-mail that is created to anyone. When you use Send, the e-mail is sent only to those people listed as attendees for the event. Your default e-mail application opens and the event is included as an attachment. The recipient can then drag the attachment, which has the extension .ics, onto Calendar to add it to her calendar.

- **If you use the Send command, you can use the event to track people's response to your invitation.** The event's block on the calendar contains the icon of a person with a question mark, which indicates that people have been invited, but have not yet responded to the event. As people accept and add the event to their calendars, you see a green check mark next to their names when you open the event's Information window. If an attendee hasn't added the event to his calendar, his name is marked with a question mark icon. This tracking doesn't occur when you use the Mail Event command.

- **Open the menu attached to meeting invitees to take an action, such as removing someone from a meeting, inviting him again, and so on.**

Working with event invitations and availability

As covered earlier, you can invite people to your events, including meetings. Calendar can help you determine whether someone is available for a meeting you are planning. Create an event and add invitees as explained earlier. Choose Window ➪ Availability Panel. When the panel opens, you see the people whom you have invited. You see whether each person is available. If not, you can click the Next Available Time button to see the next time that everyone is free.

When you receive an invitation (assuming you selected the Automatically retrieve CalDAV invitations check box on the General preferences tab), you see the Notifications button next to the Add button in the upper-left corner of the Calendar window. Click it to see the invitations you have received and information about the events. Click Maybe or Accept to add the event to your calendar, or Decline to reject it. The person inviting you is notified about your reply and sees your status in the event on his calendar.

Managing events

As you build calendars in Calendar, there are many ways you can view and manage events. The following list covers what you can do with the Calendar window to control how information is displayed:

- **If you want to focus on specific events and reminders, deselect the check boxes for the calendars that don't interest you.** Their information is then hidden.

- **There are four views for your calendars: Day, Week, Month, and Year.** You can change the view by clicking the related button.

- **The line across the calendar with a pushpin at one end shows the current time.** This appears in both the Day and Week view.

- **You can jump to the current day by clicking Today.** To move ahead or back, click the Back or Forward arrows on each end of the Today button. This moves you ahead or back by one in the manner in which you are viewing the calendar (such as by day, week, or month).

- **If Time Zone Support is enabled, you can change the current time zone by choosing one on the pop-up menu to the left of the Search tool.** Open the menu, choose Other, and the Change time zone sheet appears. Click the map near a city in the time zone you want, choose the specific time zone on the Closest city pop-up menu, and then click OK. The times and dates are adjusted according to the new time zone. From that point on, the time zone you selected appears on the menu so you can choose it to switch to that time zone.

- **Use the Search tool to search for events, notes, titles, locations, or combinations of information.** To start a search, type the search text in the Search field and, as you do, items that match your search are found. You can click an item to make it the search term. When you type search text, Calendar's Search Results pane, shown in Figure 9.7, automatically opens along the right side of the window. This pane lists all events that meet your search criterion. To see an event on the calendar, select it on the Search Results pane. The calendar view then shifts to show the event (whether it is in the past or the future).

9.7 When you search, you see the results in the pane on the right side of the Calendar window.

You can scroll the list to see all of the found events. When you are done with a search, click the Clear (x) button in the Search tool. The search is cleared and the Search Results pane closes.

Genius

To change the calendar view to by Day, Week, Month, or Year, press ⌘+1, ⌘+2, ⌘+3, or ⌘+4, respectively. To move to the next day, week, month, or year, press ⌘+right arrow. You can move back by pressing ⌘+left arrow. Press ⌘+T to jump to today or Shift+⌘+T to move to a specific date. You can refresh all of your calendars by pressing ⌘+R.

Printing Calendars

While having your calendar in an electronic format is very useful and practical (because you can take your MacBook Pro with you), there may be times when you'd like to have a hard copy. You can use the Calendar Print command to create paper versions of your calendar information. Follow these steps to print a calendar:

1. **Choose File ⇨ Print.** The Print dialog appears, as shown in Figure 9.8.

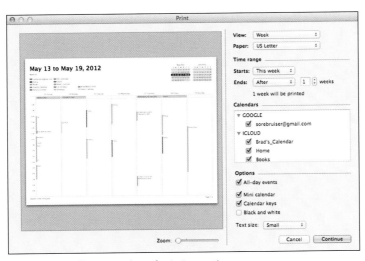

9.8 Calendar offers a number of printing options.

2. **Choose the view you want to print on the View pop-up menu.**

3. **Use the tools in the Time range section to define the time period of the printed version.**

4. **In the Calendars section, select the check box for each calendar with information you want to be included in the printed version.**

5. **Use the Options check boxes to set print options.** For example, if you are printing to a black-and-white printer, select the Black and white check box.

6. **On the Text size pop-up menu, choose the relative size of the text on the calendar.**

7. **Click Continue.** The Print dialog for the current printer appears.

8. **Use the controls in the Print dialog to configure the printer.**

9. **Click Print.**

Sharing Calendars

Calendar is designed to be a collaborative calendar tool, so you can publish or share your calendars. The difference between publishing and sharing a calendar is that when you publish it, a calendar is read-only. When you share a calendar, the people with whom you share it can make changes to it according to the permissions you set.

Note The information in this section assumes that everyone with whom you are sharing calendars uses Calendar, iCloud, and a Mac. If not, you can send a link to your calendar so it can be viewed via a website by anyone, as explained later.

Publishing calendars via iCloud

With your iCloud account and Calendar, it's simple to publish calendars for other people to view (but not change). Follow these steps to publish a calendar:

1. **Select the calendar you want to publish.**

2. **Perform a secondary click, and then choose Share Calendar on the contextual menu.** The Share sheet appears, as shown in Figure 9.9.

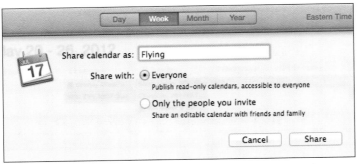

| Day | **Week** | Month | Year | | Eastern Time |

Share calendar as: Flying

Share with: ⦿ Everyone
               Publish read-only calendars, accessible to everyone

        ⦾ Only the people you invite
               Share an editable calendar with friends and family

[Cancel] [Share]

9.9 Select the Everyone option to publish a calendar with read-only access.

3. **Type the name of the calendar as you want it to appear to someone with whom you share it.**

4. **Select the Everyone radio button.**

5. **Click Share.** The calendar is shared and the sharing icon appears next to its name on the calendar list.

Follow these steps to invite people to view your shared calendar:

1. **Open the shared calendar's contextual menu.**

2. **Choose Resend Invitations.** A new e-mail message that contains a link to your calendar is created.

Note

If you open a published shared calendar's contextual menu, you see several interesting commands. These include: Stop Sharing, which removes the calendar from the web; Copy URL to Clipboard, which copies the calendar's URL to the Clipboard so you can paste it into documents; and Refresh, which publishes any changes you have made to the calendar.

3. **Complete and send the invitation e-mail.** You can send the message to everyone you want to have access to the calendar. They can then subscribe to it in their version of Calendar (explained later in this chapter) or any other compatible application.

Sharing calendars via iCloud

When you share a calendar, it becomes collaborative, meaning that people with whom you share it can also change it if you give them permission to do so. Follow these steps to share a calendar with someone:

1. **Select the calendar you want to share.**

2. **Perform a secondary click and choose Share Calendar on the contextual menu.** The Share sheet appears.

3. **Type the name of the calendar as you want it to appear to the person with whom you are sharing it.**

4. **Select the Only the people you invite radio button.** The permissions pane appears on the Share sheet.

5. **Click the Add button (+).**

6. **Type the person's name (if the person is in the Contacts application and has an e-mail address) or e-mail address.**

7. **On the Privilege menu, choose Read & Write, as shown in Figure 9.10, to allow the person to change calendar information, or Read only to prevent the person from making changes.**

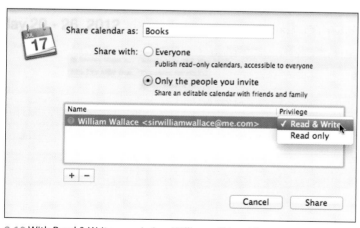

9.10 With Read & Write permission, William will be able to view and change the calendar called *Books*.

8. **Repeat steps 5 to 7 to share the calendar with more people.**

9. **Click Share.** The calendar is shared and the people with whom you shared it receive notifications. If the person accepts the shared calendar by clicking Join Calendar in the e-mail notification, or by opening the Invitation and selecting Accept Calendar in the Calendar application, the calendar you shared appears in Calendar on her computer.

Working with Published and Shared Calendars

When people publish or share their calendars with you through Calendar, you can work with them. When a calendar is published as read only, you can subscribe to it. When a calendar is shared with you, you can work with that calendar according to the privilege you are granted. You can also subscribe to public calendars.

Subscribing to published calendars

Perform the following steps to add published calendars to Calendar:

1. **Open an e-mail containing an invitation.**

2. **Click the subscribe link.** You move back into Calendar and see the Subscribe sheet in which the URL to the calendar appears, as shown in Figure 9.11.

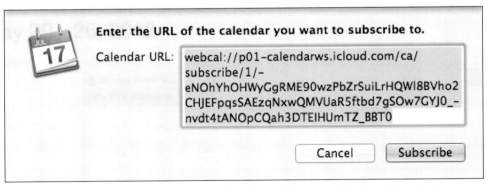

> Enter the URL of the calendar you want to subscribe to.
>
> Calendar URL: `webcal://p01-calendarws.icloud.com/ca/subscribe/1/-eNOhYhOHWyGgRME90wzPbZrSuiLrHQWl8BVho2CHJEFpqsSAEzqNxwQMVUaR5ftbd7gSOw7GYJ0_-nvdt4tANOpCQah3DTEIHUmTZ_BBT0`
>
> Cancel Subscribe

9.11 When you click the link in a subscribe to calendar e-mail, you see this subscription sheet.

3. **Click Subscribe.** The Subscribing configuration sheet appears, as shown in Figure 9.12.

4. **Here, you can change the name of the calendar, assign a color to it, choose a location for it, and specify if you do not want its associated alerts or attachments.**

5. **If you want the calendar's information to refresh automatically, select the frequency at which you want this to occur on the Auto-refresh pop-up menu.**

6. **Click OK.** The calendar is added to the Subscriptions section of your Calendar window and you can view it just like your own calendars. However, you can't add information to a calendar to which you've subscribed.

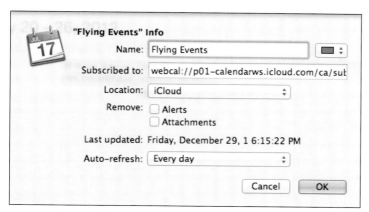

"Flying Events" Info

Name: Flying Events

Subscribed to: webcal://p01-calendarws.icloud.com/ca/sub

Location: iCloud

Remove: ☐ Alerts
☐ Attachments

Last updated: Friday, December 29, 1 6:15:22 PM

Auto-refresh: Every day

Cancel OK

9.12 Use this sheet to configure options for a calendar you are sharing.

Note

You can also subscribe to a published calendar by choosing File ➪ New Calendar Subscription. In the resulting sheet, type the URL for the calendar and click Subscribe.

Working with shared calendars

When someone shares a calendar with you, you receive an e-mail notification containing the Join Calendar button, along with a notification in Calendar. To access the shared calendar, click Join Calendar or click Accept on the Calendar notification. The calendar is added to your calendar list where you can work with it. If you have Read & Write permissions, you can add events, change events, and so on. Any changes that you make are made for everyone who is sharing the calendar.

Subscribing to public calendars

Many public calendars are available to which you can subscribe. For example, many professional sports teams have calendars that show games and other events. You can also find DVD release calendars, TV schedules, and many other types to which you can subscribe. Just like shared calendars, when you subscribe to public calendars, their events are shown in your Calendar window. Follow these steps to find and subscribe to public calendars:

1. **Go to the iCalendars Most recent page here: www.apple.com/downloads/macosx/ calendars/.**

2. **Browse the available calendars by category, such as Most recent, Most popular, or Alphabetical.**

3. **Click Download for the calendar to which you want to subscribe.** The calendar is downloaded to your MacBook Pro.

4. **Choose the calendar to which you want the events on the public calendar added, or choose New Calendar to create a new one for the events.**

5. **Click OK.** The calendar is added to the Subscriptions section of your Calendar window (if you selected the New Calendar option), and you can view it just like your own calendars. If you added the calendar's events to one of your existing calendars, you see its events when you view that calendar.

Genius

Calendar is great for tracking events associated with specific time periods, but for anything you don't want to forget, you can use the Reminders application. Reminders can be set to track just about anything. If you've used the Reminders app on an iPhone, iPad, or iPod touch, you have a good idea of how it works on your MacBook Pro because they are quite similar.

Moving Calendars to iPhones, iPods, and iPads

If you have an iPhone, iPod touch, or iPad, you can synchronize your calendars in Calendars with those on other devices. Follow these steps to get it set up:

1. **Connect the device to your MacBook Pro or put it on the same Wi-Fi network if you have enabled wireless syncing.**

2. **Move into iTunes.**

3. **Select the device on the Source list.**

4. **Click the Info tab, as shown in Figure 9.13.**

5. **Scroll down to the Sync Calendars check box and select it.**

6. **Configure iTunes to move all (or selected) calendars to your device.**

7. **If you want to prevent older events from syncing, select the Do not sync events older than check box, and then type the number of days in the field.**

8. **Click Apply.** Each time you sync your device, its calendar is updated with changes that you make in Calendar. Any changes that you make on the device's calendar are, likewise, moved into Calendar.

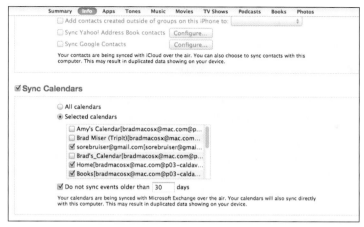

9.13 Keeping your calendars in sync with a mobile device can make them even more convenient.

Genius

If you have an iCloud, Exchange, or other account that supports calendars, you can sync your calendars on your devices wirelessly. Just configure your account on the device and ensure that the Calendars setting is On.

How Can I Make Better Use of the MacBook Pro Audio Features?

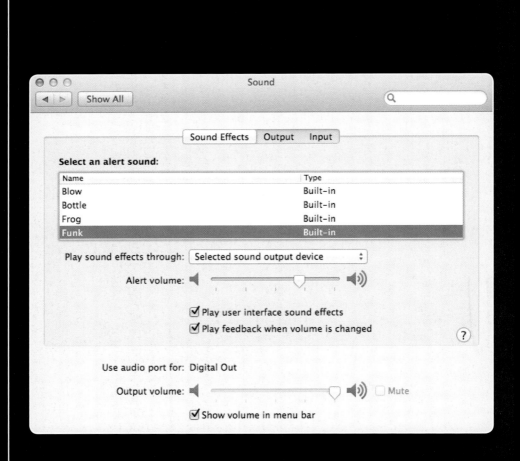

Sound is an important part of using a MacBook Pro. If you use iTunes, iDVD, GarageBand, or any other Mac digital media application, audio is a major part of the experience. Therefore, understanding how to get the most from the MacBook Pro audio capabilities is fundamental to enjoying your MacBook Pro to the fullest. On its own, a MacBook Pro has reasonable audio capabilities. If you want to invest in a bit of hardware and some additional software, you can transform your MacBook Pro into an audio powerhouse.

Getting Sound Out of a MacBook Pro

Sound is a major element of many applications that you use, including iTunes, iDVD, iPhoto, DVD Player, QuickTime, and iMovie. In this section, I cover the sound output options that are available to you. I also explain how to choose and use those options to ensure that you have a great audio experience as you work with your MacBook Pro.

Understanding sound output options

When it comes to audio, there are two fundamental options: Analog or digital. As with any other device with these options, digital is better than analog from the quality perspective. However, taking advantage of digital sound is more expensive and requires a bit more work than analog sound. With your MacBook Pro, you can use both options in different situations. On the analog side, you have the following methods for getting sound out of your MacBook Pro:

- **Built-in speakers.** The MacBook Pro includes built-in stereo speakers that actually do a decent job, considering their small size and basic capabilities. However, if the quality of the sound is important to you when you listen to music, or watch movies or television shows, it's unlikely that the internal speakers will satisfy you. They are a bit on the tinny side and their bass certainly isn't impressive compared to a home theater or car audio system.

Note Current MacBook Pros and some older models have only one audio in/out port, which is used for both input and output. This MacBook Pro automatically detects the type of device connected to this port and configures itself accordingly.

- **Headphones.** You can connect any analog headphones to the MacBook Pro audio line out port located on the left side of the computer (it's marked with the headphones icon).
- **External speakers.** You can connect any set of powered (also called computer) speakers to your MacBook Pro audio line out port.

Genius You can use the earbud headsets included with iPhones to control iTunes running on a MacBook Pro. When you listen to iTunes via these headphones, use the switch on the right side to control the tunes. For example, press the center part of the switch to play or pause. Press the upper part of the switch to increase the volume or the lower part to decrease it.

When it comes to digital music, you need to add an external speaker system (such as a 5.1 sur-round sound speaker system) to experience the best in sound quality for movies, television shows, and music. Fortunately, your MacBook Pro has the internal hardware required to support digital speaker systems so that all you need to add is the system itself.

Using external speakers

To ensure that your speakers are compatible with your MacBook Pro, you must use a powered speaker system. This is because the audio line out port on the MacBook Pro doesn't provide enough power to drive a speaker, so standard audio speakers won't work. The good news is that there are many kinds of powered speaker sets available.

Genius Many speaker systems that are designed for iPods work great with a MacBook Pro. As long as a speaker system has a jack for external input, you can connect that system to your MacBook Pro.

Connecting an analog system

Analog speakers are the simplest to install. If you have a two-speaker set, place one speaker on your right and one on your left. If you have a three-speaker system, place the bass unit on the ground or on your Desktop. Connect the input line for the speaker set (which is usually connected to one of the satellite speakers or to the bass unit) to the audio line out port on the MacBook Pro. Connect the speakers to the bass and power the system. That's all there is to it: you're now ready to control the sound (more on this later in this chapter).

Connecting a digital system

Your MacBook Pro has only one audio out port (on the 13-inch MacBook Pro and Retina models, it is also the audio in port). While this looks like a typical stereo mini jack port, its appearance is decep-tive. When you connect a typical stereo mini jack plug, it behaves like a regular stereo mini jack (like the headphones port on an iPod) and you get stereo sound output. To access the digital output from the port, you need the *Mini Toslink adapter*, shown in Figure 10.1. It connects to a digital audio cable and fits into the port in order to make the correct connections for digi-tal audio. When you buy a digital audio cable, look for one that includes this adapter or that has a Mini Toslink connector integral to it. You can also purchase the cable and adapter separately.

10.1 To connect to a digital sound system, use a digital cable with a Mini Toslink adapter, like this one from Belkin.

The input connectors on your speaker system determine the specific type of audio cable you need. There are two basic options: *Digital coax* or Toslink (which is more commonly called *optical digital*). If you use a 5.1 system, it probably includes a central control unit with the input jacks. The jacks determine the cable you need. It is likely it has more than one input, and they often also include a digital optical input, digital coax input, and analog stereo input. After you place the speakers, connect their wires together at a central point. Typically, you connect them to the bass speaker along with power. Next, connect the bass input wire to the control unit, and then use the cable you purchased to connect the control unit's input jack to the MacBook Pro audio out port.

Note

Some speaker systems connect via one of the MacBook Pro USB ports. These work like other external systems, with the exception that they don't disable the MacBook Pro internal speakers like a system connected to the audio line out port does.

Controlling sound output

When it comes to sound output, be aware that there are up to three types of volume levels:

- **System volume level.** This sets the base level of volume output for the MacBook Pro.
- **Relative volume of applications.** When you adjust volume levels within applications, such as iTunes or DVD Player, you change their volume relative to the system volume level.
- **Physical volume level of an external speaker system.** You control this with the system's volume controls. Like the system volume level, changes you make impact all the audio coming from your MacBook Pro.

Follow these steps to configure the MacBook Pro output sound:

1. **If you are using headphones or an external speaker system, connect them to the MacBook Pro audio out port.**
2. **Open the Sound pane of the System Preferences application.**
3. **Click the Output tab, as shown Figure 10.2.** On this tab, you see the available output devices on the list at the top of the pane. When you select an output device, you see controls for the selected device below the list.
4. **Select the output device over which you want your MacBook Pro to play sound.** The following are the most common options:
   - **Internal Speakers.**
   - **Headphones.** Use this option for headphones or external analog speaker systems.

- **AirPlay devices.** These include Apple TVs and speaker systems connected to an AirPort Base Station.

- **Digital Out.** Use this for an external, digital speaker system.

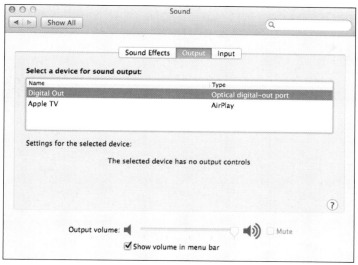

10.2 Use the Output tab of the Sound pane of the System Preferences application to configure how you hear audio.

5. **Use the controls that appear for the selected device to adjust its sound.**

6. **If the Output volume slider is enabled, drag it to its center point.** This sets the system volume at midlevel. If you are using an external speaker system, set its volume at a relatively low level.

7. **Select the Show volume in menu bar check box.**

Note

When you use the slider on the Volume menu (its icon is the speaker with waves emanating from it) or the volume function keys to adjust volume, you are changing the system volume level. Most applications have keyboard shortcuts that enable you to adjust the application's volume level. In iTunes, press ⌘+↑ or ⌘+↓.

8. **Open an application that you use to play audio, such as iTunes.** Use that application's volume slider, as shown in Figure 10.3, to set its relative volume level.

10.3 Use the volume slider on iTunes to set the application's volume relative to the system volume level.

Note If you are using a digital system and see this message: The selected device has no output controls, when Digital Out is selected, you use only the speaker system's controls to set system volume levels. You also use it to make all other adjustments, including the bass level, balance, surround sound field, and so on. You can still use an application's volume control to adjust the relative volume.

9. **Play the audio and adjust the system volume level accordingly.** Typically, you want to set the system volume at a level that allows you to control the volume with the application controls, so you can make it as loud or as quiet as you want. This sometimes requires experimentation to get the right balance between the system and application volume levels. If you use external speakers, their volume control is yet a third level to balance.

Note To mute all sound, select the Mute check box or press F10. To unmute the sound, deselect the Mute check box or press F10. You can change the system volume level by pressing F11 or F12. (If you use a digital speaker system, these controls are disabled.)

Creating and Using Sound Effects

Mac OS X includes a number of sound effects that the system uses to alert you or to provide audible feedback for specific events. You control these effects on the Sound Effects tab on the Sound pane of the System Preferences application.

Configuring sound effects

Perform the following steps to configure sound effects:

1. **Open the Sound pane of the System Preferences application.**

2. **Click the Sound Effects tab, as shown in Figure 10.4.**

10.4 Use the Sound Effects pane to configure the alert and other interface sounds.

3. **Click a sound on the alert sound list.** The sound plays and becomes the current alert sound.

4. **If your MacBook Pro can output sound through different devices simultaneously (such as internal speakers and a sound system connected to a USB port), then select the system on which you want the sounds to be played on the Play sound effects through pop-up menu.** If the MacBook Pro currently supports only one sound output device, Selected sound output device is selected on the menu automatically.

5. **Drag the Alert volume slider to the right to make it louder, or to the left to make it quieter.** This sets the volume of the alert sound relative to the system sound level. The default alert sounds have a relatively low volume level, so you'll probably have to set the slider to a high level to hear them over music or any other audio.

6. **If you don't want to hear sound effects for system actions (such as when you empty the trash), deselect the Play user interface sound effects check box.**

7. **If you don't want audio feedback when you change the volume level, deselect the Play feedback when volume is changed check box.**

Creating and using custom sound alerts

You can also create and use your own alert sounds if you want your MacBook Pro to communicate with you in a unique way. Under Mac OS X, system alert sounds are in the Audio Interchange File Format (AIFF). You can use iTunes to record or convert almost any sound into an AIFF file, and use that sound as a custom alert.

Creating a sound alert

The following are some of the ways in which you can create a custom alert sound:

- **iMovie.** You can use iMovie to create an audio track and save it as an AIFF file, or you can save part of a movie's audio track as an AIFF file. You can also record narration or other sounds to use as an alert sound. (I cover getting sound into your MacBook Pro later in this chapter.)

- **iTunes.** You can use iTunes to convert any sound in your library to an AIFF file.

- **GarageBand.** You can create a music snippet and save it as an AIFF file.

- **Record audio playing on your MacBook Pro.** Using an application like WireTap Pro from Ambrosia Software, you can record any audio playing on your MacBook Pro and use what you record as an alert sound.

Below is an example showing how to use iMovie to create and save a sound as an alert from audio stored in your iTunes library. Use this technique to add just about any sound as an alert:

1. **Move the audio you want to use as an alert sound into your iTunes library.** You can add it from the iTunes Store, download it from the Internet, or record it in another application.

2. **Launch iMovie.**

3. **Choose File ⇨ New Project.** The New Project sheet appears.

4. **Name your project.** The Theme, Aspect Ratio, and Frame Rate settings don't matter because you are only going to use the audio.

5. **Click Create.** The new project is created and appears in the project library.

6. **Click the Titles button (the button with the capital T).** The Titles Browser appears in the lower-right corner of the window.

7. **Drag a title into the project window and choose a background, if prompted to do so.** It doesn't matter which title you choose because it's not going to be seen. You perform this step because iMovie needs some video in a project to be able to work with audio content.

8. **Click the Music and Sound Effects button (the musical note icon).** The Music and Sound Effects Browser appears in the lower-right corner of the window.

9. **Select iTunes.** The content of your iTunes library appears.

10. **Search or browse for the audio you want to use as the alert sound.**

11. **Drag the audio from the Music and Sound Effects Browser and drop it in the project window.** You may need to adjust the duration of the title clip to get enough of the audio track to use as the alert sound.

12. **Open the audio clip's Action pop-up menu and choose Clip Trimmer.** The Clip Trimmer opens in the lower-left corner of the window.

13. **Edit the audio clip so that it contains only the alert sound, and then click Done, as shown in Figure 10.5.**

14. **Edit the title clip so it is the length of the alert sound.**

10.5 Use the Clip Trimmer to edit your alert sound.

15. **Choose Share ⇨ Export using QuickTime.** The Save exported file as dialog appears, as shown in Figure 10.6.

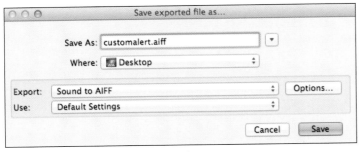

10.6 Export the alert sound as an AIFF file.

16. **On the Export pop-up menu, choose Sound to AIFF.**

17. **Name the sound file.** Append an f to the existing filename extension so it is .aiff (it is .aif by default).

18. **Choose a location in which to save the alert sound and click Save.** The file is exported from iMovie and is ready to use as an alert sound.

Adding a custom sound alert

You can add alert sounds to the system so they are available to all user accounts on your computer. To do this, you must authenticate yourself as an administrator. Follow these steps to add alert sounds to your system:

1. **Drag the AIFF file into the folder** *startupvolume***/System/Library/Sounds (where** *startupvolume* **is the name of your Mac OS X startup volume).**

2. **At the prompt, click Authenticate, provide an administrator account username and password, and then click OK.** The custom alert sound is copied into the folder.

3. **If the System Preferences application is open, quit it, and then open it again.**

4. **Click the Sound Effects tab, as shown in Figure 10.7.**

5. **Select and configure the custom alert sound just like one of the default sounds.** Alert sounds that you add to the system have the type Built-in and also behave the same as the default alert sounds, so any user can access them.

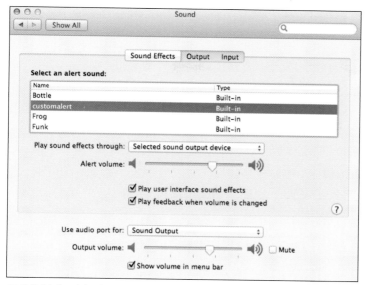

10.7 If this book had a soundtrack, you'd hear this awesome custom alert sound.

Recording and Working with Sound

There are many situations in which you may want to put sound into your MacBook Pro. For example, you might want to add narration to iMovie projects or iPhoto slide shows; you need to have audio input for FaceTime chats; if you use GarageBand, you'll want to record instruments and vocals.

On the simplest side, you can use the built-in microphone in the MacBook Pro to record voice narration or other sounds, and it is certainly good enough for most audio and video chats. On the more complex side, you can add an external MIDI (Musical Instrument Digital Interface) keyboard or other device that enables you to record sound from musical instruments and other sources.

Caution

The MacBook Pro audio in port is not powered. This means that you can't just plug a standard analog microphone into it and record sound. Whatever you connect to the port must provide amplification to be able to record sound from it. To be able to connect a microphone to it, there must be a power source for the microphone.

Recording sound with the internal microphone

Using the MacBook Pro internal microphone is easy and suitable for a number of purposes, such as audio and video chats, recording narration for iMovie and iPhoto projects, and other relatively simple projects.

Configuring the internal microphone

To record audio with the built-in microphone, you must first follow these steps to configure the internal microphone:

1. **Open the Sound pane of the System Preferences application.**

2. **Click the Input tab.** The Input tab has two default options: Internal microphone or Line In. If you are using the 13-inch model, it has only one option, the Internal microphone. Under the device list, you see the controls you use to configure the device selected on the list.

3. **Select Internal microphone.** As your MacBook Pro receives audio input through the microphone, the relative volume of the input is shown on the Input level gauge, as shown in Figure 10.8.

4. **As you speak or play the sound, monitor the input on the level gauge.** The maximum level freezes briefly so that you can see where it is.

5. **If the gauge shows input when you aren't speaking or playing a sound, select the Use ambient noise reduction check box.** This applies a filter that screens out background sound.

6. **Drag the Input volume slider to the left to reduce the level of input sound, or to the right to increase it.** The microphone should be ready to use to record sound in an application.

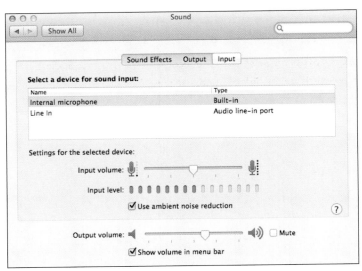

10.8 Use the Input level gauge to assess the input level of sound coming in to the MacBook Pro.

Recording sound with the internal microphone in iMovie

A common use of recorded sound is as narration in iMovie projects. Follow these steps to add your own narration to an iMovie project:

1. **Launch iMovie.**

2. **Select the project in which you want to record sound using the internal micro-phone, and then put the playhead where you want to start recording.**

3. **Click the Voiceover button (the microphone).** The Voiceover dialog appears, as shown in Figure 10.9.

4. **On the Record From pop-up menu, choose Built-in Input.**

10.9 Here, I'm recording narration for an iMovie project.

5. **Click the clip for which you want to record narration.** The timer starts a countdown. When the countdown stops, the project starts to play and iMovie starts recording.

6. **Speak in a normal conversational voice as the project plays.** As you speak, monitor the sound levels using the two input gauges under the Input Volume slider. You want the sound level to be as high as possible without going into the red. If it isn't, use the tools in the Voiceover dialog to adjust the input volume. A red bar fills the clip you are recording over, and you see a large red dot and the *Recording* message in the Preview pane.

7. **When you finish speaking, press the spacebar.** The recording stops, and an audio clip appears under the clip on which you recorded sound. The recording also stops when you reach the end of the project.

8. **Edit the recorded audio clip just like other audio clips.** For example, you can make it fade in, adjust its volume, and move it earlier or later in the project. Narration is shown in purple and is labeled with Voice Clip.

Recording sound with a USB headset

If you are going to be recording a lot of narration, or if you want better quality when you have video or audio chats, a USB headset is a good option. Like other audio input devices, you configure the USB headset to record its input, and then use it to record sound in applications.

As shown in the following steps, configuring a USB headset is similar to configuring the internal microphone:

1. **Connect the headset to a USB port.**

2. **Open the Sound pane of the System Preferences application.**

3. **Click the Input tab.** You should see the USB headset on the list of devices.

4. **Select the USB headset.** As the MacBook Pro receives audio input through the headset, the relative volume of the input is shown on the Input level gauge.

5. **As you speak or play the sound, monitor the input on the level gauge.** The maximum level freezes briefly so that you can see where it is.

6. **Drag the Input volume slider to the left to reduce the level of input sound, or to the right to increase it.** The USB headset should be ready to use to record sound in an application.

Recording sound from a USB headset is similar to recording sound with other input sources. For example, the steps to record sound in iMovie are the same as the steps described earlier for the internal microphone, except that you select the USB headset instead of Built-in Input.

Recording sound with a video camera

While it might not be obvious, a video camera can be a great way to record sound for your projects. You can then use iMovie to save that sound as a file to use in projects, add to your iTunes library, or for other purposes. The following steps walk you through the process of moving sound you've recorded on a video camera into your iTunes library:

1. **Connect the camera to your MacBook Pro.**

2. **Launch iMovie.**

3. **Choose File ⇨ Import from Camera and add the clips containing the audio to the event library.**

4. **Choose File ⇨ New Project.** The New Project sheet appears.

5. **Name your project.** Again, the options don't matter because you are only using the audio.

6. **Click Create.** The new project is created and appears on the project list.

7. **Add the clips with audio you want to save to the new project.**

8. **Edit the clips until the audio track is the way that you want it.**

9. **Choose Share ⇨ Export using QuickTime.** The Save exported file as dialog appears.

10. **On the Export pop-up menu, choose Sound to AIFF.**

11. **Choose a location and save the file.** The file is exported from iMovie.

12. **Launch iTunes.**

13. **Choose File ➪ Add to Library.** The Add To Library dialog appears.

14. **Move to and select the sound file you created in iMovie.**

15. **Click Open.** The sound is added to your iTunes library where you can listen to it, or you can select it from other applications using the Media Browser (for example, you can select it as a soundtrack for an iPhoto slide show).

Recording sound from external microphones and musical instruments

If you want to record sound from external microphones and musical instruments, you need an interface between those devices and the MacBook Pro. These devices can use either the audio or USB ports to connect to your MacBook Pro. The USB is a more common interface and, in most situations, it is the easier method with which to work.

There are a variety of USB audio devices that you can use for this purpose. Some devices include a MIDI instrument, such as a keyboard, as part of the interface device. These are convenient because you get an input source (the instrument) and the interface in one unit. To use a device like this, connect it to a USB port on your MacBook Pro. You then connect the microphones or instruments from which you want to record sound into the various ports. Once the device is configured, you can choose it as the input device in audio applications, such as GarageBand, so that you can record the output of the microphones and instruments in those applications.

Recording sound with an iPhone, iPod touch, or iPad

iPhones, iPod touches, and iPads have the Voice Memos application that you can use to record sounds. It's intended and works best for sounds spoken into the phone or into the headset mic. Follow these steps to capture sound on one of these devices:

1. **Tap Record Memos.** The application launches.

2. **Tap the Record button.**

3. **Start speaking.**

4. **When you finish recording, tap the Stop button.** The sound you recorded is captured as a clip.

To move the sound onto your MacBook Pro, connect the device to the MacBook Pro, and then select it on the iTunes Source list. Next, click the Music tab, select the Include voice memos check box, and then click Apply. The device is synced and the sound clips you recorded are moved into your iTunes library (the default name of each clip is the date and time you recorded it). You can work with these clips just like other audio in iTunes; you can add them to iMovie and other projects through the Media Browser.

Genius

You can also use the Camera app to record video, including sound. To use that sound in projects, add it to iPhoto via the sync process. Video in iPhoto is available in the iMovie Event Library. You can add this video to your projects, just like a video you import from a video camera.

Dictating to Your MacBook Pro

One of the most useful audio features of Mac OS X Mountain Lion running on a MacBook Pro is the Dictation feature. As you might suspect from its name, this feature enables you to speak to your MacBook Pro and it transcribes your spoken words into text on the screen. Even better, this capability is available to you in any application, from word processing to e-mail to messages to—well, you get the idea. Before you start talking to your MacBook Pro, follow these steps to set your dictation preferences:

1. **Open the Dictation tab of the Dictation & Speech pane of the System Preferences application, as shown in Figure 10.10.**

2. **Select On to enable dictation.**

3. **Click Enable Dictation in the resulting sheet that explains that what you say is sent to Apple to be converted into text.**

4. **On the Shortcut menu, choose the shortcut for activating dictation.** You need to activate dictation so that the software knows when you are speaking to it for dictation purposes, as opposed to just background sounds or conversation with someone.

5. **Configure the input device on the menu under the microphone icon.** You can use the information earlier in this chapter to set up the input device you want to use.

6. **Set your preferred language on the Language menu.**

Note

You can also activate dictation by choosing Edit ▷ Start Dictation.

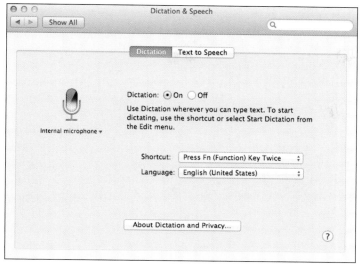

10.10 With Dictation, you can speak to your MacBook Pro instead of typing on the keyboard.

Note

You can use the Text to Speech tab to configure how Mac OS X speaks to you, such as the voice it uses, verbal announcements for alerts, and so on.

After you've enabled dictation, using it is a snap. In the document into which you want to dictate text, use your shortcut (such as pressing the Fn key twice) to activate dictation. The Dictation box appears, as shown in Figure 10.11. Speak the text you want to appear. When you are done speaking, click Done or press your shortcut again. You see the processing status as what you spoke is translated

10.11 When you see this box, you can speak to your MacBook Pro to dictate text.

into text. When the process is complete, you see the new text in the document. Edit the text as needed; you should expect to have to edit the text because, while dictation is handy, it isn't perfect. To increase the accuracy of dictation, it's best to use it in a quiet environment; a USB or other microphone that rests near your mouth also improves results.

Note

Your MacBook Pro must be connected to the Internet to dictate text because what you speak is actually transcribed by Apple.

How Do I Add and Manage Storage Space?

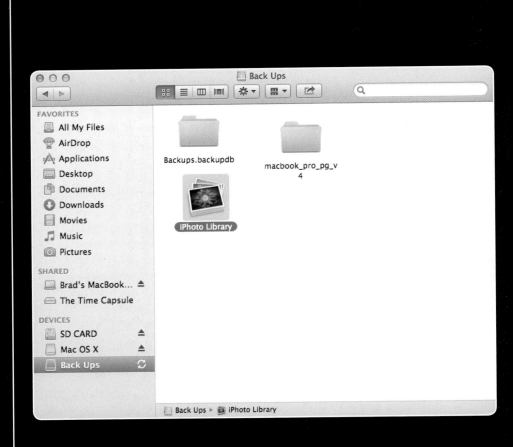

The two primary reasons to add more data storage space to your MacBook Pro are to back up your data or increase the data storage space. Time Machine, which requires an external hard drive, is the easiest way to back up data. Over time, you collect a lot of data and the MacBook Pro hard drive is only so big. Adding more storage space enables you to work with more information. You may also want to carry data with you when you don't have your MacBook Pro, and a flash drive or SD card is ideal for this purpose.

Using External Hard Drives

Adding an external hard drive to your MacBook Pro system is an easy and relatively inexpensive way of making more storage space available. It is also essential if you want to use Time Machine for backing up your MacBook Pro over the long haul. In this section, I cover how to add more space to your MacBook Pro by adding, configuring, and using an external hard drive. You should consider the following factors when choosing a hard drive to add to your MacBook Pro:

- **Which interface do you want to use to connect the drive to your MacBook Pro?** External drives that you can use with current MacBook Pro models include Thunderbolt, FireWire 800, or USB 2/3 interfaces (some support more than one of these), so you can use a wide variety of external hard drives (different models of MacBook Pros have different numbers and types of ports). Older MacBook Pros might not support Thunderbolt, but may support FireWire and USB 2. Another important interface consideration is performance. Thunderbolt drives are the fastest followed by USB 3, FireWire 800, FireWire, and USB 2. From a cost perspective, Thunderbolt drives are the most expensive. Because USB 2 is the most common technology, those drives tend to be the least expensive, all other things being equal. Drives that support more than one kind of interface are more expensive, but also provide more flexibility.

- **How many devices are you using with your MacBook Pro?** If you already use two or more USB devices, you might want to consider a Thunderbolt or FireWire 800 because it's unlikely you will use these ports for other devices. In addition, you can daisy chain Thunderbolt drives with external displays that use the Mini DisplayPort or Thunderbolt interface.

Note

Daisy chaining enables you to connect peripheral devices to each other instead of connecting them all to your MacBook Pro. For example, you can connect a Thunderbolt hard drive to your MacBook Pro, another Thunderbolt drive to the first one, and an external display that uses the Mini DisplayPort or Thunderbolt interface to the second drive. This is useful because you only use one port on your MacBook Pro to connect multiple devices.

- **What size drive do you need?** Drives come in various sizes. Generally, you should get the largest one you can afford. Hard drive prices continue to fall, and even large drives (2TB or larger) are fairly inexpensive. Smaller drives, such as a 750GB, are even less expensive. For backup purposes, I don't recommend you ever purchase a drive smaller than 1.5TB, but in all cases, a drive with more capacity is better than one with less storage space.

- **Does the drive need to meet specific performance requirements?** If you intend to use the drive for high data rate work, such as for digital video, you need to get a drive that spins at least 7200 RPM. Some drives spin even faster, which means they can transfer data at a greater rate. However, if you are primarily going to use the external drive for backing up and less for data-intense projects, speed isn't really important. Because faster drives are more expensive, you can save some money by choosing a relatively slow drive.

- **What format is the drive?** There are a variety of formats available, and all drives come formatted for one system or another. Fortunately, it doesn't really matter which format the drive comes in because you can always reformat it to work with your MacBook Pro using the Disk Utility application (which I cover later in this chapter). Drives that are formatted for Windows are generally less expensive than those that have been formatted for Macs. It's usually better to get a less expensive drive formatted for Windows, and then use Disk Utility to prepare it to work with your MacBook Pro.

- **How much can you afford to spend?** As with all things digital, you tend to get more by spending more. For most purposes, such as backing up, you should decide how much you can afford to spend, and then get the largest drive you can afford for that amount of money. If you shop around a bit, you'll be amazed at how much the cost of external hard drives varies from retailer to retailer—they are often on sale.

Installing an external hard drive

Installing an external hard drive is about as simple as it gets. Follow these steps to get yours going:

1. **Connect the power supply to the drive and an electrical outlet.**

2. **Connect the cable to the drive and the appropriate port on your MacBook Pro.**

Note

If the drive is formatted so that your MacBook Pro can access it, you might be prompted to configure Time Machine. Just click Cancel and proceed to the next section. Time Machine is covered in Chapter 13.

3. **Power up the drive.** If the drive is formatted so that it is compatible with your MacBook Pro, it mounts on your Desktop and you see it on the sidebar in the Finder windows indicated by its default name, as shown in Figure 11.1. If not, you won't see the device. In either case, you should reformat and initialize the drive before you start using it.

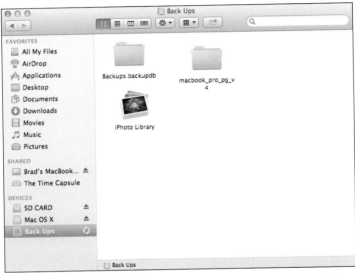

11.1 A mounted external hard drive appears in the Devices section of the sidebar, just like the internal hard drive.

Preparing an external hard drive with Disk Utility

Before you use a hard drive, you should initialize and format it. You can also partition a hard drive to create multiple volumes on a single drive so that it behaves as if it is more than one drive.

Note

I recommend that you reformat your external drive to ensure that you have the most storage space available and that it is formatted in the best way for your MacBook Pro. Some drives include software, especially if they are intended for use with Windows computers, in which case that software is a waste of space and you should get rid of it.

When you partition a hard drive, logical volumes are created for each partition on the drive. For most practical purposes, a logical volume looks and acts just like a separate hard drive. There can be some small performance advantages to partitioning a drive, or you might choose to partition it to help you keep your data organized. For example, you might want to create one partition on the hard drive for your backups and another to install Mac OS X as an alternate start-up drive.

One of the results of partitioning a drive is that all of the volumes outside of the start-up volume are also outside of the default Mac OS X organization scheme. This can be a benefit or a problem depending on what you are doing. For example, unlike documents you store within your Home folder, documents that you store on a separate volume aren't secured using the Mac OS X default permissions. If you want to provide broader access to files, this is a good thing; if you don't want people to be able to access these documents outside the control of the Mac OS X security, it isn't.

Generally, you should keep your partitions pretty large unless you create one for a very specific purpose, such as to install Mac OS X for an alternate start-up drive. If you run out of space on a partition, you have to delete files from or repartition it, which means that you must start over and reformat the drive (resulting in all files being erased). Unless you have a very specific reason to do so, you typically shouldn't partition a drive into more than two volumes. In many cases, especially if you are only using the drive for backups, one partition is the best option.

Caution

When you follow the steps to format a hard drive, all information on the drive is erased. If the hard drive came with software installed, make sure that you don't need it (you probably don't). If you do want to keep it, copy it from the external drive onto a DVD, CD, another hard drive, or the MacBook Pro internal drive before formatting the drive.

Follow these steps to initialize, format, and partition a drive:

1. **Launch the Disk Utility application, located in the Utilities folder within the Applications folder (you can get quick access to it via the Launchpad).** In the Disk Utility window, you see two panes. In the upper part of the left pane, you see the drives with which your MacBook Pro communicates, along with the MacBook Pro internal hard and optical drives. Under each drive, you see the volumes with which that drive has been partitioned. Below the drives, you see any drive images that are currently mounted on your MacBook Pro. In the right pane, you see information and tools for the drive or volume that is selected in the left pane.

2. **Select the drive you want to format.** At the top of the right pane are five tabs, each of which enables you to view data about a drive or to perform a specific action. At the bottom of the window, you see detailed information about the drive with which you are working, such as its connection bus, type, and capacity.

3. **Click the Partition tab, shown in Figure 11.2.** In the left part of this tab, you see a graphical representation of the partitions on the drive. If the drive is partitioned, you see its current partitions. If you are working with a new drive or one with a single partition, you see one partition called Untitled (if you've not yet named it). In the right part of the pane, you see information about the selected volume, such as its name, current format, and size.

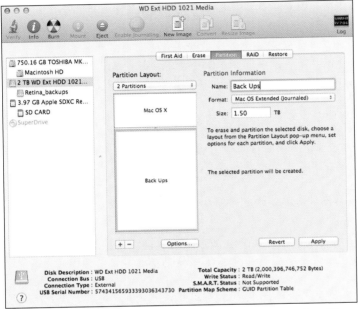

11.2 This drive will have two partitions: One called Back Ups with 1.5TB, and one called Mac OS X with 500.40GB.

4. **Select the number of partitions you want to have on the drive using the Partition Layout pop-up menu.** You can choose Current, which leaves the partitions as they are, or choose the number of partitions you want from 1 to 16. After you choose the number of partitions, each one is represented by a box in the disk graphic shown under the Partition Layout pop-up menu. The partitions are called Untitled 1, Untitled 2, and so on.

5. **Select a partition by clicking its box in the graphical representation of the drive.** The volume's partition is highlighted and information for that volume is shown in the Volume Information area.

6. **Name the selected volume by typing a name in the Name box.** As you type the name, it is shown in the partition's box. You can name the partition just about anything you want. This is how you identify the partition's volume in the sidebar and other locations, so use a meaningful name. In most cases, you want to use one that indicates the purpose of the partition.

Genius

Instead of adding a space in a partition name, use an underscore or just run the words together so the space isn't replaced by 20% in a path name.

7. **Select the format for the partition on the Format pop-up menu.** In most cases, you should choose Mac OS Extended (Case-sensitive, Journaled) to take advantage of the most sophisticated format option.

8. **Type the size of the partition in the Size box.** You can enter a size up to the maximum capacity of the drive, but it also depends on the number of other partitions on the drive and how much space is allocated to each.

Genius

You can also set the size of a partition by dragging its Resize handle in the Volumes pane.

9. **Once you've configured all of the partitions on the drive, click Options.** The Options sheet appears.

10. **If it isn't selected already, select the GUID Partition Table radio button.** The other options don't apply when you are using the drive with a MacBook Pro.

Caution

If you purchase a drive that's been formatted for Windows computers using the Master Boot Record format option, it won't mount or be usable on your MacBook Pro. You must format the drive with the GUID Partition Table format before you can use it.

11. **Click OK.** The format option is set and the sheet closes.

Caution

Before proceeding, make sure that the drive doesn't contain any data you need. Performing the next steps erases all the data from the drive.

12. **Click Apply.**

13. **If you are sure that you want to initialize and partition the drive, click Partition in the Warning sheet.** In this sheet, you see a summary of what will be done to the drive. After you click Partition, you return to the Disk Utility window and a progress bar appears in the lower-right corner of the window. You can use this to monitor the process. Once this process is completed, you should see the partitions you created under the drive's icon. The drive and its partitions are ready to use. You may be prompted to use the drive for Time Machine; choose the partition you want to use for Time Machine backups, and then click Use as Backup Disk, Decide Later, or Don't Use.

Working with external hard drives

After it's configured, you can use an external hard drive in the following ways:

- **Store files.** You can use the drive just like the internal hard drive.

- **Back up to the drive with Time Machine.** I discuss Time Machine in Chapter 13.

- **Stop using the drive.** Before you stop using a hard drive and any of its partitions, you need to eject it. This ensures that all data has been written to the drive and that all processes affecting it are stopped so that when you disconnect the drive, the data isn't damaged. To eject a drive, select one of its partitions and click Eject. If the drive has only one partition, it is unmounted and disappears from the Finder window. If the drive has more than one partition, you are prompted to eject only the selected partition by clicking Eject, or you can eject the entire drive by clicking Eject All. You should always click Eject All, at which point all of the drive's partitions are unmounted and disappear from the Finder window. You can then disconnect the drive from the MacBook Pro.

- **Use the drive again.** To start using a drive again, simply reconnect it to your MacBook Pro. After a few moments, it is mounted, you see all of its partitions in the sidebar, and it is ready to use.

Sharing an External Hard Drive

An external hard drive is a great way to share files among multiple computers. The following list includes some of the ways in which you can do this:

- **Physically connect the drive to different computers.** After a drive has been formatted, you can connect it to any Mac to access its files or write files to it.

- **Share the drive over a network.** Like other resources, you can share the partitions and files on them with other computers over a local network.

- **Share the drive from an AirPort Base Station.** If you connect a USB external hard drive to an AirPort Base Station, any computer that can access the Base Station's network can also access the drive.

Maintaining Hard Drives

Keeping your hard drives, whether internal or external, in good working condition goes a long way toward making your MacBook Pro reliable. In this section, I cover some of the more important drive maintenance habits you should practice to keep your drives in top form.

Caution You should regularly maintain your hard drives to keep them operating as long as possible. If a drive is making an odd noise, such as becoming louder, you should expect it to fail soon, if not immediately. Unusual sounds typically (but, not always) precede hard drive failure. Make sure that you get any data you need off the drive right away, or it will be a very expensive hassle to recover it. Never store important data in only one location.

Managing free space on a hard drive

You can do a lot for the performance of your drives by simply ensuring that they have a good amount of free space. The more data you have on your drive, the less room there is to store new files. If your drives get too full, their performance slows down significantly. You can also run into all kinds of problems if you try to save files to drives that are full to the brim; how full this is depends on the size of the files with which you are working.

As you use hard drives, keep an eye on their available space by choosing Apple menu ⟹ About This Mac, and then click More info. The About This Mac window appears. Click the Storage tab and scroll until you see the MacBook Pro internal hard drive, as shown in Figure 11.3. If the space available falls below 10GB, you might start running into problems when you try to save files or perform other tasks. If the space available drops below 1GB, you can count on having problems.

Learn and practice good work habits, such as deleting files you don't need, uninstalling software you don't use, keeping your files organized (no duplicates), and archiving files you are done with (such as on a DVD). Regularly removing files that you no longer need from your hard drives keeps them performing well for you, not to mention that it maximizes the room you have to store the files you do need.

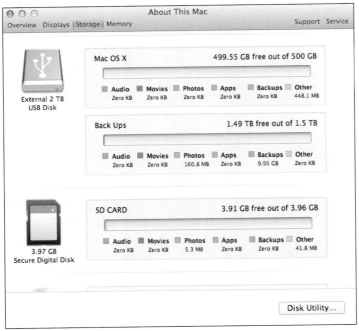

11.3 This external drive has more than 499GB available, so it is in good shape.

Genius

Application installers waste drive space. If you're sure that the application version you want will continue to be available online, delete its installation files. If you paid for an application, archive its files in case you need to reinstall it. Some companies remove older versions as newer ones are released, in which case you might have to pay an upgrade fee to download the application again. With the version you purchased safely archived, you can always get back to it.

Checking the available space on a drive with Activity Monitor

You can use Activity Monitor to get more information about how you are using a specific drive. Follow these steps to do so:

1. **Launch the Activity Monitor (Applications ⇨ Utilities ⇨ Activity Monitor).**

2. **Click the Disk Usage tab located at the bottom of the window.**

3. **On the pop-up menu, choose the drive or partition with the information you want to view.** You see a pie chart, as shown in Figure 11.4, that shows the amount of free space (in green) versus the amount of space used (in blue), along with the specific values within each category.

Genius

If you want to change the colors associated with free or used space, click the color button next to the number of bytes in each category.

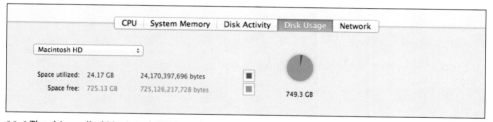

11.4 The drive called Macintosh HD has almost nothing stored on it.

Note

Each partition and drive has its own trash. If you empty the trash while an external drive that has files in its trash is disconnected, the trash can icon becomes full again when you reconnect the drive. This is because the trash associated with that drive still has files in it. Empty the trash again once you've reconnected the drive to get rid of the deleted files.

Checking or repairing an external drive with Disk Utility

Two of the tasks for which you can use Disk Utility are to check or repair an external hard drive. If you start having problems with a drive, first make sure that it has plenty of available space. If it doesn't, get rid of files until it does. If it does have plenty of free space, follow these steps to use Disk Utility to check or repair it:

1. **Launch Disk Utility.**

2. **Select the drive or partition you want to check or repair.** In most cases, you should select a drive so that the entire drive is checked or repaired, rather than just one of its partitions.

3. **Check the bottom of the Disk Utility window for information about the drive, volume, disc, or image you selected.** If you select a hard drive, you see the disk type, connection bus (such as ATA for internal drives), connection type (internal or external), capacity, write status, S.M.A.R.T. (Self-Monitoring, Analysis, and Reporting Technology) status, and partition map scheme. If you select a partition on a drive, you see various data about the volume, such as its mount point (the path to it), format, whether owners are enabled, the number of folders it contains, its capacity, the amount of space available and used, and the number of files it contains.

4. **Click the First Aid tab to see some information explaining how Disk Utility works.**

5. **Click Repair Disk.** The application checks the selected drive for problems and repairs any it finds. When the process is complete, a report of the results appears, as shown in Figure 11.5.

You can choose to verify a drive by clicking Verify Disk, rather than clicking Repair Disk. When you do so, the application finds problems with the drive and reports back to you. You then have to tell the application to repair those problems.

Note   For most drives, the S.M.A.R.T. status provides an indication of the drive's health. This is Verified if the drive is in good working condition, or About to Fail if the drive has problems. If you see About to Fail, immediately copy important data onto another drive, CD, or DVD. If a drive doesn't support S.M.A.R.T., you see the status Not Supported. Your MacBook Pro internal drive supports S.M.A.R.T., but many external drives do not.

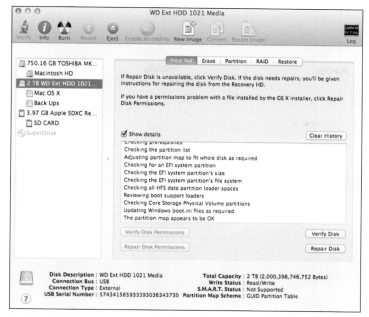

11.5 Disk Utility has checked this drive, which seems to be okay.

Checking or repairing the internal drive with Disk Utility

Because you can't use Disk Utility to repair a drive with open files, and your start-up drive always has open files, you can't use Disk Utility to repair the internal hard drive while you are started up from it. If your internal hard drive appears to have problems, you must start up from a different drive to repair them. You can use one of the following options to accomplish this:

- **Start up from an alternate drive and run Disk Utility from there.** If you have installed Mac OS X on an external drive, you can start up from that drive and run Disk Utility to repair the internal drive. (See sidebar later in this chapter to learn how to start up from an alternate start-up drive.) Once you've booted up, use the steps for checking or repairing an external drive to select and repair the internal hard drive.

- **Start up from the Recovery HD volume.** Use the information provided in Chapter 14 to start up from the Recovery HD partition and run Disk Utility from there.

Note While you can't repair the current start-up drive, you can verify it. Although this won't fix any problems, it does identify that there is a problem.

Erasing an external hard drive with Disk Utility

Perform the following steps to erase and reformat an external hard drive with Disk Utility:

1. **Launch Disk Utility.**

2. **Select a partition you want to erase.**

3. **Click the Erase tab.**

4. **Choose the format you want to use for the volume on the Volume Format pop-up menu.** The format options are: Mac OS Extended (Journaled); Mac OS Extended (Journaled, Encrypted); Mac OS Extended (Case-sensitive, Journaled); Mac OS Extended (Case-sensitive, Journaled, Encrypted); MS-DOS (FAT); or ExFAT.

Genius   You can use the Erase Free Space button to remove files that you have deleted from a drive or partition. This makes them harder (or impossible) to recover using data recovery tools.

5. **Click Security Options.** The Secure Erase Options sheet appears, as shown in Figure 11.6.

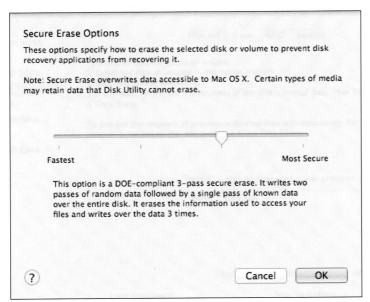

11.6 Use this sheet to select how you want data you are erasing to be handled.

6. **Select one of the following options by dragging the slider to the right to make the erase more secure but slower, or to the left to make it less secure but faster:**

- **Don't Erase Data.** This makes the data unviewable from the Finder but leaves it physically on the drive. As your MacBook Pro needs to write more files to the drive, it overwrites the erased space. Until the data is overwritten, it can be recovered (unerased) using an application designed to do so. This is the fastest, but least secure option.

- **Zero Out Data.** This option writes zeros in all sectors on the drive. This is secure because it overwrites the entire drive, making the data harder to recover. However, this is slower than the first option.

- **3-Pass Erase.** This option overwrites the drive three times. It takes even longer, but makes the data nearly impossible to recover.

- **7-Pass Erase.** This option writes data over the entire drive seven times. This takes a long time, and makes the data virtually impossible to recover (hey, if it's good enough for the U.S. Department of Defense, it should be good enough for you).

Installing Mac OS X on an External Hard Drive

You can install Mac OS X on an external hard drive and start up from it, which is very useful for troubleshooting. Perform the following steps to do so:

1. **Configure a partition or external hard drive on which you want to install Mac OS X.**

2. **Open the App Store application, click the Purchased tab, and download the latest version of Mac OS X.** After the application downloads, the Mac OS X installer will launch.

3. **Click Continue, and then agree to the license.**

4. **Click Show All Disks.**

5. **Select the partition or external hard drive you configured in step 1.**

6. **Click Install, and then authenticate yourself.**

7. **Click Restart.** The installation process begins. Your MacBook Pro restarts and you see the installation progress. When installation is complete, you're prompted to restart your MacBook Pro or wait and let it restart automatically. The MacBook Pro starts up from the external drive.

8. **Work through the screens of the Mac OS X Setup Assistant to complete the installation.** This is the same process as when you first started your computer.

Note

The purpose of the three overwrite options is to prevent data on the drive from being restored after you erase it. If you are transferring a drive to someone else, you should use one of these options so the data on the drive can't be recovered. If you are maintaining control of the drive, you probably don't need to do this. However, using the Zero Out Data option doesn't take a lot of time, so it's not a bad idea.

7. **Click OK.** The option you selected is set and the sheet closes.

8. **Click Erase.** The confirmation sheet appears.

9. **If you are sure you want to erase the drive, click Erase in the sheet.** The data on the drive or partition is erased and formatted with the option you selected.

Working with SD Cards and Flash Drives

Your MacBook Pro has an SDXC (Secure Digital Extended Capacity) card slot so it can read and write to an SD card. These cards are commonly used in digital cameras, so you can just pop the card into your MacBook Pro and import the photos it contains to your iPhoto library. However, you can also use these very compact storage devices in the same way that you would a drive, to transport or even back up files.

Follow these steps to use an SD card on your MacBook Pro:

1. **If the memory card includes an SD adapter (most do), install the card into the adapter.**

2. **Insert the card/adapter into the SD slot on the left side of your MacBook Pro.**

3. **Use Disk Utility to reformat/partition the drive, as shown in Figure 11.7.** In most cases, you'll only have one partition because these cards are usually pretty small relative to an external drive (4GB or 8GB).

When the process is complete, the card is mounted on your Desktop, as shown in Figure 11.8, and you can use it like any other storage device.

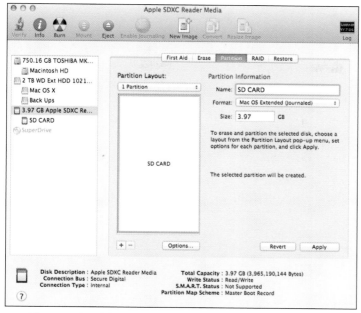

11.7 Like a new hard drive, you can use Disk Utility to reformat an SD card.

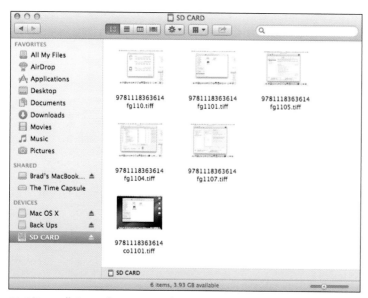

11.8 Its small size makes carrying data on an SD card very convenient.

USB flash drives are another popular way to move files around. Because they have flash memory, they are very small and easy to carry. The capacity of these drives continues to increase rapidly; at this writing, you can get them in up to 256GB. However, large-capacity flash drives are quite expensive when compared to external hard drives. A smaller flash drive, such as a 32GB, is very inexpensive and can be quite useful. A flash drive can be a good way to transfer files among computers or to back up data when you are on the move.

To use a flash drive on your MacBook Pro, simply plug it into one of the USB ports. The drive is then mounted on your MacBook Pro for you to use. However, for best results, you should prepare the drive for use by reformatting it with Disk Utility using the same process used with a hard drive or SD card.

Genius

If you also want to use a flash drive on Windows computers, select the MS-DOS (FAT) format. This makes it easy to move files between Macs and Windows PCs.

How Can I Run
Windows Applications?

Some of us live in two worlds: The Mac world and the Windows computer world. Windows computers dominate certain areas, particularly midsize and large organizations, and there are a number of applications that run only on Windows. With your MacBook Pro, you can run the Mac OS and Windows on the same computer, which means you really can have the best of both worlds. In this chapter, I cover the options available to run both operating systems on your MacBook Pro, including Boot Camp and using a virtual machine.

has its advantages and disadvantages, and you can use both of these methods when you need to.

Boot Camp is the Apple technology that transforms Mac hardware into a fully capable Windows PC. You can choose to boot up your MacBook Pro in the Mac OS or in Windows. When you boot up in Windows, you have a fully functional Windows PC on your hands. The strengths of Boot Camp include great performance, maximum compatibility for hardware and software, and a lower cost because your only expense is a copy of Windows. A minor downside is that it can be a bit more complicated to share data between the two operating systems because they can't be running at the same time. Also, you have to restart your computer to switch between the operating systems.

Under virtualization, an application provides a virtual environment (also called a virtual machine) in which you install and run Windows. You install the virtualization application and then install a version of Windows in a virtual machine. When you want to run Windows, you launch the virtualization application. Within its windows you run Windows and Windows applications. Using a virtual approach has a number of benefits. One is that you can run Windows and the Mac OS at the same time because the virtualization software is just another application running on your MacBook Pro. Other benefits include the good performance (it isn't noticeably slower than running it under Boot Camp) and easy data sharing because the Mac OS and Windows are running at the same time.

Obtaining Windows

To run Windows on a Mac, you have to purchase a full copy of Windows 7 to install, whether you use Boot Camp or a virtualization application (or both). You can't use an upgrade (unless of course, you've previously installed a version of Windows on your Mac). The cost for this varies, depending on the version of Windows you purchase and how you purchase it. When you purchase Windows, try to get a version that is designed for builders, also called the Original Equipment Manufacturers (OEM) version. This version is significantly less expensive than the full retail version and is ideal for installing Windows on a MacBook Pro.

There are several types of Windows 7, such as Home, Professional, and Ultimate, and the differences are somewhat difficult to understand. For most MacBook Pro users running Windows as a second operating system, the Home version is likely to be sufficient. However, you should compare the versions to make sure one doesn't offer something you need to have. Visit http://windows.microsoft.com/en-US/windows7/products/compare for Microsoft's explanations of the differences between versions.

Virtualization does have two points against it: The cost of the virtualization software and the fact that it may not be compatible with all of the hardware and software you want to run. While I've explained Boot Camp and virtualization as two distinct options, if you chose the virtualization application, I recommend VMware Fusion. This way, you can use both options and switch between them easily.

Running Windows with Boot Camp

To get Windows running under Boot Camp, use the Boot Camp Assistant, which creates a partition on your hard drive for your Windows installation. Once the Assistant finishes its work, you install Windows in the partition it creates. During the process, the Assistant creates a DVD that you use to install the required drivers for your MacBook Pro hardware. Once the installation is complete, you can run Windows at any time.

Configuring Boot Camp and installing Windows

Running the Boot Camp Assistant is mostly a matter of following the on-screen steps to work through the Assistant, and then using the Windows installer.

Note If the MacBook Pro hard drive is already partitioned into two or more volumes, the Boot Camp Assistant won't be able to create a partition for Windows, or even download the software you need. This process only works if the MacBook Pro hard drive has one partition (which is almost always the case).

The following steps demonstrate how to install Windows 7 Professional; if you use a different type, the details might be slightly different, but the overall process is the same:

1. **Launch the Boot Camp Assistant application located in the Utilities folder in the Applications folder.** You see the first screen of the Assistant.

2. **Click Continue.** You see the Select Tasks screen.

3. **Select Download the latest Windows support software from Apple and the Install Windows 7 check boxes and click Continue.** The Assistant downloads the Windows drivers and other software to your Mac so Windows can work with the Mac hardware. Next, the Assistant creates the Windows partition and installs Windows in it.

4. **If your MacBook Pro has an internal DVD drive or you have an external one, select Burn a copy to CD or DVD.** Insert a blank disc into your MacBook Pro, and then click

Continue; if you don't have a drive available, click Save a copy to an external drive. The rest of these steps focus on using a DVD. The Assistant downloads the software and looks for the drive.

5. **When the software has been downloaded and the disc is found, click Burn.** The software is written to the disc. When the process is complete, the disc is ejected. You're prompted to authenticate yourself.

Note

If you have an external hard drive connected to your MacBook Pro or if you have a flash drive, you can save the software to one of those instead, as long as the drive is formatted as MS-DOS (FAT). The save process is faster and you won't have to use a blank DVD. As explained in Chapter 9, you can use Disk Utility to format an external or flash drive in the MS-DOS (FAT) format.

6. **Type your administrator password and click Add Helper.** You see the Create a Partition for Windows screen. On the left, you see the partition for Mac OS X, while on the right you see the partition for Windows, which is a minimum of 20GB.

7. **Perform one of the following actions to set the size of the Windows partition:**

   ● **Drag the Resize handle (the dot) between the two partitions to the left to increase the size of the Windows partition, as shown in Figure 12.1.** You can set the partition to be any size you want, but you have to trade off drive space for Windows versus what is available for the Mac OS. I recommend that you allocate at least 50GB to Windows. If you plan to install a lot of Windows applications and create large documents, you may need a larger partition.

   ● **Click Divide Equally to divide the drive into two equally sized partitions.** I don't recommend this option, as it significantly reduces the amount of space available to you under Mac OS X.

Caution

After you've partitioned your drive, you won't be able to make the Windows partition larger without repartitioning the drive and reinstalling Windows, which is a time-consuming process. Make sure that you give the Windows environment plenty of space.

8. **Insert your Windows installation disc.**

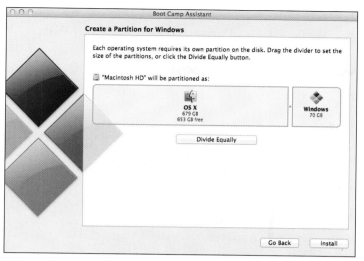

12.1 Use the Create a Partition for Windows screen to set the size of your Windows environment.

9. **Click Install.** The Assistant creates the Windows partition on the MacBook Pro hard drive.

10. **At the prompt, enter your username and password, and then click Restart.**

The MacBook Pro restarts and boots from the Windows installation disc. The installation application starts installing files and you see the progress at the bottom of the Windows Setup screen. You see the Windows Starting message as the Windows Installer opens. Follow these steps to work through the install process:

1. **At the prompt, choose the language, time and currency format, and keyboard method, and then click Next.**

2. **Click Install Now.** The Setup process begins.

3. **Accept the license and click Next.**

4. **Select the new installation option.**

Caution

Make sure that you select the correct partition on which to install Windows. If you don't, you might overwrite a partition with Mac OS X or your data on it, in which case that data is lost.

5. **Select the Bootcamp partition.** If you see an error message stating that Windows can't be installed on the selected partition, you need to format that partition by performing steps 6 and 7. If you don't see this error message, move to Step 8.

Note If you have to reformat the partition, it may not be called Bootcamp after you do so. Note what it is called so that you can select the correct partition.

6. **Click Show Details, and then click Format.** You see a warning about files that may be installed on the partition.

7. **Click OK.**

8. **Click Next.** The installation process begins on the partition you selected. You see progress information in the Install Windows window and in the status bars at the bottom of the window. The install process can take quite a while and your MacBook Pro may restart multiple times. Eventually, you see the Set Up Windows screen.

9. **Work through the various screens of the Setup Windows application to configure Windows.** For example, you need to create a username and password, type the Windows product key, choose how Windows handles updates, and set the time and date. The computer may need to restart during the process as well. When the process is complete, you see the Windows Desktop.

10. **Eject the Windows installation disc.**

11. **Insert the Support Software disc you created earlier.**

12. **Click Run setup.exe, and then click Yes to allow it to install software in Windows.** The Boot Camp Installer application opens.

13. **Follow the on-screen instructions to complete the installation of various drivers and other software that Windows needs to work with the MacBook Pro hardware.**

14. **When the Boot Camp Installer is complete, click Finish.**

15. **Click Yes at the prompt to restart your MacBook Pro.** It starts up in Windows.

Note You may be prompted to configure various Windows options (such as choosing a network location) while the Boot Camp Installer runs. You can minimize those until the Boot Camp Installer process is complete, or let the Boot Camp Installer run in the background and configure Windows while it runs.

16. **Type your password to log in to your Windows account, and then press Return.** Windows is ready to use, but you should apply all available updates before doing so.

17. **Open the Windows menu and choose Control Panel ⇨ System Security ⇨ Windows Update.**

18. **Click Check for updates.**

19. **Follow the on-screen instructions to install all available updates.**

20. **To return to the Mac OS, choose Windows menu ⇨ Shut down, as shown in Figure 12.2.**

21. **Restart the MacBook Pro and hold the Option key down while it starts up.**

22. **Select the Mac OS X startup volume and press Return.** The Mac starts up under Mac OS X again.

12.2 To shut down Windows, use the Shut down command on the Windows menu.

Note

When Mac OS X restarts, you may return to the Boot Camp Assistant because Mac OS X restores open windows by default. Because you've already completed the Assistant, just quit it.

Running Windows using Boot Camp

After you install Windows, you can perform the following steps to transform your MacBook Pro into a Windows PC:

1. **Open the Startup Disk pane of the System Preferences application, as shown in Figure 12.3.**

2. **Select the Bootcamp Windows startup disk.**

3. **Click Restart.**

4. **At the prompt, click Restart again.** The Mac restarts and the Windows Login screen appears.

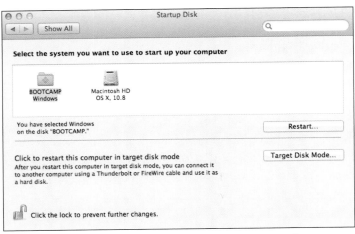

12.3 Use the Startup Disk pane of the System Preferences application to choose a default operating system.

 Genius Right-clicking is a fundamental part of using Windows. To right-click with your MacBook Pro when running Windows, hold two fingers on the trackpad and click the trackpad button.

5. **Log in and use Windows.**

6. **When you're ready to switch back to the Mac OS, shut Windows down.**

7. **Restart the MacBook Pro and hold the Option key down while it starts up.**

8. **Select the Mac OS X startup volume, and then press Return.** The Mac starts up under Mac OS X again.

 Caution Windows is constantly under attack from viruses, Trojan horses, and other attempts to steal or damage data. Running Windows on a MacBook Pro doesn't protect you from these threats when you use the Windows environment. It's susceptible to the same attacks it would be if you were running Windows on a PC. You should use security software under Windows as soon as you get your Windows environment running, especially if you're accessing the Internet from it.

Windows Activation

You must activate a copy of Windows to keep it running for more than 30 days. When you do this, the copy of Windows you run is registered to the specific computer on which you activate it as a means to limit illegal copies of Windows. Don't activate your copy of Windows until you've used it long enough to ensure that it is configured the way that you want and you can run it under Boot Camp, in a virtual environment, or both. Once activated, if you make a significant change, there's a chance you'll have to reactivate it. This usually isn't a big deal, but if it is, you might have to try to explain the situation to Microsoft to get the previous activation undone so you can activate it under a different environment. Running a non-activated version of Windows doesn't limit you in any way, although you do get annoying reminders that it needs to be activated along the way. Once you hit the 30-day mark, you have to activate it to continue using Windows.

Running Windows Virtually with VMware Fusion

As covered earlier in this chapter, running Windows under a virtual environment has the significant advantage of allowing you to run Windows and the Mac OS simultaneously. This makes it fast and easy to switch between the two environments. The following general steps will help you get started running Windows under a virtual environment:

1. **Purchase and install the virtualization software.**
2. **Configure a virtual environment and install Windows.**
3. **Run Windows in the virtual environment.**

There are several virtualization applications available, but the one that works best for me is VMware Fusion. This application is simple to install and configure, and performs very well. It has a lot of great features, including the ability to easily share data and files between the Mac OS and Windows. You can download and try it before you purchase the application. At this writing, it cost about $50 to continue using the application beyond the 30-day trial period. It also has the benefit of being able to use Windows installed under Boot Camp, in which case you don't need to install Windows again, and you retain the option of running Windows under Boot Camp any time that you want. The remainder of this chapter focuses on using VMware Fusion using a Boot Camp installation of Windows. If you choose a different application or install a version of Windows directly under VMware Fusion, your details may vary.

Installing VMware Fusion

Perform the following steps to download and install VMware Fusion:

1. **Navigate to www.vmware.com/ products/fusion/overview.html.** Click Try for Free.

2. **Create a VMware account by following the on-screen instructions.** You have to follow an activation process to be able to download the application.

3. **Download VMware Fusion.**

4. **When the download process is complete, move back to the Desktop and drag the VMware Fusion application into your Applications folder to install it, as shown in Figure 12.4.** You're ready to launch VMware Fusion and configure a virtual environment.

12.4 Drag the VMware Fusion application into your Applications folder to install it.

Note

One of the great things about VMware Fusion is that the Windows environment gets its network settings from the Mac. If the Mac on which you install Fusion is connected to a network and the Internet, so is the Windows environment—no further configuration is necessary. Also, any protection the Mac has from hacking through the network (such as NAT protection from an AirPort Extreme Base Station) is also applied to the Windows environment.

Running Windows under VMware Fusion

VMware Fusion automatically detects and uses a Boot Camp installation of Windows, so there's no additional configuration, unless you have selected to run Windows from some other environment.

Follow these steps to run Windows:

1. **Launch VMware Fusion.** The application launches and you see the Boot Camp environment has been selected. If you have more than one virtual machine, you see the Virtual Machine Library window, shown in Figure 12.5.

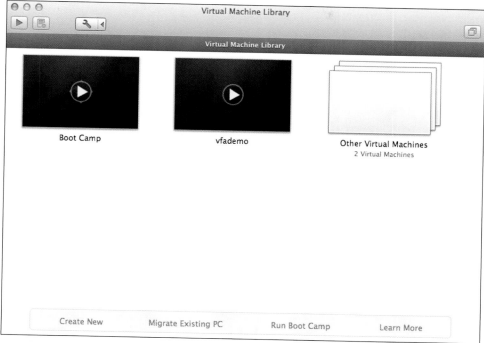

12.5 Starting Windows is as easy as clicking the Play button.

2. **Click the Play button.** The first time you start Windows, some additional preparation has to be done, but for subsequent times, the process is much faster.

Note The first time that you run Windows under VMware Fusion, you should install the VMware Fusion tools. The VMware Tools Installer launches automatically and begins the installation process. When the process is complete, click Restart to restart the Windows environment.

3. **If prompted, type your Mac OS X username and password, and then click OK.**

   Windows starts up in the VMware Fusion window, as shown in Figure 12.6.

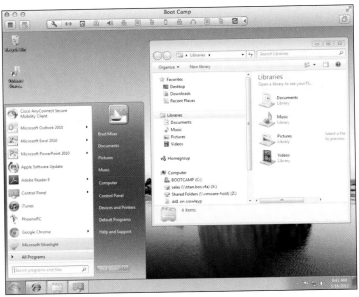

12.6 Here Windows is running inside the VMware Fusion window.

There isn't much difference between running Windows in a virtual machine and running it on a Windows PC. The following are some points of interest to consider:

- **You can move from the Windows OS to the Mac OS by pressing Control+⌘, clicking in an application's window, choosing it on the Dock, or any of the other standard ways of switching between applications.**

- **You can copy files from Windows to the Mac or vice versa by dragging them from one environment to the other.** You can also copy information from one environment to the other with standard copy-and-paste commands.

- **Only one environment can be using a CD, DVD, flash drive, iPhone, and so on at the same time.** When you insert a disc or connect a device, you are prompted to choose the OS that should use it. If you've inserted a CD or DVD, or connected another device but don't see it on the Mac Desktop, the odds are that Windows is running, and the disc or device is mounted there, making it unavailable to the Mac. Stop the Windows environment and the disc or device appears on the Mac Desktop.

- **You can use the Unity mode so that the Fusion window disappears.** All that you will see on the Mac Desktop is the VMware Fusion menu on the menu bar and any Windows applications you are running. To try this, choose View ⇨ Unity when the VMware Fusion application is active. You then access Windows applications by opening the VMware Fusion menu on the menu bar, and navigating to and selecting the application you want to run. It appears in a new window on your Mac Desktop.

- **You can view the Windows OS in Full Screen mode to have it fill the screen and hide the Mac OS.** In this mode, a toolbar appears at the top of the screen. To change the view, open its View menu. Even in Full Screen, you can move into the Mac OS as needed. The Full Screen Windows environment moves into the background.

- **For the ideal situation, if you have two displays, you can also run VMware Fusion in Full Screen mode.** This is especially useful because you can run the Mac OS on one display and have the Windows environment fill the other. To try this, run Windows in the Single Window view, and then drag the window onto a display. Click Full Screen. The Windows environment fills that display and each OS has its own display.

When you finish running Windows, shut it down by choosing Windows menu ⇨ Shut down. After Windows shuts down, you can quit the VMware Fusion application.

My MacBook Pro?

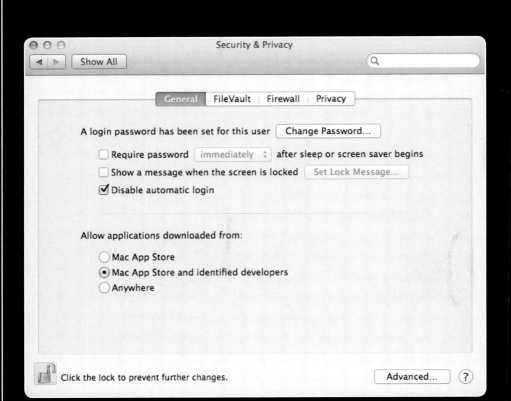

Your MacBook Pro is valuable and protecting it is important, but this chapter is about protecting the *data* on your MacBook Pro, which is even more valuable. If you lose a document on which you've been working, all of the time and effort you've invested is lost. While you can redo work on documents, you can't replace photos. Think about how bad it would be if you lost your photo library. Then there's personal data, such as financial information, that needs safeguarding. For all of these reasons, you should take precautions to secure your MacBook Pro and its data.

Keeping Software Current

There are two good reasons to keep the software that you use current. One is that software developers frequently develop revisions to improve the features of their applications and remove bugs. The other (and the reason this topic is included in this chapter) is that many applications, and most definitely Mac OS X itself, play a large role in how secure your MacBook Pro and its data are. The bad guys—people who develop viruses and attempt to hijack your computer or steal your data—are always working on new ways to penetrate your computer. Most software developers try to limit your exposure to attacks in their software as much as possible. To keep up with all new attempts to compromise your computer, take advantage of the security improvements that are part of software updates.

There are two basic categories of software that you need to keep current: The kind that is updated via the App Store and third-party software. The first category is updated via the App Store application, which includes Mac OS X, along with any applications you have downloaded from the App Store. The second category is the third-party software you have installed in some other way, such as from an installer you downloaded from the Internet, or from a DVD or CD.

Keeping App Store software current

The App Store application makes it easy to find, download, and install applications from Apple and third-party developers. There are thousands of applications available. The App Store application also tracks all of the applications you download and notifies you when updates are available. You can also use the application to update any software that you've downloaded from the App Store.

Because it is the largest factor in how secure your MacBook Pro and its data are, Mac OS X is the most important software to keep current. The good news is that you can also use the App Store application to keep Mac OS X and other system software current. You can either use the App Store app to manually check for updates, or you can configure Software Update to check for them automatically.

Updating App Store software manually

As demonstrated by the following steps, you can check for, download, and install updates easily:

1. **Launch the App Store application.** When it opens, it checks the status of all of the applications you've downloaded. If updates are available, you see the number available on the App Store icon on the Dock and the Updates tab.

You can also check for updates by choosing Apple menu ⌂ Software Update. The App Store application opens, and then checks for updates for your applications and Mac OS X.

2. **If updates are available, click the Updates tab.** You see a list of available updates, as shown in Figure 13.1. Next to the application's icon, you see the version of the update, when it was released, and a summary of the changes.

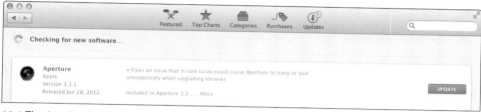

13.1 The App Store application has found updates to an application.

Note The number of available updates is also shown on the App Store icon on the Dock.

3. **To install an application's update, click Update.** To install all updates, click Update All.

4. **If prompted, type the Apple ID and password under which the application was obtained, and then click Sign In.** The updates you selected begin to download to your MacBook Pro. You can see the progress next to the updates, as shown in Figure 13.2. When the process is complete, the update is removed from the Updates tab and the number of updates available is reduced by the number you installed.

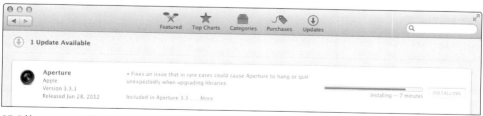

13.2 You can monitor the status of an update on the Updates tab.

If a restart is required, your MacBook restarts and continues the installation process. When the Desktop reappears, you are using the updated software.

Updating App Store software automatically

Checking for software updates is easy enough, but why not have your MacBook Pro handle it for you automatically? Follow these steps to get it set up:

1. **Open the Software Update pane of the System Preferences application.**

2. **Select the Automatically check for updates check box as shown n Figure 13.3.**

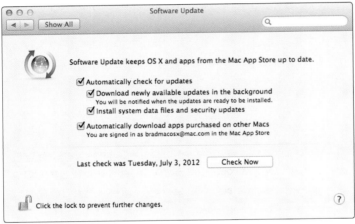

13.3 Use the Software Update pane to check for software updates automatically.

3. **If you want updates to be downloaded automatically, select the Download newly available updates in the background check box.** I recommend that you select this check box so updates are downloaded as soon as they are found. If you don't select this, you're prompted to download updates when they are available.

4. **To automatically install system data files and security updates, select that check box.** I recommend that you leave this check box selected.

5. **To automatically download applications you've purchased on a different Mac onto your MacBook Pro, select the Automatically download apps purchased on other Macs check box.**

6. **Quit the System Preferences application.** Software Update will manage updates according to the settings you selected.

Genius

You can manually check for updates by clicking Check Now. This does the same thing as choosing Apple menu ➪ Software Update.

Keeping other software current

It's likely that your MacBook Pro has software installed on it that you didn't get from the App Store. You also need to keep this software current. Each of these applications provides its own tools to download and install updates. Most also support manual or automatic updates. The details of updating a third-party application that you obtained outside of the Mac App Store depend on the specific application. The two examples included here cover how to manually update Microsoft Office applications and how to configure Snapz Pro X from Ambrosia Software to automatically update. The process for updating other third-party applications is similar.

To Install or Not to Install?

Updates are also software and, like other kinds of software, they can have bugs, security problems, and other issues. Some experts recommend that you delay installing updates until it's clear that they don't cause more problems than they solve. There is some logic to this approach, as there have been occasions in which an update has proven to be problematic. However, those occasions are rare, especially for Apple software. Additionally, if an update is released to correct a potential security issue, you continue to be exposed to that issue until you install the update.

Personally, I install updates to Apple software as they become available. In the rare cases that an update with problems is released, it is typically immediately followed by one that corrects the problems. If you prefer a more cautious approach, you should disable automatic software updates and use the manual approach. However, you'll need to keep up on Mac-related news to determine when updates are released and if there are problems with them before you install them. This is too much work with too little return for most people, though.

Manually updating Microsoft Office applications

Most Mac users are also Office users. Follow these steps to manually update an Office application:

1. **Launch the Office application.**

2. **Choose Help ⇨ Check for Updates.** The Microsoft AutoUpdate application opens, as shown in Figure 13.4.

13.4 You can use the Microsoft AutoUpdate tool to check for and manually or automatically install updates.

Can't Find an Update Command?

While most modern applications provide either a manual update command or an automatic update setting, not all of them do (if you obtain an application through the App Store, you can use the App Store application to check for updates). Whether an application doesn't support updates via a command, you have to manually determine whether an update is available. To do so, go to the website for the software and determine the current version. Compare the version installed on your MacBook Pro with the most current one shown on the website. If a new version is available, download and install it.

For most applications, when you download and install them, you have an option to sign up for e-mails related to the application. This is a good way to remain informed about new updates because information about, and links to them are usually included in the e-mail. Some e-mails, though, are purely for marketing, so determine the purpose of any e-mails before you agree to receive them.

3. **Click Check for Updates.**

4. **Follow the on-screen instructions to complete the update.**

Genius

You can configure Microsoft Office applications to automatically check for updates by choosing Help ➪ Check for Updates. In the Microsoft AutoUpdate window, select the Automatically radio button, and then select the frequency at which you want to check for updates on the Check for Updates pop-up menu. The application checks for updates according to the schedule you set; when an update is found, you are prompted to download and install it.

Automatically updating Snapz Pro X

Snapz Pro X from Ambrosia Software (www.ambrosiasw.com) is the best screen capture application for the Mac (in fact, many of the figures in this book were captured with it). Follow these steps to configure it to automatically check for updates:

1. **Launch Snapz Pro X.**

2. **Click the Preferences tab.**

3. **Select the Check for new versions at launch check box.** Each time you launch the application, it checks for a newer version. When one is found, you are prompted to download and install it.

Preventing Internet Attacks

When you use your home network, you should shield your MacBook Pro from Internet attacks through an AirPort Extreme Base Station or Time Capsule. When you use networks outside of your control, such as one available in public places, you should use the Mac OS X firewall to prevent unauthorized access to your computer.

Caution

Never connect your MacBook Pro directly to a cable or DSL modem without first enabling the Mac OS X firewall.

Shielding your MacBook Pro with a base station

You can protect the computers on your local network from attack by placing a barrier between them and the public Internet. You can then use a Dynamic Host Configuration Protocol (DHCP) server that provides Network Address Translation (NAT) protection for your network. You can also add or use a hub that contains a more sophisticated firewall to ensure that your network can't be violated. A benefit of these devices is that you can also use them to share a single Internet connection.

One of the easiest (and best) ways to protect machines on a local network from attack and simultaneously share an Internet connection is to install an AirPort Extreme Base Station or Time Capsule. These devices provide NAT protection for any computers that obtain Internet service through them. For most users, this is an adequate level of protection from hacking. That's because the addresses of each computer on the network are hidden from the outside Internet. The only address exposed is the one assigned to the base station by the cable or DSL modem. This address is useless to hackers because there isn't any data or functionality exposed to the Internet from the base station.

Note

For more details about how to configure a base station to protect your network and computers, see Chapter 3.

Shielding your MacBook Pro with the Mac OS X firewall

Whenever your MacBook Pro isn't protected by a base station or other firewall, make sure that you configure its own firewall to protect it from Internet attacks. Common situations are when you travel and connect to various networks, such as in public places and hotel rooms. Most of these networks are configured to limit access to your computer (similar to how a base station shields it), but you shouldn't count on this. Instead, perform the following steps to protect your MacBook Pro with its firewall:

1. **Open the Security & Privacy pane of the System Preferences application.**

2. **Click the Firewall tab.**

3. **Click Turn On Firewall.** If the button is disabled, click the Lock icon and authenticate yourself as an administrator to enable it. The firewall starts running with the default settings.

4. **Click Firewall Options.** The Firewall Options sheet appears, as shown in Figure 13.5.

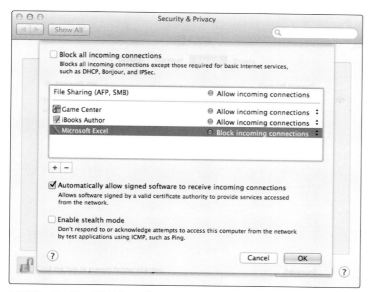

13.5 Use the Mac OS X firewall to protect your computer from Internet attacks.

5. **To provide the maximum protection, select the Block all incoming connections check box.** This prevents all connections, except the most basic ones required for network access, such as DHCP and Bonjour. After configuring the firewall, if an action you normally perform doesn't work, deselect this check box and perform step 6 instead.

6. **Add any applications you are sure you want to allow incoming connections.** To block all incoming connections, click the Add (+) button below the action list, select the application you want to add, and then configure its pop-up menu to Allow or Block incoming connections. Applications that are allowed have a green status, while those that are blocked have a red status. Any blocked applications are unable to receive incoming traffic, and functions associated with receiving communication from outside your MacBook Pro are prevented. When you've not allowed a specific application through the firewall and it tries to communicate, you're prompted to allow or prevent it.

7. **To allow applications that have a valid security certificate to receive incoming connections, select the Automatically allow signed software to receive incoming connections check box.**

8. **Select the Enable stealth mode check box.** This further protects your MacBook Pro by making sure that uninvited connection requests aren't acknowledged in any form so that the existence of your computer is hidden.

9. **Click OK.** Your settings are saved and the sheet closes. Your MacBook Pro is protected by the firewall.

Genius

If you have trouble with some network or Internet services after configuring the firewall, make sure that you check the firewall configuration to ensure that it isn't preventing the service you are trying to use. As long as the service is configured within Mac OS X, this shouldn't be the case, but it's a good thing to check if you have a problem.

Protecting MacBook Pro with General Security

Mac OS X includes a number of general security settings that are particularly useful if you use your MacBook Pro in a variety of locations, some of which might allow it to be accessed by someone else. Do the following to configure these settings:

1. **Open the Security & Privacy pane of the System Preferences application.**

2. **Click the General tab, as shown in Figure 13.6.**

3. **Select the Require password after sleep or screen saver begins check box to require a user to type his login password to stop the screen saver or wake the MacBook Pro.** On the pop-up menu, choose the amount of time the computer is asleep or in screen saver mode before the password is required.

4. **To show a message on the screen when the MacBook Pro is locked, select the Show a message when the screen is locked check box.** Click Set Lock Message, type the message you want to be displayed, and then click OK.

5. **To prevent someone from being able to use your computer just by starting it, select the Disable automatic login check box.** This prevents a user from being automatically logged in. To use your MacBook Pro, someone must know the password for at least one user account.

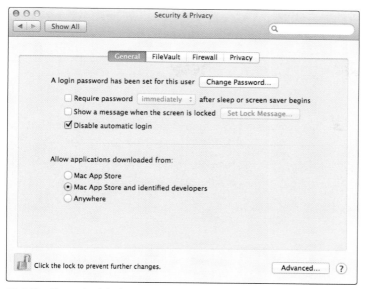

13.6 The General tab helps you protect your MacBook Pro from unauthorized access.

Note On the Privacy pane, you can disable sending diagnostic and usage information to Apple. You can also enable or disable location services (which identifies the current location of your MacBook Pro) for the entire system or specific applications. You also see applications that have accessed location services; those that have done so within the past 24 hours are marked with the arrow icon.

6. **Choose the Gatekeeper option you want to use.** Gatekeeper is designed to prevent malicious applications from being downloaded and run on your computer. Select one of the following radio buttons:

   - **Mac App Store.** This is the safest option because it allows only applications that you've obtained from the App Store to be used.

   - **Mac App Store and identified developers.** This is a relatively safe option as it limits applications to those you've either downloaded from the App Store or that are provided by recognized developers.

   - **Anywhere.** This option allows any application to run. Unless you are quite sure of your ability to monitor applications being downloaded and run on your computer, I don't recommend this option as it provides no protection.

Are Viruses a Big Deal?

I believe that viruses are less of a problem than they appear to be from the tremendous amount of media hype they receive, especially for Mac users. Most of the time, you can protect yourself from viruses by being very careful about the files you receive in e-mail or download from the web. Because the most common way for a virus to get onto your machine is for you to accept a file in which it is contained, you can protect yourself from most viruses by using common sense. For example, if you receive an e-mail containing an oddly titled attachment (such as the famous I Love You file), you should either request more information from the sender before you open the file or simply delete the message.

There are cases in which malware has reportedly been downloaded when users browse certain websites. Make sure you keep Mac OS X current because Apple releases updates to address those types of security threats. When you see a prompt asking if you want to open an application (which happens the first time you open an application downloaded from the Internet), make sure that application is one you intended to open. Also, use Gatekeeper to limit the applications that can be downloaded and run on your MacBook Pro.

Adding and using an antivirus application makes your machine even safer, but if you are very careful about downloading files, you might find that you can get by just fine without one. It's mostly a matter of whether you are consistently careful about moving files onto your computer or whether you would benefit from an application helping you avoid viruses. An antivirus application is definitely a good idea if you share your computer with inexperienced users who are more likely to accept viruses.

Protecting Data with Time Machine

The most important thing you can do to protect your MacBook Pro and its data is to back it up. To back up simply means that you have at least one copy of all of the data on your computer in case something happens to it. What could happen? Lots of things: An accidental deletion of files, a hardware or software problem that makes the data unavailable, liquid being spilled on the MacBook Pro that causes it to be damaged such that you can't start it up, and so on. There shouldn't be any question in your mind that something like this will happen, because no matter how careful you are, at some point data you want to keep is going to disappear from your computer. If you have everything backed up properly, this is a minor nuisance. If you don't have good backups, this could be a disaster.

To drive this point home, consider the photos that you manage in iPhoto or Aperture. Many of those are irreplaceable, but without a backup in place, you could lose them and never get them back. Then, there are documents you've created, financial records, and so on. The point is that you have lots of information on your MacBook Pro that would either be difficult or expensive to replace or that simply can't be replaced. You should have a reliable, easy-to-use backup system to protect your data.

The good news is that with an external hard drive, you can use Mac OS X Time Machine to back up with minimal effort on your part. In fact, once you set it up, the process is automatic. Time Machine makes recovering files you've lost easy and intuitive. When your MacBook Pro isn't connected to a backup drive, it stores backups on the MacBook Pro hard drive so that you can recover files from there. While you don't want to rely on this long-term because the backed up data is on the same physical drive as the original data, it can be useful when you are away from your backup disk because it provides some level of protection for your data.

Time Machine backs up your data for as long as it can until the backup hard drive is full. It stores hourly backups for the last 24 hours, daily backups for the last month, and weekly backups until the backup drive is full. Once the drive is full, it deletes the oldest backups to make room for the new. To protect your data for as long as possible, use the largest hard drive you can, and exclude files that you don't need to back up (such as system files for Mac OS X) to save space on the backup drive. To use Time Machine, you need to gain access to an external hard drive, and then configure Time Machine to use it. You should also know how to use Time Machine to restore files, should (I mean when) you need to.

Preparing a backup drive

To use Time Machine, you need to be able to store data on an external drive. You can use one of the following options to accomplish this:

- **Time Capsule.** This Apple device, shown in Figure 13.7, is a combination of an AirPort Extreme Base Station and a hard drive. With capacity options of 2TB or 3TB, you gain a lot of backup storage space. Additionally, a Time Capsule is also a fully featured AirPort Extreme Base Station, so you can also use it to provide a wireless network. It also makes an ideal backup drive for any computer connected to the AirPort network it provides. The downside of Time Capsule is that it is more expensive than a standard hard drive, but if you don't already have an AirPort Extreme Base Station, it is slightly less expensive than buying the base station and hard drive separately.

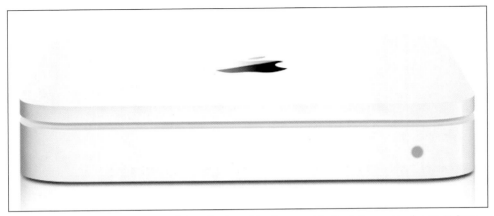

13.7 The Apple Time Capsule is useful as a backup drive for your MacBook Pro and is also an AirPort Base Station.

- **Hard drive connected through USB, FireWire 800, or ThunderBolt.** You can use a hard drive directly connected to your MacBook Pro as a backup drive. This provides the fastest performance of any option, and hard drives are also inexpensive and easy to configure. (See Chapter 11 for more details about connecting your MacBook Pro to an external hard drive.)

- **Shared hard drive.** You can back up to a hard drive that you access through File Sharing over a local network.

Caution

It's best if you don't use a backup hard drive for any purpose beyond backing up your data. You want to keep as much space as possible available for your backups. Using the drive for other purposes leaves less room for backing up, which means that your backups don't go as far back in time as they might. You can share a backup drive among multiple computers, but if you do this, make sure it is a very large one.

Backing up with Time Machine

After you gain access to a backup hard drive, you can configure Time Machine to back up your data. In an ideal world, your backup hard drive is large enough to save copies of all of the files from the MacBook Pro drive, so you can restore any file on your machine. However, unless you have a relatively small amount of data on your computer or a very large backup hard drive, making a complete backup will limit the time over which backup data is stored. You might want to exclude certain files (such as system software files) to make your backups smaller so that they can be stored longer.

Caution If your backup drive fails, it is no longer protecting your data. If you don't discover this until you need to restore files, you're out of luck. Back up important files in a second way, such as on DVDs, and store them in a separate location just to be safe. It's also a good idea to back up critical (if not all) files online through a backup service.

Perform the following steps to configure Time Machine:

1. **Open the Time Machine pane of the System Preferences application.**

2. **Drag the slider to the On position.** Time Machine activates and the select drive sheet appears, as shown in Figure 13.8.

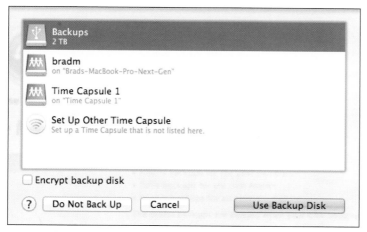

Backups
2 TB

bradm
on "Brads-MacBook-Pro-Next-Gen"

Time Capsule 1
on "Time Capsule 1"

Set Up Other Time Capsule
Set up a Time Capsule that is not listed here.

☐ Encrypt backup disk

(?) [Do Not Back Up] [Cancel] [**Use Backup Disk**]

13.8 Use this sheet to select the drive Time Machine uses to store your backed-up data.

3. **Select the drive on which you want to store the backed-up information.**

4. **Click Use Backup Disk.**

5. **If you selected a Time Capsule or another location that is protected by a password, type the password, and then click Connect.** The sheet closes and you return to the Time Machine page. The drive you selected appears at the top of the pane and the timer starts the backup process, which you see next to the text *Next Backup*.

6. **Click Options.** The Exclude items sheet appears. This sheet enables you to exclude files from the backup process. For example, you can exclude the System Files and Applications if you have those files stored elsewhere, such as on a DVD.

Note

If you encrypt your data with the Mac OS X security features, you also need to encrypt your backups or anyone who gains access to your backup drive may be able to recover its data. If you want the backed-up data to be encrypted, select the Encrypt backup disk check box. This prevents the data from being used without the encryption passcode. If you do select it, make sure that you never lose the password.

7. **Click the Add (+) button.** The select sheet appears.

8. **Move to and select the folders or files you want to exclude from the backup and click Exclude.**

9. **If you selected system files, click Exclude System Folder Only to exclude only files in the System folder, or Exclude All System Files to exclude system files no matter where they are stored.** If you exclude system files, you should choose to exclude them no matter where they are located.

10. **If you don't want the backup process to run when you are operating on battery power, deselect the Back up while on battery power check box.**

11. **If you want to be warned as old backups are removed from the backup drive, select the Warn after old backups are deleted check box.** This is a good idea, as it lets you know when your backup drive fills up.

12. **Click Save.** You return to the Time Machine pane, which displays information about your backup, as shown in Figure 13.9. The timer starts and when it expires, the first backup is created. From then on, Time Machine automatically backs up your data to the selected drive. New backups are created every hour.

13. **Select the Show Time Machine in menu bar check box.**

Genius

After you disconnect an external backup drive or move out of range of a Time Capsule, the next time you connect to it a backup is performed automatically. Make sure that you connect to the hard drive or Time Capsule frequently because your backups are only as fresh as the last time you connected to the backup drive. Time Machine also backs up your files onto the MacBook Pro hard drive while it isn't connected to the backup disk.

13.9 The progress of the current backup is shown in the Backing up progress bar.

Time Machine backups happen automatically, but you should follow these suggestions to ensure that things are working properly:

- **Every so often, open the Time Machine pane of the System Preferences application and check the status of your backups.** This includes the name of the current backup drive, the amount of drive space available, the oldest backup stored on the drive, the latest backup, and the time at which the next backup will be performed. The latest backup date and time tell you how fresh your current backup is; it shouldn't be more than one hour old unless there is a problem, you've disabled Time Machine, or you haven't connected the backup drive to your MacBook Pro in a while.

- **As the backup drive gets full, you see warnings when old backups are deleted if you enabled that preference.** Make sure that there aren't files in the old backups that you might need. This can happen if you delete a document or folder from your MacBook Pro but don't restore it for a long time. Eventually, the only copy left might be in the oldest backup that gets deleted when the backup drive gets full.

- **When your backup system has worked for a while, check the status of the backup hard drive.** If it is filling up rapidly, consider removing some of the system and application files that might be part of it to reduce the space required. The most important files to protect over a long time are those you've created, changed, or purchased. Files that are already on a disc are relatively easy to recover, so there's no need to include them in a backup unless the disc is the only place that they exist.

- **If there are files you want to keep, but don't use any more, consider moving them onto a DVD or CD for archival purposes.** Then, delete them from the MacBook Pro hard drive and, over time, they'll be removed from the backups or you can exclude them from Time Machine to reduce the amount of drive space required. If the files are important, you should archive them in a couple of ways in case the disc you saved them on is lost or damaged.

- **Test your backups periodically to make sure that things are working properly by attempting to restore some files (which is explained later in this chapter).** If you don't discover a problem until you need to restore important files, it is too late, so make sure your backup system is working properly. Create a couple of test files for this purpose and let them exist long enough to get into your backups (at least one hour, assuming you are connected to your backup drive). Delete some of the test files and empty the Trash. Make and save changes to some of the test files. Then, try to restore both the deleted files and the original versions of the files you changed. If you are able to restore the files, your data is protected. If not, you have a problem and need to solve it so that your data isn't at risk.

- **Use the Time Machine menu on the Finder menu bar to quickly access commands and information.** At the top of the menu, you see the date and time of the most recent backup. You can use the Back Up Now command to start a backup at any time. Select Enter Time Machine to restore files. Select Open Time Machine preferences to move to the Time Machine pane of the System Preferences application.

Restoring files with Time Machine

If you only have to use the information in this section to test your backups, it's a good thing. However, there may come a day when you need to use this information to recover files that are important to you. These might be photos from your last vacation, favorite songs you purchased from iTunes, or even documents you've put a lot of work into. Maybe you accidentally deleted files, realized that you wanted a previous version of a file, or something just went haywire on your MacBook Pro and you lost some important files.

The reason this function is called Time Machine is that you can use it to go back in time to restore files that are included in your backups. You can restore files and folders from the Finder and recover individual items from within some applications (such as photos from iPhoto).

Restoring files in the Finder

If the folders or files you want to restore are included in your backups and available in the Finder, you can perform the following steps to restore them:

1. **Open a Finder window showing the location where the files you want to recover were stored.** This can be the location where files that have been deleted were placed, or

it may be where the current versions of files are stored (if you want to go back to a previous version of a file).

2. **Launch the Time Machine application in one of the following ways:**

   - **Click its icon (the clock with the arrow showing time moving backward) on the Dock if it is installed there (it isn't by default).**

   - **Double-click its icon in the Applications folder.**

   - **Choose Time Machine menu ⇨ Enter Time Machine.**

Genius

You can launch Time Machine first and then navigate to the location from which you
want to recover files using the Finder windows you see while in Time Machine.

3. **The Desktop disappears and the Time Machine window fills the entire space, as
   shown in Figure 13.10.** In the center of the window, you see the Finder window that
   you opened in step 1. Behind it, you see all of the versions of that window that are stored
   in your backup, from the current version to as far back in time as the backups go. Along
   the right side of the window, you see the timeline for your backups starting with today
   and moving back in time as you move up the screen. Gray bars indicate backups stored
   on the MacBook hard drive, while the magenta bars indicate backups stored on your
   backup drive. At the bottom of the screen you see the Time Machine toolbar. In the center of the toolbar, you see the time of the window that is currently in the foreground. At
   each end, you see controls that you use to exit Time Machine (Cancel) and the Restore
   button (which is active only when you have selected a file or folder that can be restored).

13.10 You can use Time Machine to travel back in time to when the files
you want to restore were available.

4. **Move back in time by doing one of the following:**

   - **Click the time on the timeline when the files you want to restore were available.** As you hover over a line, the time and date of the backup is shown.

   - **Click the back arrow (pointing away from you) located just to the left of the timeline.**

   - **Click a Finder window behind the foremost one.**

5. **When you reach the files you want to restore, select them.**

6. **Click Restore.** The files and folders you selected are returned to their locations in the condition they were in the version of the backup you selected, and Time Machine quits. You move back to the Finder location where the restored files were saved. You can resume using them as if you'd never lost them.

Genius

To restore a previous version of a file and keep the current version, rename the file before you launch Time Machine. Then, restore the version of the file you want and you'll have both versions in the Finder window.

Restoring files in applications

Some applications that work with individual files, such as iPhoto and iTunes, provide Time Machine support so that you can restore files from within those applications instead of by selecting the files in the Finder. This makes restoring files from certain kinds of applications easier because you can find the files to restore using the application's interface instead of using the Finder (which is difficult for some applications, such as iPhoto files because of the way that application names and organizes your photos). The following steps cover how to restore photos in iPhoto (the process for restoring files in other compatible applications is similar):

1. **Open iPhoto.**

2. **Launch the Time Machine application by doing one of the following:**

   - **Click its icon (the clock with the arrow showing time moving backward) on the Dock if it is installed there (it isn't by default).**

   - **Double-click its icon in the Applications folder.**

   - **Choose Time Machine menu ⇨ Enter Time Machine.**

3. **The Desktop disappears and the Time Machine window fills the entire space.** In the center of the window, you see the iPhoto window. Behind it, you see all versions of that window that are stored in your backup from the current version as far back in time as the backups go.

4. **Move back in time by doing one of the following:**

   ● **Click the time on the timeline when the photos you want to restore were available.** The higher on the timeline you click, the farther back in time you go.

   ● **Click the back arrow (pointing away from you) located just to the left of the timeline.**

   ● **Click an iPhoto window behind the foremost one.**

5. **As you move back in time, you see the versions of the window that are saved in the backup you are viewing, and the date and time of the backup in the center of the toolbar.**

6. **Use the iPhoto controls to move to the photos you want to restore and select them.**

7. **Click Restore.** The files are returned to iPhoto, and you can use them as if they'd never been lost.

Genius

A portable hard drive is an ideal accessory for your MacBook Pro so you can back up your data when you are on the move. A flash drive or SD card is a good option to back up specific files when you can't access your regular backup system. You can also use a full-fledged online backup service and your data is backed up whenever you are connected to the Internet.

Using the Mac OS X Document Protection Features

Mac OS X includes two features designed to preserve versions of documents that you are using: Auto Save and Versioning. These features ensure specific documents with which you are working are protected while Time Machine protects groups of documents. You use both at the same time to provide as much protection as possible.

Note

Applications have to be written to support Auto Save or Versioning. Not all applications support these features.

Using Auto Save

Applications designed to work with Mac OS X automatically save your open documents every hour and as you make substantial changes to them, so, you don't need to bother saving documents manually. To determine whether an application supports Auto Save and Versioning, open its File menu. If you see Save As, the application does not support these features. If you see Save a Version or Duplicate, it does.

Genius

If you want to create a new version of a document, choose File ⇨ Duplicate. A copy of the file is created. Save the copy with a new name. You now have two documents and changes you make in one will not affect the other.

Restoring documents with Versioning

As documents are automatically saved, each save results in a version of the document. Versions are saved every hour and as you make significant changes. Hourly versions are kept for 24 hours and early versions are available daily until they are a month old, from which point they are maintained weekly. When you delete a document, all of its versions are deleted, too.

Genius

You can create a version of a document at any time by choosing File ⇨ Save a Version.

Perform the following steps to visit or recover a version of a document:

1. **Choose File ⇨ Revert to ⇨ Browse All Versions.** The application disappears and the version viewer screen appears. On the left side, you see the current version of the document, labeled Current Document. On the right side, you see a stack of all of the saved versions. The date and time of the version currently being displayed is shown under the front document window. To the far right, you see the document's timeline.

Note

Time Machine maintains as many versions of your documents as you have room to store on the backup drive or on the MacBook Pro hard drive.

2. **Click an older version of the document to bring it to the front or use the timeline to move back to a specific version, as shown in Figure 13.11.**

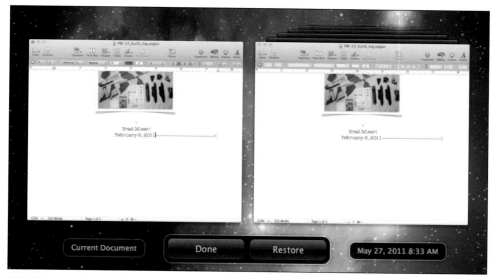

13.11 You can view all of the saved versions of a document and return to a previous one if you choose.

3. **Compare the two versions of the document.** You can scroll and navigate within each document.

4. **Find the version of the document that you want to restore.**

5. **With the version you want to restore on top of the version stack on the right, click Restore.** That version of the document replaces the one you had been working on and you return to the application.

Note

To keep the current version of the document instead of restoring an older version, click Done.

Protecting Data with Online Backup Services

Time Machine is great because it is easy to set up and use to recover files. However, it does have several significant downsides. One is that no matter how large your backup drive is, it does have limited space. Another is that your backup drive has to be in the same general location as your

MacBook Pro. This means that if something catastrophic (such as a fire, flood, or theft) happens, both your MacBook Pro and the backup drive may be damaged, leaving you without your data. Your MacBook Pro also has to be in range of your backup drive (either within cable length or your wireless network) for your files to be backed up. When you are away, your files aren't backed up.

Note

Most online backup services allow you to configure the software so that it works in a low-priority . This is so the backup process doesn't significantly slow down your other activities. You may also be able to set the backups to only occur at specific times, such as the middle of the night when you aren't using your connection (you should be using Time Machine, too, so that backups are created more frequently).

To address Time Machine's weaknesses, you may want to consider using an online backup service as another means of backing up your data. These services usually offer unlimited backup space for a relatively low annual fee. When you sign up for a service, you download and install a pane in the System Preferences application that enables automatic backups of the data you select and restores of your data. The first time you back up, it can take a long time, depending on how much data you are backing up and your connection speed. After that, only incremental changes are backed up so the process is much faster.

Two providers of online backup services for Mac users are Carbonite (www.carbonite.com) and Mozy (www.mozy.com). Both offer free trials, so you might want to try them out, and then sign up for the one that best suits your needs.

Protecting Data with Encryption

If you travel with your MacBook Pro, the data it contains is vulnerable because your computer can be carried away by other people. If you store important data on your computer, you can encrypt your data so that it can't be used without an appropriate password. This way, even if someone is able to mount the hard drive in your MacBook Pro, he must have the password to access the data in your Home folder.

Caution

If you use your MacBook Pro in public, you should disable automatic login whether or not you use FileVault. With automatic login enabled, anyone who starts your computer can use it. With this feature disabled, a password is needed to access it, which provides some level of protection. You should also require a password to wake the computer or stop the screen saver if you leave your MacBook Pro for any period without logging out.

The Mac OS X FileVault feature encrypts your drive using a password that you create so that this data can't be accessed without the appropriate password. To do this, Mac OS X creates a copy of your data during the encryption process. This means that you must have free space that is at least the size of the information in your Home folder before you can enable FileVault.

Caution To use FileVault, the associated user account must have a password. If you didn't configure a password for your own or any other user account, you must do so before you can activate FileVault for that user.

Perform the following steps to activate FileVault:

1. **Open the Security & Privacy pane of the System Preferences application.**

2. **Click the FileVault tab, as shown in Figure 13.12.**

13.12 FileVault encrypts the data in your Home folder to prevent unauthorized access to it.

3. **Click Turn On FileVault.** You see a sheet listing all of the user accounts on your MacBook Pro. Each user's password must be entered for that user to be able to unlock the drive. Users who are able to unlock the drive are marked with a check mark. If users cannot unlock the drive, you see the Enable User button. The account under which you are working is automatically enabled.

4. **Click Enable User for the user you want to allow to unlock the drive.**

5. **Type that user's password and click OK.**

6. **Repeat steps 4 and 5 until you've enabled all of the users you want to be able to unlock the drive.**

7. **Click Continue.** You see a sheet containing your recovery key. This key is needed if you forget your password. You can use the key yourself to recover data, and you can provide it to Apple to get help recovering your data. If you don't have this key and forget your password, all of your data will be lost. Record your recovery key by writing it down or taking a screenshot and storing it in a secure location. Then, click Continue.

8. **On the resulting sheet, choose to store the key with Apple by selecting Store the recovery key with Apple.** You can elect not to by selecting Do not store the recovery key with Apple. Click Continue.

9. **If you elected to store the key with Apple, configure your security questions on the resulting sheet, and then click Continue.** If not, skip this step.

10. **Click Restart.** Your MacBook Pro restarts.

11. **Log back into your user account.** The encryption process begins.

While the encryption process runs, you may not notice anything. The process can take quite a while depending on how much data you have on your MacBook Pro. To see the status of the process, open the FileVault pane again. You see that the FileVault is turned on, and if you sent a recovery key to Apple you see a confirmation that it was sent. Below that, you see the encryption status bar.

After the process is complete, you also won't notice any difference because data is decrypted as needed when you log in. The difference occurs when someone tries to access the drive without the password; all of the data on the drive is useless. For example, suppose someone steals your MacBook Pro. Although she can't access your user account without your login password, she can connect the computer to a FireWire drive with Mac OS X installed and start up from that volume. Because the files on your MacBook start-up volume are no longer protected (the OS on the computer to which the MacBook is connected is running the show), they are accessible. If FileVault is not on, these files are not encrypted and can be used. However, if FileVault is on, these files are encrypted and useless without the correct password.

Protecting Information with Keychains

Many times, you can select a check box that causes Mac OS X to remember the passwords you type. These passwords are remembered in the keychain associated with your account. Just by using the remember check box, you get a lot of value from the keychain because it stores the various usernames and passwords for you. All you have to remember is the password for your user account to unlock the keychain, which in turn, applies the appropriate usernames and passwords so you don't have to type them.

When you have applications, like Safari, remember usernames and passwords (such as those for websites you visit), they are also stored in your keychain so that you don't have to type this information each time you need to log in. Each kind of username and password is stored as a specific type in your keychain. Before you can use a keychain, it has to be created. A keychain is created automatically for each user account you create. However, you can create additional keychains for specific purposes if you need to.

To use a keychain, it must be unlocked. To unlock a keychain, type its password when you are prompted to do so. When you log in to your user account, the default keychain for that account is unlocked automatically because its password is the password for the user account with which it is associated. While typing a keychain's password can be annoying because it is a fairly common requirement, you should remember that at least you only have to remember the keychain's password instead of remembering a separate password for each resource. Many types of resources, including the following list, can be added to your keychain so you can access them:

- **AirPort network passwords**
- **File sharing passwords**
- **Internet passwords**
- **iCloud password**
- **Secure notes.** You can store information that you want to protect using secure notes. For example, if you want to store your credit card information so that it can't be accessed unless you are logged in to your user account, you can add it to your keychain. When you need that information, you can open the secure note containing your credit card information in your keychain.

Viewing and configuring keychains

Note   Your default keychain is called the login keychain. You'll also see a System keychain.

Follow these steps to view and configure your keychain:

1. **Open the Keychain Access application, shown in Figure 13.13, located in the Utilities folder within the Applications folder.** In the top-left pane is a list of all keychains that your account can access. In the lower-left pane is a list of categories for all of the keychains installed under your user account. Select a category and the keychain items it contains appear in the lower-right pane of the window. You see information related to each keychain item, such as its name, kind, the date it was last modified, when it expires, and the keychain in which it is stored. When you select a keychain item, detailed information about that item appears in the upper part of the window.

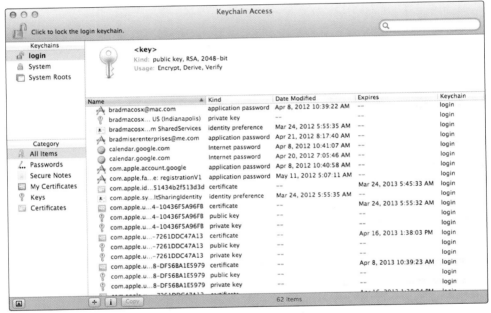

13.13 As you can see, a number of items are stored in my keychain.

2. **To see what items are included in your default keychain, select login.**

3. **Select the All Items category.** Each item in your keychain appears in the list.

4. **To get summary information about a keychain item, select it.** A summary of the item appears at the top of the window, including the kind of item it is, the user account with which it is associated, where the location to which it relates is, and the modification date.

5. **Double-click a keychain item.** Its window appears. This window has two tabs: Attributes and Access Control. The Attributes tab presents information about the item, such as its name, its kind, the account, the location of the resource with which it is associated, comments you have entered, and the password (which is hidden when you

first view an item). The Access Control tab enables you to configure how the item is used.

6. **To see the item's password, select the Show password check box.** You are then prompted to confirm the keychain's password.

7. **Confirm the password by typing it at the prompt and choosing to allow access to the item.** When you return to the Attributes tab, you see the item's password.

8. **Click the Access Control tab.** Use the access controls in the pane to control which applications can access this keychain item and how they can access it.

9. **To allow access to the item by all applications, select the Allow all applications to access this item radio button.** If you want to configure access for specific applications, continue with the rest of these steps.

10. **To allow access by specific applications but require confirmation, select the Confirm before allowing access radio button.** Select the Ask for Keychain password check box if you want to be prompted for your keychain's password before access is allowed.

11. **To enable an application not currently on the list to access the keychain item, click the Add (+) button located at the bottom of the list, and then select the application to which you want to provide access.**

12. **Click Save Changes.** Your changes are saved, and you return to the Keychain Access window.

Adding items to a keychain

You can add items to a keychain in any of the following ways:

- **When you access a resource that can provide access to a keychain, such as a file server, select the Remember check box.**
- **Drag a network server onto the Keychain Access window.**
- **Drag the Internet Resource Locator file for a web page onto the Keychain Access window.**
- **Manually create a keychain item.**

Genius If a particular application or resource doesn't support keychains, you won't be able to access that resource automatically. However, you can still use Keychain Access to store such an item's username and password for you, thus enabling you to recall that information easily.

One useful thing you can add to a keychain is a secure note. This protects the information you type with a password so that it can only be viewed if the appropriate password is provided, which is the password that unlocks the keychain. Follow these steps to add a secure note to a keychain:

1. **Open Keychain Access.**

2. **Select the keychain to which you want to add the note.**

3. **Choose File ⇨ New Secure Note Item.** The New Secure Note sheet appears, as shown in Figure 13.14.

4. **Type a name for the note in the Keychain Item Name box.**

5. **Type the information you want to store in the Note box.**

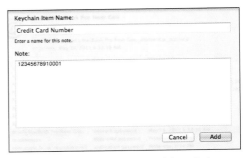

6. **Click Add.** The note is added to your keychain and you return to the Keychain Access window where you see the new note you added.

13.14 Here's a secure note containing vital information.

Follow these steps to view a secure note:

1. **Select the Secure Notes category.** Your secure notes appear.

2. **Double-click the note you want to read.** The note opens, but the information it contains is hidden.

3. **Click the Show note check box (if you have not displayed the note before, you need to allow keychain to access it).** You see the note in the window.

Working with keychains

When an application needs to access a keychain item and it is not configured to always allow access, you see the confirm dialog that prompts you to type a keychain's password and choose an access option. When prompted, choose one of the following options:

- **Deny.** Access to the item is prevented.
- **Allow.** A single access to the item is allowed.
- **Always Allow.** Access to the item is always allowed, and you don't see the prompt the next time it is used.

If you want to become a keychain master, check out the following information:

● **Choose Edit ➪ Change Settings for Keychain** *keychainname* **(where** *keychainname* **is the name of the keychain).** You can set a keychain to lock after a specified time or lock when the MacBook Pro is asleep.

● **Choose Edit ➪ Change Password for Keychain** *keychainname* **(where** *keychainname* **is the name of the keychain) to change a keychain's password.**

● **Choose Keychain Access ➪ Preferences.** On the General tab, select the Show keychain status in menu bar check box. This adds the Keychain Access menu to the menu bar. From this menu, you can lock or unlock keychains, and access security preferences and the Keychain Access application.

● **Choose Edit ➪ Keychain List.** You see the Configure Keychain sheet, which you can use to configure keychains for a user account or the system. For example, you can select the Shared check box to share a keychain between user accounts.

● **Choose Keychain Access ➪ Keychain First Aid.** You see the Keychain First Aid dialog, which you can use to verify keychains or repair a damaged one.

How Do I Solve MacBook Pro Problems?

While MacBook Pros are among the most reliable and easiest-to-use computers available, they are still complex systems that involve advanced technology, intricate software, and connections to networks, the Internet, and other devices. To put it in analog terms, there are a lot of moving parts. You can expect that every once in a while, something is going to go wrong. However, with a bit of preparation and some basic troubleshooting, you should be able to recover from most common problems relatively easily.

Looking for Trouble

You should build a MacBook Pro toolkit to troubleshoot and solve problems. This way, a lot of time and energy won't be wasted trying to locate or create the tools you need to solve problems. Instead, you can simply put them into action. Here are a few of the most important tools you should have in your toolkit in case of an emergency:

- **Current backups.** Backups are a critical part of your toolkit because restoring your data is the most important task that you need to be able to do. Having a good way to restore your data limits the impact of drastic problems (like your MacBook Pro not working) and makes less significant problems (like the accidental deletion of a file) trivial to solve. Once you have an automated backup system that updates frequently (see Figure 14.1) and you store your backups in at least two ways (Time Machine and an external hard drive, on CD, DVD, or an online backup service), you are protected against the loss of your data. Test your backup system periodically by restoring some files to make sure that your backed-up data is ready when you need it (refer to Chapter 13 for more information about backing up).

14.1 If your backup process includes Time Machine (which it should), the only data at risk is that which has changed since the last backup, which shouldn't be more than one hour ago.

Note Mac OS X automatically saves snapshots of your files every hour. You can use these to recover previous versions of documents. However, you should not rely on this capability as it only protects your documents for a limited time. You should always have a complete backup of all of your files so you can recover them when you need to.

- **Alternate system software.** Your MacBook Pro system software is all important because the OS is what makes it run. If your startup volume/drive or the system software it contains has a problem, you might not be able to start up, which reduces your MacBook Pro to being a very cool-looking piece of technology art. Mac OS X includes the Recovery volume that enables you to start your MacBook Pro using its software so you can perform some important troubleshooting tasks. These tasks include using the Disk Utility application to repair a drive or volume, reinstalling Mac OS X, and so on. Your toolkit should also include an alternate startup hard drive on which Mac OS X is also installed. This allows you to troubleshoot and solve problems that prevent your MacBook Pro from starting up on its internal hard drive (in which case, the Recovery volume will not help).

Note

You should start up from your external startup drive and run Software Update periodically to keep the alternate startup drive's OS software current. Plus, this tests the drive to ensure that you can actually start up from it before you need to actually do so, such as when there is a problem with the MacBook Pro hard drive.

- **Alternate user accounts.** Because some problems can be related to preferences and other files specific to a user account, having an alternate user account, as shown in Figure 14.2, is important for troubleshooting. If you haven't created an alternate test user account, you should do so now.

14.2 A troubleshooting user account can help you identify a problem that is related to your primary user account.

● **Application installation files.** If you purchase an application on disc, keep it where you can easily access it when necessary. If you purchase and download applications from the Internet, burn the installation files to a DVD or CD, and keep them with your other application discs.

● **A record of important information.** Consider devising a secure way to record passwords, usernames, serial numbers, and other critical data so you don't have to rely on memory. Although keeping such information in hard copy is usually not advised, some people find it safer to develop and use a code for this information, and then keep a hard copy of the encoded information handy. You can also store this data in a keychain, because it is protected with your user account password. If you allow website and account usernames and passwords to be remembered, this information is automatically stored in your keychain. You can also store application registration information as secure notes (see Chapter 13). As long as you can get to your keychain, the information it contains is easily accessible. However, you should back up your keychains, too, to use for troubleshooting.

● **System report.** Consider maintaining a system profile generated by the System Information application, shown in Figure 14.3. This information can be very helpful when troubleshooting problems.

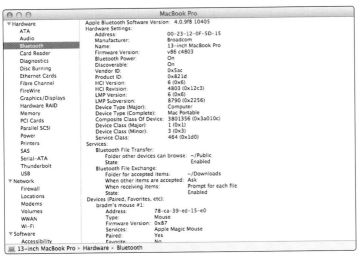

14.3 A detailed system report can be useful when troubleshooting.

Note

Applications that you purchase from the Mac App Store don't need to be saved on a CD or DVD because, should you need to, you can always download any that you've purchased again.

Caution

If you have to purchase upgrades to an application that you originally downloaded from a website, be aware that the version you purchased might not always be available. If you lose the application because of a hardware or software problem, you might have to purchase it (or an upgrade) again to download it. Make sure that you store application update installers on a DVD or CD, too, so you can return to them in the future.

Understanding and Describing Problems

When you start to troubleshoot, the most important thing you can do is understand a problem in as much detail as possible. This enables you to know what you need to do to correct the problem or, at least, it gives you ideas of things you can try. As you gain insight into your problem, you should be able to describe it in detail, so you can get help from others if you are not able to solve it yourself. Recognizing the symptoms of various kinds of problems also helps you identify what the problem is, which puts you in a position to try solutions.

Recognizing user errors

One common source of problems is your own mistaken (or lack of proper) actions. Recognizing a problem that you've caused is a bit tough, because user errors can have many consequences. The most common one is software or hardware not doing what you expect it to. In such cases, a common cause is a failure to do things in the recommended way. The following are some common user errors:

- **Not following instructions.** Sometimes taking a few minutes to read directions can save minutes or hours of troubleshooting.

- **Not performing proper maintenance on your system.** Mac OS X Software Update can automatically keep your operating system and applications you've downloaded from the App Store current.

- **Not keeping enough free space on your hard drives.** If a drive is full, or very close to it, you might have problems when you try to store more data on it.

Recognizing software problems

Software problems manifest in a number of ways, but the most common symptoms are hangs and unexpected quits. A hung application is one that has stopped responding to your commands and appears to be locked up. Hangs are usually accompanied by the spinning color wheel icon, which indicates that a lot of processor activity is happening, but the process being attempted isn't moving ahead. Fortunately, because Mac OS X has protected memory, a hung application usually affects only that application and your others continue to work normally. You may lose some unsaved data in the hung application, but at least your losses are limited to changes you've made within a single application, within the last hour through the Mac OS X snapshots (you can go even further back in time if you use Time Machine to back up).

Before deciding that an application is hung, wait a couple of minutes. Sometimes, the application can complete what it was trying to do and recovers on its own, which is a good thing. It won't hurt anything to let the application sit in a hung state for a few minutes, and you might avoid losing data should the application recover on its own. After you've decided that the application is definitely not going to recover on its own, the only immediate solution is to force it to quit. After forcing an application to quit, you should look for updates for it in case the issues that caused it to hang have been solved.

Caution

When you force an application to quit, you lose any unsaved data with which you are working. You shouldn't do this until you're sure the application is actually hung.

Sometimes the application you are using suddenly quits. The application windows that were open simply disappear. That's bad enough, but the worst part is that you lose any unsaved data with which you were working, and there's nothing you can do about it. Some of the likely causes of unexpected quits include software bugs, and conflicts between applications or applications and hardware. You should always restart your MacBook Pro after an unexpected quit and, like a hang, you should check to see whether an update to the application is available.

Unexpected behavior is obvious because an application starts not doing what you are telling it to, or doing things you aren't telling it to. Likely causes of this problem are bugs, or using the application other than how it was intended. Internet attacks or viruses can also be the cause of unexpected behavior.

When an application starts acting oddly, quit it and perform a restart of your MacBook Pro. Then, check for updates to the application that is misbehaving, as shown in Figure 14.4.

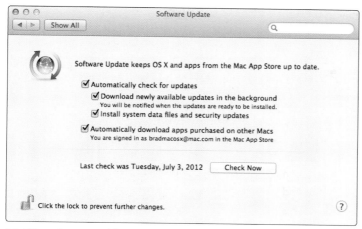

14.4 If you have a problem with an Apple application, open the Software Update pane and click Check Now. An update might easily and immediately solve the problem.

Note   Applications that support the Mac OS X Autosave automatically save versions of your documents so you can recover them should the application or your MacBook Pro have a problem. If you use an application that doesn't support this feature, save your work frequently and (if it has the capability) configure the application to save automatically.

Recognizing hardware problems

As odd as it might seem, the most unlikely cause of a problem is a hardware failure. Although hardware does fail now and again, it doesn't happen very often. Hardware failures are most likely to occur immediately after you start using a new piece of hardware or close to the end of its useful life. Sometimes you can induce a hardware failure when you upgrade a machine or perform some other type of maintenance on it.

Symptoms of a hardware problem are usually pretty obvious. You have a piece of hardware that just won't work as you expect it to, or at all (hopefully, that hardware isn't your MacBook Pro). If the cause of a hardware problem is software, you can often solve the problem by updating the software associated with the device. If the problem is actually with the hardware, though, you probably need help solving it, such as having it repaired.

Describing problems

Being able to accurately describe a problem is one of the most fundamental skills for effective troubleshooting. To describe a problem accurately, you must take an in-depth look at the various aspects of the problem. This puts you in a better position to solve it because effectively describing your problem is critical to help someone help you. The following are some questions you need to answer:

- **Which specific applications and processes (not just the one with which you were working) were running?**
- **What were you trying to do (print, save, format, and so on)?**
- **What specifically happened?** Did an application unexpectedly quit or hang? Did you see an error message?
- **Have you made any changes to the computer recently (installed software or changed settings)?**

The answers to these questions provide significant clues to help you figure out what is triggering the problem, which is integral to identifying its cause. As strange as this may sound, when a problem occurs, you should recover the best you can, and then immediately try to make the problem happen again. Open the same applications and follow your trail the best that you can, repeating everything that you did when the problem appeared. You can use the Activity Monitor application, shown in Figure 14.5, to see what happens when you re-create the situation that led to the problem.

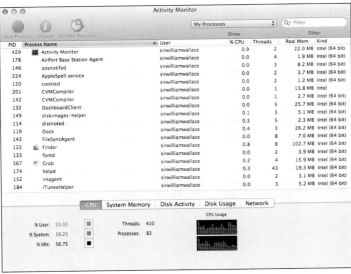

14.5 Use the Activity Monitor application to see what processes are running at any point in time, such as when you are trying to re-create a problem.

When you attempt to re-create a problem, there are two possible results—and both of them are good if you think about them correctly. One result is that you can't make the problem happen again. In this case, all you can do is go about your business and hope that you just got unlucky with some combination of events (if there is an underlying problem, don't worry about missing it because it will likely happen again at some point).

The other result is that you are able to replicate a problem. While this is painful because you don't really want to be dealing with a problem, being able to replicate it makes figuring out what is happening much easier. The hardest problems to fix are those that occur only occasionally or intermittently. If you can re-create a problem, it is much easier to describe and also more likely that you'll be able to get help with it if you can't solve it on your own.

Trying Fast and Easy Solutions

For proper troubleshooting, you should learn to recognize and describe problems. However, in reality, your first step when solving a problem is often one of the techniques described in this section. The amazing thing is that one of these solves many of the more common problems you might encounter, at least temporarily. However, if the fast and easy solutions fail, you have to move on to more complicated efforts. For each of these solutions, I also cover in what situations you should think about trying it and the steps to follow.

Forcing applications to quit

When to try: An application is hung and isn't responding to commands. The spinning color wheel appears on the screen and remains there.

What it does: The command causes the OS to forcibly stop the application and its processes.

Caution

You will lose any unsaved data in the application that you force to quit.

1. **Perform one of the following actions to activate the command:**

   - **Choose Apple menu ⇨ Force Quit.**

   - **Control+click the Dock icon of the hung application and select Force Quit.**

   - **The Force Quit Applications dialog appears.** In this dialog, you see the applications that are running. The name of the application that is hung appears in red with the text (Not Responding) next to it.

2. **Select the hung application.**

3. **Click Force Quit.** The warning sheet appears. Click Force Quit again.

4. **If there were open windows in the application, you may be prompted to restore them.** Select this option if you want Mac OS X to attempt this. The application is forced to quit and closes. If it doesn't work, try again; sometimes it can take a few times to get a hung application stopped. Forcing an application to quit leaves it unstable. Save your changes in any open documents and restart your MacBook Pro before you continue working. This minimizes the chances of additional problems. If you selected the restore windows option, the next time that you open the application, the windows that were open when you forced it to quit open again.

Forcing the Finder to relaunch

When to try: The Finder isn't responding to commands. The spinning color wheel appears whenever you try to select or work with something on your Desktop, such as a Finder window.

What it does: The command stops and starts the Finder again.

Caution

Relaunching the Finder is a hit-or-miss proposition, so don't be too surprised if it doesn't work.

1. **Perform one of the following actions to open the Force Quit Applications dialog:**

   ● **Choose Apple menu ⇨ Force Quit.**

   ● **Control+click the Finder's Dock icon and select Force Quit.**

2. **Select the Finder.** If the Finder is hung, its name appears in red and the text (Not Responding) appears next to it. If it isn't in red, you don't need to relaunch it.

3. **Click Relaunch.** A warning sheet appears. Click Relaunch again and your MacBook Pro attempts to relaunch the Finder. Like a hung application, it can take a few tries to get the Finder to relaunch. If successful, you are able to work on the Desktop again. If not, you need to perform the steps outlined later in this section. Forcing the Finder to relaunch leaves it in an unstable condition. Save any open documents and restart your MacBook Pro before continuing to work.

Genius You can also relaunch the Finder by clicking its icon in the Dock while holding down the Control and Option keys, and then selecting Relaunch.

Restarting or restoring

When to try: When your MacBook Pro or an application isn't working the way you expect, you've forced an application to quit, or relaunched the Finder.

What it does: Shuts down all applications, processes, and your MacBook Pro, and then restarts it.

1. **Perform one of the following actions:**

   - **Choose Apple menu ⇨ Restart.**

   - **Press the Power key once, and then click Restart (this bypasses the Restart dialog).**

2. **If the Restart dialog, shown in Figure 14.6, appears and you want to restore your Desktop to its current condition (with the same applications and documents open), select the Reopen windows when logging back in check box.** This is a good option to use when troubleshooting because it returns MacBook Pro to the condition it was in when the problem happened, making describing and diagnosing it easier.

14.6 Restart your MacBook Pro when applications aren't behaving themselves.

3. **Click Restart.** MacBook Pro shuts down, restarts, and then you can get back to work.

Genius If a restart isn't the specific cure to a problem, it is almost always one step in the process. When in doubt, restart.

Shutting down soft

When to try: When your MacBook Pro or an application isn't working the way you expect, or you've forced an application to quit or relaunched the Finder and normal behavior isn't restored with a restart.

What it does: Shuts down all applications and processes, and your MacBook Pro.

1. **Perform one of the following actions:**
   - **Choose Apple menu ⇨ Shut Down.**
   - **Press the Power key once, and then click Shut Down.**
   - **Press the Power key once, and then press Return.**

2. **If you want to restore your Desktop to its current condition (with the same applications and documents open), select the Reopen windows when logging back in check box.** This is a good option to use when troubleshooting because it returns MacBook Pro to the condition it was in when the problem happened, making describing and diagnosing it easier.

3. **Click Shut Down.** The MacBook Pro shuts down.

Shutting down hard

When to try: When your MacBook Pro appears to be locked up and doesn't respond to any of your commands.

What it does: Shuts down the MacBook Pro, regardless of any running processes.

You will lose all unsaved data in all open applications.

Caution

Press and hold down the Power key until the MacBook Pro screen goes dark and you hear it stop running. The MacBook Pro turns off. Press the Power key again and your MacBook Pro starts up.

Using a troubleshooting user account and deleting preferences

When to try: When an application isn't performing as you expect and restarting your MacBook Pro doesn't solve the problem.

What it does: Determines whether the problem is related to your specific user account or is more general.

Caution

1. **Perform one of the following actions:**

   - **Choose Apple menu ➪ Log Out accountname (where *accountname* is the currently logged-in account).**

   - **Press Shift+⌘+Q.**

2. **When the Log Out dialog appears, click Log Out.** (The log out occurs automatically when the 60-second timer counts down to zero.) The Login window appears.

3. **Log in to your troubleshooting account.**

4. **Repeat what you were doing when you experienced the problem.** If the problem goes away, it is most likely related to the previous user account. In most cases, this means that a preferences file is corrupted.

5. **Log out of the troubleshooting account.**

Application preference files are stored in the Preferences files within the Library file in the user's Home folder. By default, the Library folder is hidden.

Genius

To unhide a user's Library folder, open the Terminal application (located in the Utilities folder), and type the following: chflags nohidden /Users/*username*/Library (where *username* is the Account Name of the user account), and then press Return. The Library folder in the user's Home folder appears and you don't need to hold the Option key to see it on the Go menu.

If the problem persists, perform the following steps:

1. **Log in to the previous account, under which the problem occurred.**

2. **Hold the Option key down and choose Go ➪ Library.** The Library folder opens.

3. **Open the Preferences folder.** Locate the preferences files for the application that has the problem. Preferences files have the extension .plist and include the application name somewhere in the filename, as shown in Figure 14.7. Some preferences files are stored within the company's or application's folder within the Preferences folder.

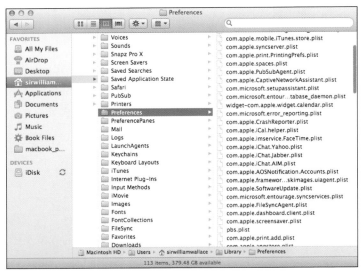

14.7 Removing a preferences file can sometimes restore an application to normal behavior.

4. **Delete the preferences files for the application.**

Caution Deleting a preferences file can remove any personalized information that is stored in it, such as registration information. Make sure you have this information stored in another location before deleting an application's preferences files.

5. **Restart the application and reconfigure its preferences.** If the problem doesn't recur, you are good to go. If it does, you'll need to try a more drastic step, such as reinstalling the application.

Genius An easy way to find all of the files related to an application is to use AppCleaner (www.freemacsoft.net/AppCleaner/). When an application is dropped on the AppCleaner icon, it finds and displays all related files and allows you to delete them.

Repairing external hard drives

When to try: You see error messages relating to a hard drive or you are unable to store data on it (and it isn't full).

What it does: Attempts to verify the drive's structure and repair any data problems.

1. **Quit all applications.**

2. **Launch Disk Utility (Applications ⇨ Utilities).**

3. **Select the drive you want to check or repair.**

4. **Check the bottom of the Disk Utility window for information about the drive you selected.** You see the drive's type, connection bus (such as ATA for internal drives or FireWire for an external drive), connection type (internal or external), capacity, write status, S.M.A.R.T. status, and partition map scheme. If you select a partition on a drive, you see various data about the volume, such as its mount point (the path to it), format, whether owners are enabled, the number of folders it contains, its capacity, the amount of space available, the amount of space used, and the number of files it contains.

5. **Click the First Aid tab to see some information explaining how Disk Utility works.**

6. **Click Repair Disk.** The application checks the selected drive for problems and repairs any it finds. When the process is complete, a report of the results appears.

If Disk Utility is able to repair any problems it found, you're done and the drive should work normally. If the problems can't be fixed, you can try a different drive maintenance application. In some cases, you might need to reformat the drive, which erases all of its data.

Repairing the internal hard drive

When to try: You see error messages relating to the internal hard drive or you are unable to store data on it (and it isn't full).

What it does: Attempts to verify the drive's structure and repair any data problems.

1. **Start your MacBook Pro from the Recovery volume (more on this later in this section).**

2. **Select the main language you want to use, and then click the right arrow button.**

3. **Click Disk Utility, and then click Continue.** The Disk Utility application opens.

4. **Select the MacBook Pro internal hard drive in the Disk Utility application.**

5. **Follow the steps in the previous task to repair the drive.**

Repairing permissions

When to try: When you get an error message stating that you don't have permission to do something for which you should have permission, or when you are experiencing unexpected behavior.

What it does: Repairs the security permissions associated with the files on a selected drive.

1. **Quit all applications.**

2. **Launch Disk Utility (Applications ➪ Utilities).**

3. **Select the drive on which you want to repair permissions.**

4. **Click Repair Disk Permissions.** The application starts searching for permission problems and repairs those that it finds. When the process is complete, you see the results in the information window on the First Aid tab, as shown in Figure 14.8.

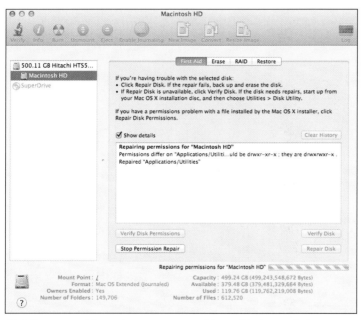

14.8 If you see odd security errors, try repairing a drive's permissions.

Reinstalling applications

When to try: You're using the current version (all patches and updates have been applied) of an application, but it's not working correctly, and you've tried restarting and shutting down soft.

What it does: Restores the application to like-new condition.

Caution You will lose any updates or patches that were released after the installer you have was produced. You may also lose all of your preferences for that application, including registration information, so make sure that you have it stored elsewhere.

How you do this depends on how you installed the application on your MacBook Pro. Perform the following steps if you installed the application through the Mac App Store:

1. **Delete the application.**

2. **Launch the Mac App Store.**

3. **Click the Purchased tab.**

4. **Click the Install button for the application you deleted.**

5. **Type the Apple ID and password under which the application was purchased, and then click Sign In.** The application is downloaded and installed. The benefit of this option is that you always get the most current version of the application you purchased.

Follow these steps to reinstall an application that wasn't installed through the Mac App Store:

1. **Perform one of the following actions to delete the application:**

   - **Run the uninstallation application (if one was provided) for the application you want to remove.**

   - **Drag the application's files and its preferences files to the Trash, and then empty it.**

2. **Run the application's installer, as shown in Figure 14.9.**

14.9 Reinstalling an application can restore it to its proper behavior.

Genius You can reinstall many applications using the receipt that was created when you first installed it. To do this, open the following folder: *startupdisk*/Library/Receipts (where *startupdisk* is the name of your startup disk). To reinstall an application, double-click its PKG file in this folder.

3. **Update the application to its latest version.**

4. **Reset your preferences.** If the application still doesn't work normally, the cause is likely a conflict between the application and either the version of Mac OS X you are using or some other part of your system, or the application might just be buggy. Possible solutions are to use a different application, avoid the functionality of the application that causes the problem, or live with the problem until an update fixes it.

Starting up from the Recovery partition

When to try: When you start your MacBook Pro and the normal startup sequence stops with a flashing folder icon on the screen, or MacBook Pro behaves oddly and you want to isolate the problem to your current startup drive.

What it does: Starts up your MacBook Pro from the Recovery HD volume.

Mac OS X includes a Recovery partition that you can use when your primary system software has an issue or you need to perform a repair on your startup hard drive. Follow these steps to start MacBook Pro from its Recovery partition:

1. **Restart your MacBook Pro.**

2. **As it restarts, hold down the Option key.** After a few moments, each valid startup drive appears.

3. **Select the Recovery volume.**

4. **Press Return.** Your MacBook Pro starts up, using the Recovery volume and software.

5. **Choose one of the following options, and then click Continue:**

   - **Restore From Time Machine Backup.** This option enables you to recover data from your backup.

   - **Reinstall Mac OS X.**

- **Get Help Online.** This option enables you to access the web to find a solution to the problem you are having.

- **Disk Utility.** This launches the Disk Utility application so you can repair your primary startup drive.

6. **Use the resulting tools to try to solve the problem.** For example, attempt to repair your startup drive with the Disk Utility application.

Note Additional options appear on the Utilities menu. These are Firmware Password Utility, Network Utility, and Terminal.

Starting up from an alternate external drive

When to try: When you try to start up your MacBook Pro and the normal startup sequence stops with a flashing folder icon on the screen, or MacBook Pro is behaving oddly and you want to isolate the problem to your current startup drive.

What it does: Starts up your MacBook Pro from the software installed on the external drive.

Caution You must have an alternate external startup drive created (see Chapter 11 for more details) because you must use the version of the OS that installed it. Also, make sure that the version of OS installed on the external drive is the latest version.

1. **Connect the external drive to your MacBook Pro.**

2. **Restart your MacBook Pro.**

3. **As it restarts, hold down the Option key.** After a few moments, each valid startup drive appears.

4. **Select the external hard drive from which you want to start up.**

Genius To set the default startup drive, use the Startup Disk pane of the System Preferences application. Select the drive that you want to be the default. To restart from that drive, click Restart or quit the System Preferences application and that drive will be used the next time you restart or start your computer. When it starts up, if the selected drive is not valid, your MacBook Pro selects one of the other valid drives to start up.

5. **Click the arrow pointing to the drive you selected.** Your MacBook Pro starts up, using the OS installed on the external drive.

6. **Use the MacBook Pro.** If things work as expected, you know the problem is related to the previous startup drive, in which case, you'll have to take more drastic action, such as reinstalling Mac OS X on your normal startup drive. If the problem recurs, you know that it is related to a specific application, hardware device, or the MacBook Pro itself, in which case the likely solutions are to reinstall the application or get help with the problem.

Note
If you ever start up your MacBook Pro and it stops with a flashing disk icon, it means that the computer can't find a valid startup drive. This either means there is a problem with the drive itself or something has happened to critical Mac OS X files, which is preventing the system from operating. Try reinstalling Mac OS X. If it can't be reinstalled on the drive, the drive has a problem you'll have to fix.

Getting Help with MacBook Pro Problems

We all need a little help once in a while. When it comes to your MacBook Pro, there's a wealth of assistance available to you.

Using the Mac Help system

Mac OS X includes a sophisticated Help system that you can use to find solutions to problems, or to get help with a specific task. In addition to Mac OS X, many other applications also use the same Help system. Follow these steps to search for help:

1. **Choose Help.** The Help menu opens.

2. **Type the term for which you want to search in the Search box.** As you type, matches are shown on the menu, as shown in Figure 14.10. These are organized into two sections. In the Menu Items section, you see menu items related to your search. In the Help Topics section, you see links to articles about the topic.

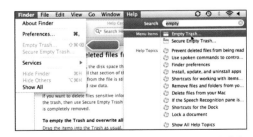

14.10 The Mac OS X Help system is, well, helpful.

3. **To see where a menu item is located, select it.** The menu opens and the item is highlighted. Figure 14.10 shows the Empty Trash menu item being selected.

4. **To read an article, click its link.** The Help window opens, and you see the article in the window. Figure 14.10 shows an article about preventing deleted files from being read in the background.

Genius

When you move away from the Help window, it closes. However, your most recent search is saved so you can return to the results just by opening the menu again. To clear a search so you can perform a new one, click the Clear (x) button in the Search bar when it contains a search term.

Describing a problem in detail

If none of the fast and easy solutions presented earlier result in a problem being solved, you may have to create a more detailed description. This increases the odds that someone will be able to help you. This section covers tools that can help you increase the level of detail in your problem descriptions.

Profiling a MacBook Pro

Your MacBook Pro is a complex system of hardware and software, in which each element has numerous technical specifications. Fortunately, you can use the System Information application to capture all of the details about your system so that you have them when you need to get help. Perform the following steps to create a profile for your MacBook Pro:

1. **Choose Apple menu ⇨ About This Mac.** The About This Mac window appears. In the upper part of the window, you see information about the version of Mac OS X installed on the MacBook Pro. In the lower part of the window, you see information about the MacBook Pro hardware.

2. **Click More Info, and then click System Report.** The system report window appears. In the left pane, you see various categories of information about your MacBook Pro, such as hardware components, and network and software information.

3. **Select an area about which you want detailed information.** The details appear in the right pane of the window. With some categories, you see more options at the top of the window. For example, when you select USB, you see the various USB ports on your MacBook Pro. You can select one of these to get more information about the device connected to it.

371

4. **When you see the information that you need, choose File ⇨ Print.** The application builds a printable version of the system report.

5. **When the Print dialog appears, click PDF to open the PDF menu.**

6. **Choose Save as PDF.** Name the report and choose a save location.

7. **Click Save.** The report is saved with the name and at the location you selected.

Genius

After you click More Info, click the related button in the About This Mac toolbar that appears to get more info about specific components. In the lower-right corner of each pane that appears, a button providing further information or more actions related to the item you selected appears. For example, when you select Storage, the Disk Utility button appears along with information about storage devices with which your MacBook can communicate.

Monitoring MacBook Pro activity

When a problem occurs, Mac OS X doesn't provide a lot of direct feedback. However, you can use the Activity Monitor application to get a closer look at what's happening in the background. Follow these steps to do so:

1. **Open Activity Monitor (Utilities folder within the Applications folder).**

2. **Click the CPU tab.** In the upper part of the window, you see a list of all running processes on the MacBook Pro. For each process, you see a variety of information, such as how many CPU resources it is using and the amount of memory. At the bottom of the window, you see a graphical representation of the current thread and process activity in the processor, as shown in Figure 14.11.

3. **Click the % CPU column heading to sort the list of processes by the amount of processor activity.**

4. **Click the Sort triangle so it is pointing down, indicating that the processes consuming more resources appear at the top of the list.** When a process is consuming a large amount of CPU resources or a lot of drive activity over a long period, it can indicate that the process is having a problem or is the cause of problems you are experiencing. In most cases, problems you are experiencing are caused by applications. You can limit the processes shown in the window to just applications, which can make the information easier to interpret.

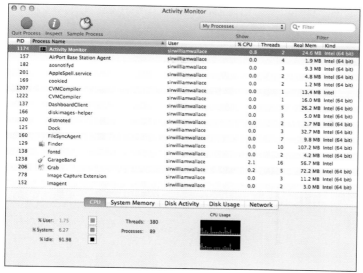

14.11 If CPU activity is maxed out for a long period, then a process is hung. You probably need to force it to quit, and then restart your MacBook Pro.

5. **On the pop-up menu at the top of the window, select Windowed Processes.** The list is reduced so that it includes only processes associated with applications.

6. **Use the tabs at the bottom of the window to explore other areas of the system.** You can use the Disk Usage tab to assess how much free space your drives have, or the System Memory tab to assess the status of the MacBook Pro RAM and its virtual memory.

Genius

When you select a process and click the Inspect button, the Inspect window opens and you see several tabs of process information, such as memory use, statistics about how a process is working, and the files and ports it has open. This information is sometimes useful when troubleshooting. You can also stop a process by selecting it, and then clicking Quit Process, which is similar to a force quit.

Capturing screenshots

When you experience a problem, capturing a screenshot is a great way to describe and document it. It's even more useful when you ask for help because you can give the person helping you all of the detailed information she needs. For example, if an error message appears on the screen, you can capture it in a screenshot. There are two built-in ways to capture a screenshot in Mac OS X. You can use keyboard shortcuts or the Grab application.

Perform the following steps to use a keyboard shortcut to capture the screen:

1. **When you want to capture the entire screen, press ⌘+Shift+3.** An image file is created on the Desktop. Move on to step 4.

2. **When you want to capture part of the screen, press ⌘+Shift+4.**

Genius To capture a window, press ⌘+Shift+4 and the spacebar. Move the pointer to the window you want to capture. When it is shaded in blue, click to capture a screenshot containing only that window.

3. **Drag over the area of the screen you want to capture and release the trackpad button when the area is highlighted.** An image file is created on the Desktop.

4. **Open the image file you created.** It is named Screen Shot *X* (where *X* is the date and time at which the screenshot was captured). The file is now ready to use.

Mac OS X also includes the Grab application, which enables you to capture screenshots in a slightly more sophisticated manner.

Genius In addition to the Timed Screen option on the Capture menu in Grab, you can also use Selection to capture part of the Desktop by drawing a box around it, use Window to capture the active window, or use Screen to capture the entire Desktop.

Follow these steps to capture a screen with Grab:

1. **Launch the Grab application by double-clicking its icon in the Utilities folder within the Applications folder.** The application opens, but you don't see any windows until you capture a screenshot. You do see the Grab menu.

2. **Choose Capture ⇨ Timed Screen.** The Timed Screen Grab dialog appears, as shown in Figure 14.12.

3. **Organize the screen as you want to capture it.** Switch back to the Finder or application that shows what you want to capture, and then configure the windows as you want to capture them.

14.12 Once you click Start Timer, you have 10 seconds until the screen is captured.

4. **Click Start Timer.** Grab's timer starts. After 10 seconds, the capture is taken.

5. **Save the image file.** The screen capture is ready to use.

Note If you are serious about screenshots, you should consider using Ambrosia Software's Snapz Pro X (www.ambrosiasw.com/utilities/), which was used for almost all the figures in this book. It gives you a lot of control over the screenshots you take. You can even capture motion and make movies of your Desktop activities.

Getting help from others

After you've tried the fast and easy solutions and the various Help systems on your MacBook Pro, your next stop should be the Internet. The following are some helpful websites you should check out:

- **www.apple.com/support.** The Apple support pages are a great source of information. You can also download system and software updates. You can search for specific problems by product, application, or just by running a general search. You can also read manuals and have discussions about problems in the forums. If the problem you are having seems to be related to the OS, Apple hardware, or an Apple application, this should be your first stop.

- **www.google.com.** Type a description of the problem you are having. The odds are good that someone else has had, and hopefully solved, the same issue. Explore the results until you find the help that you need.

- **www.macintouch.com.** This site offers a lot of news that can help you solve problems, especially if they can be solved by a software update of which you may be unaware.

Note You can also e-mail me at: bradmiser@me.com to ask for help. I will do my best to provide a solution, or at least point you to a more helpful source if I can't help you directly.

Starting Over

Hopefully, you'll never need to perform any of the tasks described here because they apply only when you have a significant problem. They also either take a lot of time and effort or can be expensive. Still, you have to do what you have to do.

Reinstalling Mac OS X

If you discover that your system has major problems, such as when your internal drive is no longer recognized as a valid startup drive, you might need to reinstall Mac OS X. Because it takes a while, and you might lose some of the installation and configuration you've done, you shouldn't make this decision lightly.

Caution If you don't have your data backed up, be aware that reinstalling the operating system can damage or delete your data. That doesn't usually happen, but you should always have a good backup just in case.

If you determine that you do need to reinstall Mac OS X, follow these steps to go about it:

1. **Back up your data.** Make sure that it backed up by trying to recover a file or two if you can. Some problems prevent this. In those cases, you'll just have to trust that your backup system has worked.

2. **Start up from the Recovery volume.** When your Mac starts up, you see the Mac OS X Utilities screen.

3. **Select Reinstall Mac OS X, and then click Continue.**

4. **Click Continue again.**

5. **Click Continue at the prompt.** This sends your MacBook Pro serial number to Apple.

6. **Follow the on-screen instructions to complete the installation.** When the process is complete, your MacBook Pro restarts.

7. **Update your software (see Chapter 13) so that you are running the most current version of Mac OS X.**

8. **Reinstall any applications that don't work correctly.** Mostly, these are applications that install software into the system. They need to be reinstalled because their software was removed when Mac OS X was reinstalled.

Genius When you are installing Mac OS X, you can click Customize to choose specific options to install. For example, to save some drive space, you can deselect languages that you don't use. When you've selected or deselected options, click OK and the files you excluded won't be installed.

Hopefully, your MacBook Pro has returned to prime condition and is working like you expect. Because the installer doesn't change the contents of your Home folder, the data you had stored there should be intact, including your application preferences and iTunes content, so you can get back to what you were doing quickly. In rare cases, these data might have been disturbed, in which case you'll need to restore them from your backups.

Melting and repouring

Sometimes, things get so bad that you just need to start over. This goes even farther than simply reinstalling Mac OS X because you erase the internal hard drive. This means that all of the data on it is deleted, including the system and all of the files stored on it. This is drastic action, and should only be taken if you really need to do it. Also expect the initial process to take a long time.

Caution

If you follow these steps, all of the data on your hard drive is erased. If you don't have it backed up, it's gone forever. Don't do this unless you are sure your data is protected.

Follow these steps to wipe your hard drive and start over:

1. **Back up your data and test your backups to make sure they work if you can.** In some cases, you won't be able to do this, such as if you can't start up your computer. In those cases, you'll have to rely on your existing backups. If they are out of date, you shouldn't perform these steps unless it is your last and only recourse.

2. **Start up from the Recovery volume.** After your Mac starts up, you see the Mac OS X Utilities screen.

Genius

If you don't have a recovery volume, press ⌘+R while your MacBook Pro restarts. This will allow you to reinstall Mac OS X.

3. **Choose Disk Utility, and then click Continue.** The Disk Utility application opens.

4. **Use Disk Utility to erase the internal hard drive.** (See Chapter 11 for the details.) When the process is complete, quit Disk Utility. You move back into the Mac OS X Utilities screen.

5. **Select Reinstall Mac OS X, and then click Continue.**

6. **Follow the on-screen instructions to complete the installation.** When the process is complete, your MacBook Pro restarts. When it does, it is in the same condition as when you first took it out of its box and turned it on.

7. **Follow the on-screen instructions to perform the initial configuration.** Again, this is just like the first time you started your MacBook Pro.

8. **Create the user accounts you need (see Chapter 2).**

Genius

If you use Time Machine for your backups, you can restore your data into the appropriate user accounts.

9. **Update your software (see Chapter 13).**

10. **Reinstall your applications.** You can use the Mac App Store application to reinstall any you purchased from the store, installers you downloaded from the web, or discs on which the software came.

11. **Restore your data from your backups.** Your MacBook Pro should be back to its old self, but without the problems you were having.

Professional Repairs by Apple

If your MacBook Pro has hardware problems, you probably need to have it repaired by Apple. You can do this by taking it to a local Apple Store or using Apple's website to arrange technical support. Follow these steps to get started with the web approach:

1. **Go to https://selfsolve.apple.com/GetWarranty.do.**

2. **Type your MacBook Pro serial number.** This number is on the MacBook Pro case and in your system report document. You can also get your serial number by opening the About This Mac window and clicking the Mac OS X version information twice.

3. **Select your country, and then click Continue.** On the resulting screen, you see warranty information about your MacBook Pro, along with links to various resources you can use to have Apple repair it for you.

Index

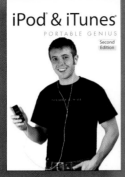

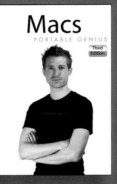